AF593454

Encounters with Artists

JASPER JOHNS
BRIDGET RILEY
CORNELIA PARKER
SARAH LUCAS HELE
ANISH KAPOOR RO
ANTONY GORMLE
CLAES OLDENBURG
LUC TUYMANS
DAMIEN HIRST
HOWARD HODGKIN
TRACEY EMIN
FRANK STELLA

Encounters with Artists

Richard Cork

Foreword by Cornelia Parker

T&H

Contents

Foreword

Cornelia Parker

Some years ago I took part in a symposium at the Tate, *Intention in Making Art*, and I titled my presentation 'Avoiding the Object on Purpose', which was me being deliberately evasive about the content of my work. I likened intention to describing a hole in a piece of wood. How do you describe a hole? You usually characterize it by describing the host material – in this case, wood, which has a rough, splintery edge. If the hole was made in marble, you might describe its properties as smooth and cool. But the stuff of the void, of the actual hole itself, is very difficult to define without resorting to metaphysics. There again, intention might just have something to do with metaphysics, with mind, matter and everything in between. And then again it might simply be announcing a course of action that an artist intends to follow.

I recently listened to an old recording of an interview between curator Stuart Cameron and myself in 1996. I was talking about my upcoming Chapter Art Centre exhibition (and ongoing body of work) 'Avoided Object', which was a work in progress at the time. Memory plays tricks on you; the ideas I touched on that were realized came into sharp focus, and those that were not disappeared into mist. It was as if by actually making the work, it became a conscious part of my history. For me it seems important that I allow my unconscious to make content; after all, it knows much more than my conscious mind. When being interviewed by a skilful art critic who wants to know the mechanics and possible meanings of the work (preferably in layman's terms), I find myself hesitating.

I always think the practice of making work is like archaeology: the first thing is having a hunch about where to dig. You find a fragment which you know has been a small part of an intact object. You dig up another fragment and another till you have the semblance of a whole thing, which might turn out to be just a small part of a much bigger picture, perhaps one of many related objects. Obviously the longer you dig, the greater the knowledge. That which emerges is a rich body of work, plucked from oblivion by your efforts.

Critics might opine about an artist's work, bringing their own preferences and specialisms to bear, but in an interview the artist is boss. Artists like reading conversations with other artists rather than pieces of conjecture written by onlookers. With an interview there is always an element of surprise – the artist inevitably remembers something long buried and gains new insights through the questioning process. That is when the experience is transformational, and the knowledge newly gleaned becomes part of the artist's story.

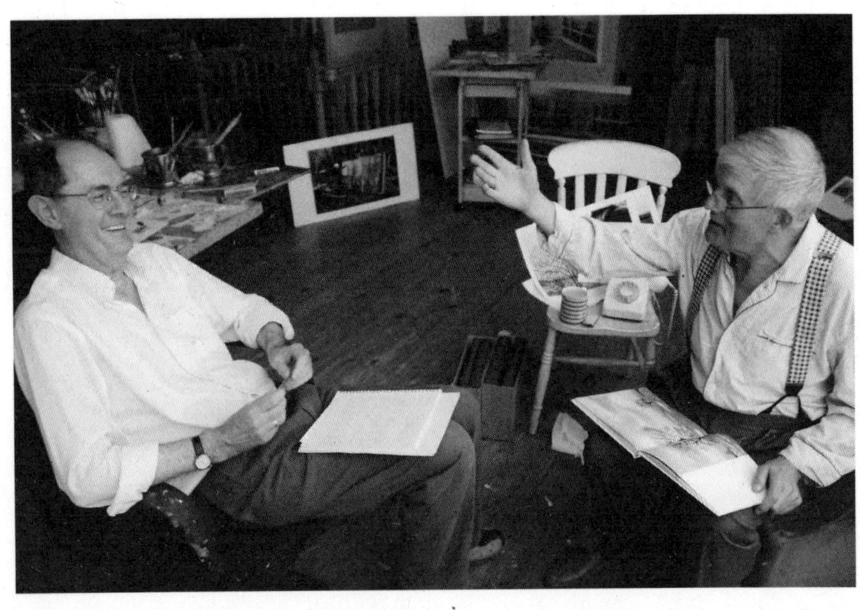

Introduction

Some artists abhor the prospect of finding their privacy invaded by an eager, relentless interviewer who bombards them with intrusive questions. When I started researching my first book, on vorticism, in the early 1970s and attempted to contact surviving members of this explosive avant-garde movement, one prominent painter steadfastly refused to acknowledge my letters. Although he lived nearby and was still producing plenty of work, William Roberts proved an extreme recluse. I tried hard to persuade this incorrigible hermit to share his memories of the feisty 1914 art rebellion in London. But he hardly ever saw anyone except his wife and son, and she told me that Roberts never even allowed her to enter his studio. He was very reluctant to open the front door of his house when the doorbell rang, or do anything except mutter curtly through the letterbox. Roberts loathed social interchange, as the distinguished curator Anne Goodchild discovered when she encountered him on the top deck of a London bus. After she enquired in suitably respectful tones if he was William Roberts, an interminable pause followed. Then, with his gaze defiantly averted, Roberts replied: 'I really do not know.'

Fortunately, my subsequent attempts to interview artists have often proved far more fruitful. True, visiting the octogenarian Duncan Grant in his haven at Charleston Farmhouse in Sussex turned out to be frustrating. He received me very warmly, dispensed tea on a hand-painted Omega table and listened with avid interest as I asked him about key moments in his early Bloomsbury career, before the First World War. But he could not recall any of the events I was describing, and finally thanked me with a wry smile for reacquainting him with so much that he had forgotten. On the whole, though, talking to artists can in my experience be surprising, revealing, salutary, testing, provocative and stimulating. Such conversations are capable of overturning all my preconceptions about the individuals I encounter.

The violent paintings produced by Francis Bacon, whom I first visited as an anxious young critic back in 1971, had led me to expect an intensely difficult occasion. So I was both relieved and amazed to discover just how friendly Bacon turned out to be. The only problem lay in the champagne. The first bottle was uncorked soon after my arrival at ten in the morning, and later on he suggested that we go off together and have lunch at his favourite Soho restaurant. To my surprise, Bacon declared that we would travel there on the Tube, even though he could easily afford to go everywhere by taxi. He told me with excitement: 'I *love* shooting through dark tunnels in a metal cylinder!' Our meal proved delightfully convivial, but Bacon kept ordering more and more wine. Oddly, I had no idea how drunk he made me while the conversation proceeded. My hand raced across page after page of my notebook, jotting down his very quotable and still surprisingly coherent remarks. Bacon then insisted that we move on to the nearby Colony Room, his cherished haunt, where he at once ordered champagne for everyone who happened to be there. The place soon filled with garrulous and inebriated people. After being importuned by one of Bacon's very randy East End gangster friends, I realized it was probably time for me to descend the Colony's perilously narrow staircase and leave. Only the following day did I notice, despite my monumental hangover, that the notes I had scribbled during our tipsy lunch were all incomprehensible.

Subsequent visits to Bacon's mews proved just as memorable, but he was usually reluctant to show me the studio where his latest paintings could be assessed. Some artists are almost superstitious about letting anyone see work in progress. They feel, perhaps, that it would reveal too much. Howard Hodgkin, who was fortunate enough to possess one of the most spectacular all-white studios I have ever seen, did allow some visitors to enter this luminous space but never let them see the unfinished paintings housed there. They remained hidden behind large stretchers – a tantalizing sight for anyone hoping to discover how Hodgkin was developing.

Louise Bourgeois went even further, forbidding me to penetrate the industrial building in Brooklyn where she defied old age and continued her work with such astonishing, disciplined resilience. This need for privacy must be respected, and I relished the eloquent way in which Bourgeois talked to me just before her major installation was revealed in the Turbine Hall at the newly opened Tate Modern. Still haunted by childhood memories of her French father's philandering, Bourgeois emphasized with understandable irony, 'England is very, very important to me, because in my family the English could do no wrong. When my father picked a mistress, it was always an English girl: if he made her pregnant, she could be shipped back to England and he would not be held responsible. It never happened. But since then I've made a lot of work called *The English Can Do No Wrong*.' Hence her decision, after moving to New York in 1938, to make an installation entitled *The Destruction of the Father*. And when I asked her if the psychological wound inflicted by him continued to plague her now, Bourgeois admitted, 'My memories still bother me....All the art I make comes from my childhood and adolescence.'

I relish the opportunity to see what artists are producing at the time when they talk to me about their activities. Work is, after all, their *raison d'être*. So it makes absolute sense when they allow me access to the contents of the studio. Gerhard Richter showed no hesitation in leading me through to a large, airy space in his converted Cologne factory. New paintings lined the walls in prodigious numbers, and he made clear that they thrived on each other's company. 'Each learns from the others,' Richter explained.

Some artists favour astonishingly small, rudimentary studios. I could hardly believe Luc Tuymans when he showed me the cramped, cold, leaking and decayed room in central Antwerp where he had insisted on painting for almost thirty years. But it had become a source of perpetual stimulus, and he clung to this unlikely little chamber in the belief that, as he said, 'my work was dependent on it.' Painters, of course, can operate in modest premises more readily than sculptors, who often need plenty of space to test out their more epic ideas. When Antony Gormley moved to his spectacular new London studio, custom designed by David Chipperfield, it 'completely changed my life'. At last, he found, 'I can do things properly, and there's no longer any excuse for not doing so.'

A car journey provided the climax of my visit to David Hockney in his native Yorkshire. After showing me some expansive new landscape paintings in his mother's former house at Bridlington, he donned a white peaked cap and scarf, climbed into the driving seat of a gleaming open-top Mini Cooper S, and invited me to sit down on the black leather seat beside him. Our destination was the countryside he had recently been painting with such energy and commitment. 'You won't believe this road through the mad valleys,' he promised. 'I've allowed well over two hours for it, and the evening light is perfect.' He was right. Driving through Thwing, Uncleby, Pocklington and Bugthorpe, I marvelled at this empty, little-known and wholly beguiling northern world. We stopped to explore the special places Hockney scrutinized in all seasons, and on the edge of a very dramatic drop he said: 'I get very thrilled here. I could sit for hours, on a chair, right there.'

Few artists want you to watch them at work. But when I visited the Chapman brothers, who shared their space with a ping-pong table, a heavy punchbag, a yapping little boxer and a bull terrier, Jake Chapman could not resist seizing a pen and drawing a man with very thin, predatory arms. 'It's Jay,' he explained – referring to their dealer, Jay Jopling. 'He's got long, dangling hands for reaching deep into people's pockets.' Rachel Whiteread went so far as to suggest, in 2001, that I meet her at the colossal South London workshop where her major sculpture for the empty plinth in Trafalgar Square was being made. After wandering through the skylit interior, I discovered Whiteread standing inside half of her immense resin work, spraying the sides with methylated spirits while a masked colleague operated a machine to smooth out the base of the sculpture. Her hands-on involvement reflected considerable anxiety about this ambitious project. After using a ladder to climb out, Whiteread confessed with a sigh that she was worried about 'the material cracking', adding that the whole process was 'behind schedule'.

Whiteread replied decisively when I asked her if she was influenced by the historic surroundings of Trafalgar Square: 'My relationship with Trafalgar Square has nothing to do with all the bombastic militarism.' She relished the opportunity to display her *Monument* there, although she didn't want to create a work which blatantly called attention to itself. 'I hate public sculpture that's in your face – I absolutely loathe it,' she said forcefully, insisting that *Monument* would be 'my response to what I found in the square. I started off as a sculptor responding to humble places, and in its low-key way the plinth is like this.' She hoped that *Monument* would be scrutinized by 'an enormous number of people who are not interested in art.'

Lucian Freud did not let me observe him in the act of painting, yet he invited me round to his top-floor studio in Holland Park late one evening. The unfinished work on the easel showed a reclining nude with her legs apart. And the model, Alexandra Williams-Wynn, was standing by a well-lit bed in the middle of the room. The walls were encrusted with paint, its thickness testifying to the amount of hard labour Freud expended on his art. He had been working on this image for several months, and when I asked him why it was taking so long he admitted: 'I'm suspicious of everything I do, and when it's quick, I think, oh, that must be wrong.' Eventually, after we talked, drank green tea and ate handfuls of almonds and cranberries, Freud went back to work with Alexandra. It was very late, but he habitually painted until past midnight and then got up again at four in the morning.

Roy Lichtenstein seemed even more dynamic. At seventy-three, he was almost ten years younger than Freud, and remained tirelessly on the move throughout my visit to his converted ironworks building in Greenwich Village. The large new paintings ranged around the spacious, tranquil studio proved that he had no desire to slow up as an artist. He even had energy left over for roller-booting round the nearby streets, and had recently started learning to play the saxophone.

'I've always felt optimistic,' he told me. 'I don't know why. I know it would be much more interesting if I wasn't. I've never done an anguished painting.' He certainly appeared in harmony with himself, and I felt deeply shocked when, weeks later, he died suddenly from pneumonia. This was his last interview. Lichtenstein's death, so unexpected, sadly deprived both him and us of the chance to find out how he might have developed in his old age. The loss was immeasurable.

Francis Bacon also died soon after our final meeting. I remember feeling astonished that someone so vital had succumbed without warning to terminal ill-health. But he was considerably older than Lichtenstein, and his achievement as an artist seemed complete; so I did not suffer the same sense of shock, even if it always feels unsettling to realize that an artist who recently talked to you with such energetic animation is now dead. Ian Hamilton Finlay, whom I visited for the last time not long before failing health brought his life at Stonypath to an end, was no exception. The garden he had created in the Lanarkshire countryside, on the southern slopes of the Pentland Hills, looked more breathtaking than ever. Yet Finlay himself appeared frail, if defiantly impervious to the rigours of the Scottish climate. An outburst of heavy rain coincided with my arrival, so I asked if he could lend me an umbrella. 'I don't think I have one,' he said.

After exploring Stonypath, where sculpture, landscape, poetry and philosophy had been brought together in a superbly orchestrated unity, I joined him for tea in his cottage conservatory. A benign bust of Rousseau presided over us, and I was impressed by Finlay's stoicism. Describing how a herd of cattle had 'broken into part of the garden one day and eaten everything', he appeared poised between playfulness and inscrutability. 'I thought the inscribed works in the garden would last a lifetime,' he said, 'but some of them are illegible already.' He seemed far quieter than I recalled from my previous visit in the 1980s. 'I used to talk a lot,' he said with a rueful smile, 'but now I say far less. I leave the garden to do the talking for me.'

Helen Frankenthaler might well have sympathized with Finlay's sentiments. She was the most guarded and reluctant artist I have ever interviewed – partly, perhaps, because we met in the formal surroundings of her suite at the Savoy Hotel in London. If I had visited her studio, she might have been less withdrawn. Eventually, Frankenthaler did speak with considerable eloquence about her work. I was aware throughout our time together that talking about art compared poorly in her mind with the act of painting, but what she said was revealing. She looked back with intense feeling at the extremely difficult moment when her radical *Mountains and Sea* was first exhibited in 1952: 'I think there were about five people who were very excited and puzzled by it and said: "Do more like that." And this, besides myself alone, was the only support. When I did show the picture about a year or two later, one of my best-known and beloved former teachers saw it and said: "My God, she's using a giant paint-rag!"'

Courageous enough to wave aside such patronizing hostility, Frankenthaler told me that only one visionary course of action was open to her: 'I had to follow what I had to do,' she insisted. 'And I was very puzzled, in a way, when I first saw it myself. Yes. But I think one evolves, and one's work evolves, and one's dreams evolve, and you become what you become.'

The hostility Frankenthaler encountered among so many early viewers of her work contrasts absolutely with the positive response experienced by Bettina Pousttchi to her potent and poignant *Echo Berlin*, intended as a memorial to the Palast der Republik, the former East German parliament building demolished in the early 2000s. She took many photographs and won a commission to make an enormous pictorial simulation of the Palast on the facade of the Temporäre Kunsthalle, newly erected on a neighbouring site. 'I had a stressful time producing all the nine hundred and seventy paper posters,' she recalled with a smile, 'and putting them on the Temporäre Kunsthalle took two weeks.'

Soon enough, however, Pousttchi felt 'overwhelmed by the public's response. It started while I was installing. Everyone could take a picture, and I had all kinds of reaction from spectators, commentators and journalists. They were enthusiastic as well as critical, and people started telling me their memories.' When *Echo Berlin* was completed in 2009, everyone realized they could 'see this fake facade in the context of Berlin. I didn't want to evoke sadness, but memory and respect towards the past.'

Pousttchi eventually came to realize that the whole project had transformed her own vision as an artist. 'Looking back now, I realize it's where everything came together in my work. Photography and sculpture became architecture in a very special place. I'm more sensitive to locations now, and my major projects are site-specific.'

When I first met Richard Long in 1971 at the Whitechapel Art Gallery, we talked about the work he had installed here for this, his very first UK solo show. I soon realized that Long, an intensely private young man, felt uneasy about the whole notion of explaining his art. But it was not an interview: I was simply attempting, as a twenty-four-year-old critic, to discover more about the first artist of my own generation whose work had excited me on a profound level. The review I wrote in the *Evening Standard* quoted Long at one point: after describing the meditative pleasure he had derived from reconstructing a maze design cut into a giant Irish stone in around 2,000 BC, he told me that his re-enactment of this ancient ritual 'provided me with my best walk to date'. But the review focused principally on my own response to the work of an audacious young artist whose most arresting Whitechapel exhibit was an immense circular pathway he had trodden out with clay across the gallery floor. It invited us to set off along such a path as well, and connected with Long's love of early legends by measuring precisely the length of a straight walk from the bottom of prehistoric Silbury Hill in Wiltshire to the top.

Over the decades, Long gradually became far more relaxed about art talk. In 2004, when we met at the Royal Academy to discuss his special show in the Central Hall, he interrupted the installation process to share a fascinating range of insights. He emphasized how important it was, in the desert or the wilderness, to cherish silence. Even a mobile phone 'spoils the walk. I don't want to interrupt the concentration: I'm in a private zone.' When

I asked if he ever felt lonely, he shook his head. 'Urban loneliness, yes, but never in a landscape.' Why? 'Because solitude is rare, and something to be savoured.'

So far as Long's student contemporaries Gilbert and George are concerned, city life is the prime focus of their art. In 1971, when I first visited them in the East End of London, they only owned a modest flat within a capacious 18th-century house overshadowed by Nicholas Hawksmoor's titanic Spitalfields church. But I advised the *Evening Standard*'s readers: 'If you fight your way through the markets of Spitalfields and knock on their door, you can expect to receive a very correct cup of tea in an environment that links up in an almost hallucinatory way with the character of their work. Here, in this small, bare room, life really does threaten to clash headlong with art; and only Gilbert and George could ever, conceivably, manage to push this unlikely conjunction so far.'

By the time I interviewed them in 1993, they owned the whole of the calm, dark-panelled house. Seated round a hexagonal tea-table on Pugin-designed chairs, they both seemed remarkably buoyant. Devon-born George, bald, bespectacled and a heavy smoker, could hardly be more removed in his background from the smaller, darker Gilbert, who grew up in an area of the Dolomites where art was equated solely with 'a school of religious wood-carvers famous throughout the valley'. But having lived and worked together in London for a quarter of a century, the neatly besuited duo spoke with one unrepentant voice about reviewers' hostility over here. 'A lot of young people feel liberated by our work,' they said, 'but the kind of British critic who believes in a very classist structure for culture has a low opinion of the general public. Nobody else is making art so easy to attack. We bring out the bigot from inside the liberal, and vice versa. Critics abroad are much more prepared to praise our work – but here, good art always has to come from a wine-growing country.'

From the moment I started talking to Steve McQueen while he was vigorously preparing his first major British show of films, sculpture and photography, the twenty-nine-year-old artist spoke very frankly about the tension he felt. Although widely hailed as an outstanding young talent, he noted: 'I get a better response in the US, maybe because Black artists are more noticeable over there and gain a broader acceptance.'

McQueen's eager involvement with film made life difficult for him as a student at Chelsea School of Art and Goldsmiths College, where he had to 'beg, steal or borrow from the film department. Goldsmiths was a tricky time: you had to find your own way. It was only when I saw a contemporary show at the Whitney during a visit to New York in 1993 that the wide variety of possibilities in art really blew me away.' This was a revelatory experience, very unlike his forbidding time at Goldsmiths, 'where I had no tutorials in my last year. Then, after leaving, a friend and fellow student who was Black committed suicide.' As McQueen explained at the heartfelt end of the interview, art 'enables you to work things out in public, creating your own world. Otherwise you're powerless: it would be terrible.'

Artists can undoubtedly feel wounded if they find themselves traduced. When the young Bridget Riley attracted highly publicized attention in New York, she felt appalled. The year was 1965; driving down Madison Avenue, Riley was astonished to pass shop-windows filled with 'Op' dresses blatantly based on her paintings. Then, at the opening of an exhibition titled 'The Responsive Eye' at the Museum of Modern Art, she was even more distressed to find half the guests wearing those dresses. Far from basking in such notoriety, she felt that her work had been falsified. It upset her so much that she attempted to take legal action against the rampant plagiarism, but she discovered that no copyright protection existed at that time for artists in the US. When Riley boarded the plane back to London she felt convinced that it would take 'at least twenty years before anyone looks at my paintings seriously again'.

This traumatic episode marked something of a watershed in Riley's career. She deliberately retreated from her fame, and to this day remains extremely reluctant to give interviews or submit herself to the disturbing level of invasive attention she experienced in New York. Besides, artists often decide as they get older that their work must take priority over self-promotion. When visiting Lucian Freud again, just before his major Tate retrospective opened in 2002,

I realized how zealously he now guarded his time. Explaining why he refused most requests for interviews, Freud insisted that the demands of work in progress must be met. 'I don't know how much time I have left, and I'm full of aches and pains,' he said. 'So I want to paint as much as possible. I'd like, ideally, to die in the studio, with brush in hand.'

Rebecca Horn might well agree. When she took me round her white studio at Bad Konig in Germany, several immense paintings filled with her vibrant mark-making transmitted an impressive sense of vitality. She told me that they were called 'cosmic maps', declaring enthusiastically, 'They're all to do with the pulsation of my own body and how far I can stretch my arms to use these fantastic Korean brushes!' The studio itself had once been part of a textile factory built by her grandfather, and she had installed an ancient Chinese statue within the workspace. When I asked her why, she explained, 'It protects the house.' Horn had retired from teaching in 2009, and she was devoting a lot of her energy to converting some of the old factory buildings into 'a village with a museum, an archive, a space for concerts and studios for artists in residence'.

As well as painting, drawing and body-extension sculpture, Horn explores film, poetry and photography. This freewheeling approach is quite unlike Henry Moore's lifelong commitment to sculpture and drawing. But ultimately, what unites these disparate individuals is a fundamental, fiercely held belief in the indispensability of art. I will never forget Moore clutching the flesh around his own stomach while emphasizing how 'central' the umbilical area was in his own sculpture. Since it clearly mattered a great deal to him, I asked him why the umbilical area was so important. He answered very directly: 'Because that's where we were attached to our mothers.' Like Francis Bacon, Moore backed up everything he said with restless physical gestures, as if expressing thoughts deeply felt within his own body.

Many artists I have interviewed seemed charged with an unusual amount of physical dynamism. Anthony Caro became instantly concerned when I happened to mention that my back had been strained the previous day. 'Oh, God,' he cried, 'is it terribly painful?

All sculptors suffer from back problems, you know.' He asked me to take off my jacket, and pressed an elaborate electrical appliance against my back. My aching body responded well to his ministrations, and I realized that his massaging prowess probably owed a great deal to his skills as a sculptor.

Doris Salcedo was acutely aware of distress, but in her case it seemed to be focused primarily on suffering in 'concentration camps as well as contemporary versions of them, places where civilians are kept without trial'. Her experience of life in Colombia, where she spent most of her time, underlined the need to protect herself against possible danger. 'The spread of kidnapping means that I no longer travel around the country as much as before,' she told me. 'But it's important to have a perspective, and I see everything from the vantage of the Third World. It's not enough to look from a comfortable position, and in Colombia they're getting poorer all the time. I think it's going to get much worse.' Turning to her own work, though, Salcedo stressed that she was 'not a message artist. I see reality in a raw, naked way, so I have to respond with my work. That's why I adore art over politics, obviously: it's where our humanness resides. But I don't think art will save us.'

Jasper Johns appeared to me more light-hearted than Salcedo. Before meeting him, I imagined that he might be aloof and unforthcoming, but he overturned all my expectations. Johns is a highly complex individual: his later art has become increasingly concerned with tragic themes, and yet he can still erupt with affectionate laughter when recalling his grandmother in South Carolina playing the piano while singing 'Red Sails in the Sunset'.

Childhood memories are equally potent for Jenny Saville, who told me she had moved around so much during her childhood that 'I've been to fourteen schools. My bedroom became hugely important to me, I made things all the time. Today my studio is an extension of all that.' It is not, however, a place where she allows herself to be cosy or complacent. 'I'm stubborn with my paintings,' she declared, 'and this new one is driving me crazy!' Looking at the 18-foot-wide canvas, I could see three female figures. 'I'm there at the top,' Saville said, 'but we're all overlapping and bits of us are in each other. I'm trying to loosen up and avoid being too academic-looking.' After I told her that the painting had, for me, the impact of a cinema screen, Saville mentioned that she was 'a massive filmgoer'. 'I go to the London Film Festival now and watch lots of good movies in the middle of the night. I can work until four a.m., so I'm a night person.'

Tracey Emin views nocturnal experience in a more alarming way. When I visited her studio, a large amount of space had been given to a formidable iron-frame Victorian bed that would serve as the centrepiece of her upcoming show in New York. Urgent messages had been applied to its pillows, blankets and sheets, the words charged with highly distressed feelings. 'I'm petrified of the dark,' Emin revealed. 'I've always been intensely frightened of it, like a phobia. I still have terrible nightmares.'

Emin has never been afraid to explore and disclose the darkest aspects of her consciousness. She even invited me to scrutinize a plaster cast of her 'death mask', which she intended to exhibit in a gold version at her New York show. 'People have said they've never seen anything more alive,' she told me with an ironic grin. But Emin herself does not view mortality as in any way laughable. She also explained that some of her current work was focused on her father. 'My dad is eighty-two,' she said, 'and I'm really scared about him dying. I made these films in Cyprus of him waving to me. So when my dad dies, I'll have all these films of him waving.'

As it happened, I interviewed Sarah Lucas in the same month as my visit to Emin. At an early stage in their careers they had worked closely together, but Lucas revealed that their friendship had now come to an end. She smoked profusely, telling me: 'I do intend to give up, but I've smoked since I was nine.' An enormous self-portrait made from filter cigarettes could be seen in her study, its playfulness darkened by a warning. 'There's a sense of death in my work,' Lucas said. 'The early things are quite dejected, and I do find that getting older is, in general, much tougher than I imagined. Life makes less and less sense. You can already begin to see it's going to get more frightening. When you're young, you have no notion of how short your time will be.' When her father died at the age of sixty-four, his loss was for Lucas 'a devastating experience. I like to be alone, but everyone is scared of being old and getting to the stage where you start losing your friends.'

The stimulating company of her friends was enormously important to Lucas, and she had even turned down an invitation to be placed on the Turner Prize shortlist because of the threat it could pose to friendships. 'I think it's a lot of aggravation for very little. I would hate it, being pitted against my friends. I hate the whole circus.' Lucas was convinced that all the publicity surrounding the prize nourished the UK's preoccupation with celebrity. 'I love Berlin partly because my good gang of friends there don't have this stupid interest in personal life,' she said. 'I find it really oppressive.'

Sam Taylor-Wood revealed at the outset of our interview that she did not like telling journalists her own feelings about life and work. When I visited her enormous East London studio in 2004, she was still an artist and had not yet become the film director Sam Taylor-Johnson. She surprised me by disclosing that in her opinion, 'being interviewed is like having root-canal treatment. I just want to hit some of the people who come and see me. They ask such insensitive questions, like a thud in the gut, to do with my illness. Sometimes I feel too open.'

I could see why she might be reluctant to discuss her experience of cancer, which began when she was twenty-nine years old. Although she had recovered her health, it was a truly shocking ordeal. But during our conversation she wanted to share her memories of it, explaining, 'It's important for me to talk about cancer. When I had it, there was no one willing to discuss their experiences as a patient, because it's a fucking tough thing to go through. But if I can help other people, by showing them you can conquer it and survive, I will.' She felt immensely stimulated by the new studio, a converted stable. And her energy was self-evident: 'I'm much more prolific than I was: this is a place to work hard and think in. You can breathe more. It's quite calming, and brought about a phenomenal change in my life.'

Annette Messager likewise has unforgettable memories of the time she spent in hospital. In her case, they go back to childhood experiences when 'people were X-rayed and spoke only about the body. I like all the things inside me!' Hence her long-term involvement with 'the body and books of anatomy'. When I met her at the Hayward Gallery preparing for a major London exhibition, Messager was intent on recreating part of a spectacular and highly disturbing installation that won the Golden Lion Award at the 2005 Venice Biennale. While there, I had seen lengthy queues of visitors eagerly waiting to visit this work. She was the first woman artist ever selected to represent France at the Biennale, and told me that her intensely dramatic Hayward show would contain 'a red curtain, and Pinocchio has become human. There is some kind of birth, with a lot of blood and inside plenty of organic elements and wind. You see, Pinocchio was eaten by a whale.'

When I asked her to speculate about the origins of her long-lasting obsessions, she exclaimed: 'Ah, Dr Freud! It's difficult to say, but I compare Pinocchio to an artist who wants to travel and be free. When young I didn't ever want to work in an office.' Nor did Messager yearn to stay in Berck-sur-Mer, the town near Boulogne where she spent her childhood.

Eva Rothschild grew up in Ireland, and although now happily based in London, she told me that she thought about going back to her native country 'every week. I had a very secure childhood in a happy family, and our house was near the sea in Dún Laoghaire near Dublin.' She misses the sea: 'It gives you a sense of focus, and when you go outdoors it's like a compass....Having a good place does affect your work.'

Rothschild showed me a sculpture called *Women of the World* in which seven ball forms balanced perilously on top of one another. When I commented on its acute sense of precariousness, she smiled and said: 'I'm happy about that. It's an improbable physicality, almost like being on a tightrope. It could fall apart, like the Leaning Tower of Pisa.' Acutely aware of ever-worsening global instability, Rothschild mentioned that she had recently attended a climate change demonstration where 'it felt overwhelmingly bad' because 'there were far too many police'.

When I interviewed Cornelia Parker in 2009 she expressed similar concerns, declaring that 'the sense of the apocalyptic' in her work was now focused on climate emergency across the planet. It filled her with 'terror and fear. I've been around enough scientists who are at the cutting edge to realize that it's much more serious than people think. We could be seeing the extinction of the species.' In response, Parker exhibited at the Royal Academy a work called *Heart of Darkness*, its name taken from the novel by Joseph Conrad. 'My piece contains the burnt remains from a forest in Florida,' she told me.

Her voice filled with emotion, Parker described how 'As an artist, I feel powerless in some ways and vocal in other ways. When you've got kids of your own, the enormity of it all seems even more staggering. I've not thought about much else for the last few years. We are the first species to know that we are becoming extinct, but we're not doing enough about it.' Even if Parker still felt 'quite ambivalent about what artists can do', she was adamant that 'creativity on every possible level is what will get us out of this shit'.

I interviewed Sonia Boyce at the resplendent Piccadilly headquarters of the Royal Academy, in the lofty and luminous Academicians' Room – a setting far removed from the surroundings in which she spent her childhood. Boyce's mother and father were immigrants from Barbados and Guyana respectively and Boyce became, in her words, 'aware of racism from a very, very young age'. She would later become the first Black British woman artist to have her work purchased by the Tate, but growing up near Brick Lane in London's East End was often extremely tough.

By the time she made her first visit to Barbados, at the age of twenty-seven, Boyce had become actively involved with the Black Art Movement. She was delighted in particular by carnival culture, and loved the exuberant moments when 'Folk figures would suddenly appear at events, and everyone accepted them. I was amazed! Why is nobody batting an eyelid, I wondered.' Later in her ceaselessly inventive, prolific and multifaceted career, Boyce made a major two-screen video piece called *Crop Over*, named after the Barbados carnival. Some scenes rejoice in the spectacular vivacity of carnival performers, who even invade a grand mansion once inhabited by members of the shamelessly lavish white Caribbean plantocracy. Boyce juxtaposes them with poignant sequences shot at Harewood House in Yorkshire, where all the colossal wealth derived from the family's involvement in Barbados during the 18th century. A lone carnival figure makes his way round the immense estate, soberly meditating on the deplorable origins of Harewood's splendour.

While growing up in a small house outside Delhi adorned with paintings, Anish Kapoor became aware of ancient history. He remembers enthralling family trips to explore great Indian temples where architecture and sculpture combine in exuberant harmony. When I first interviewed him in the 1980s, he also vividly recalled his sense of fear and wonder as a boy when a pair of cobras appeared in his family's back garden. Anxious to get rid of them, Kapoor's parents hired a snake charmer, who promptly 'made a search of the garden. When he had decided where he thought the cobras might be, he placed some bowls of milk around the spot. He then got out his flute and began to play. He played all day, trance-like. Well, snakes can't hear so he also did a sort of dance, tapping his foot on the ground so that the snakes could feel the vibrations. Eventually the snakes came up out of the undergrowth towards the bowls of milk, and he was quick enough to be able to catch them without getting bitten. There was a mystical kind of communication between this very simple person and these vicious animals. India is full of things like that.'

When Kapoor later came across the work of Joseph Beuys, who saw the artist as a shaman-like figure, he immediately felt in sympathy with such a view. I once spent a whole afternoon listening to Beuys after he installed his final, intensely memorable exhibition at the Anthony d'Offay Gallery in London. He was already very ill, yet remained irrepressibly committed to the importance of talking about his limitless hopes for art. The television camera crew who were with me carried on recording his voice long after their supply of film ran out, but nothing of that mesmerizing session has been preserved in the archive. The complete, unaccountable disappearance of Beuys's eloquent words makes me even more glad that so many of my other encounters with artists were saved, and can now be published here. They affirm, in all their stimulating diversity, the fundamental reason why art matters so much to the men and women who produce it.

Pablo Picasso

1965

By an astounding piece of luck, the first artist I ever met was Pablo Picasso. It happened way back in 1965. At that time, nobody had heard of the phrase 'gap year', but I certainly made good use of the fallow months leading up to my first term at Cambridge. After working on a building site and in a brewery, I saved enough to set off with some adventurous teenage mates on an overland trip to Morocco. We travelled in a battered old Bedford van, and after reaching Marrakesh decided to head for the Côte d'Azur. Arriving at Cannes, we ran out of money. So I struggled to earn a precarious living, first as a disastrous waiter and then by drawing portraits of tourists down by the harbour in the old quarter.

That is why, one warm and lazy lunchtime, I was carrying an ample sketchpad when my school friend Tim Curry nudged me excitedly and said: 'Look, isn't that Picasso over there?' I laughed, imagining he was merely pulling my leg. But he pointed at a nearby cafe table out in the summer sunshine, where a short, powerfully built and deeply tanned man sat with some companions. I recognized him at once. Picasso proved easy to identify from a thousand photographs, and so was his wife Jacqueline. They must have driven down for lunch from their villa outside Mougins, high in the hills above Cannes. Gazing at him from a distance, I marvelled at how spry and energetic this irrepressible octogenarian looked in his summer shirt boldly patterned with blue and white stripes. Although he and Jacqueline were accompanied by a French couple, as well as an extravagantly attired American lady studded with large jewels, Picasso did not seem very aware of them. He behaved as if he was alone, staring out gravely towards the sea, sky and Mediterranean light.

'Well, what are you going to do about it?' said Tim. I shrugged, feeling far too shy to go and introduce myself to this man I had revered for so long. But Tim, showing the persistence that would later land him the plum role of Frank-N-Furter in *The Rocky Horror Show*, pointed out that I would never have such an extraordinary opportunity again. 'Why don't you ask him for his autograph or something?' he said, gesturing at my sketchpad. The sheer effrontery of his suggestion must have made me laugh. At any rate, I began to relax a little and entertain the possibility of taking Tim's advice. But I will never quite understand how I managed to propel my eighteen-year-old body in the direction of Picasso's table.

Once there I introduced myself, cursing my inadequate command of French. But the American lady, who called Picasso 'the Maestro' and looked like the wealthy trustee of a grand New York museum, acted as our interpreter. So I was able to tell Picasso how much I loved art, how I intended to study it at Cambridge, how I drew incessantly, how his work enthralled me and how gratified I had felt when, quite recently, he sold his convulsive painting of *The Three Dancers* to the Tate for a very reasonable price. He asked the questions and I provided answers, so I didn't learn much about what Picasso was up to in 1965. But he must have felt genially disposed towards this eager young student and was prepared, for a while at least, to humour me. He even grinned when I asked him for his autograph.

There was no reason why Picasso should have been willing to interrupt his meal and grant my presumptuous request. After all, he had by this time become a fairly reclusive figure who spent most of his time working at his villa. But he gave me a generous nod. Nervously handing over my sketchpad and black pen, I watched him appraise the size of the page and then, with phenomenal speed, write his surname along the top. Fortunately, the sheet was large enough to tempt him further. As if unable to resist the inviting blankness offered by the space beneath his signature, he drew with an exuberant flourish right across this expanse of whiteness. For years I saw his high-spirited, billowing forms as a purely abstract image. But Picasso's art, even at its least representational, was usually anchored in observed reality. So the high-spirited curves may refer to a cloud, the wind-rippled water or the shape of Cannes harbour itself, stretching away from his lunchtime vantage.

Delighted with my acquisition, I thanked Picasso and took the sketchpad back to the harbour, where we had been given a boat-painting job. Tim inspected the artist's expansive signature. To my astonishment, he said: 'Is that all?' Feeling indignant, I asked him what the hell he meant. 'I just don't understand why you've come away so soon,' Tim explained. 'I mean, he's still there, the lunch isn't finished yet. You should go back there and draw his portrait.' I was incredulous. 'What? Draw Picasso's portrait? You must be out of your tiny mind.' But Tim remained adamant. 'He obviously likes you, so go and do it, while you still have the chance. In a few minutes, it'll be too late.'

He was right, and I suddenly felt emboldened enough to find out whether Picasso would allow himself to be drawn by an importunate English invader. Approaching his table once more, I began to fear that my reception would be distinctly less cordial this time around. Might it be wiser to stop a few yards off? After all, if I asked his permission and he refused, the whole delicate enterprise would be ruined. So I quietly propped my sketchpad up against an ironwork screen, took out my Conté crayon and started to draw him. Right away, Picasso spotted me. But he did not seem affronted by the bizarre spectacle of this tall, slender adolescent, striving to produce a portrait of the world's most venerated living artist. Instead, he was hugely amused. Within an instant, Picasso the grave and intent gazer transformed himself into an outrageous clown.

He grinned at me, stuck out his tongue, rolled his eyes and brandished both hands in fantastical shapes at either side of his forehead. My embarrassed response made him laugh out loud. He pulled and twisted his malleable features with instinctive gusto.

The distortions became more and more outrageous. I found myself staring, gobsmacked, at an extended sequence of grotesque and hilarious apparitions who might well have strayed from Picasso's most unfettered paintings. His lunch companions were immensely entertained by his performance. So I was tempted to give up the unequal contest and lapse into mirth as well. But the sheer inventiveness of my theatrical 'sitter' seemed tantamount, finally, to a challenge. However obstructive his antics may have been, I felt he was testing my persistence in order, possibly, to find out the true extent of my determination to defy his quicksilver shifts of mood.

I still felt absurd as my hand continued with the struggle to make sense of his ceaseless parade of imbecilic grins, pouts, leers, scowls, winks and sneers. But instead of becoming overwhelmed by Picasso's bravura antics and conceding that there was no point in drawing any longer, I tried to continue. And then, just as I was about to abandon the portrait, he relented. For the last, unforgettable minutes of his mealtime, he gave me the chance to study him without impediment.

It proved profoundly rewarding. I noticed how tough and alert Picasso appeared, still taut and as compact in build as a wrestler. He resembled an athletic sixty-year-old rather than a man who would soon be celebrating his eighty-fourth birthday. Several months later, he underwent a serious operation at the American Hospital in Neuilly. But he showed no sign of incipient illness to me. I marvelled at the youthfulness of his clear black eyes, set with such startling intensity in features remarkably free from the folds of slack flesh encumbering so many elderly faces. The eyes were mesmerizing, and I struggled to capture their forcefulness. Sombre now, Picasso seemed to devour everything he scrutinized. His prodigious appetite for looking made him stare far longer, and with a great deal more hungry concentration, than anyone I have ever encountered, before or since.

After fastening themselves with a fierce directness on whatever he chose to study, his eyes did not waver or blink until he decided to train his gaze elsewhere. Most of us are far less disciplined about the way we look randomly around, yet Picasso surveyed his surroundings with magisterial deliberation. He stared at his chosen subjects with intense watchfulness, making me appreciate just how completely focused his way of seeing really was. I also recall thinking that he seemed curiously removed and isolated, even though there was plenty of company nearby. His engaging show of buffoonery, which had both entertained and flummoxed me for a while, could not disguise an underlying gravity of mood. Content to let Jacqueline and their friends do most of the talking, he sat in a very private, absorbed silence which enabled him to pursue his own interests undisturbed.

Eventually, the lunch was over before I had completed my drawing. Conscious above all of its inadequacy, I closed the sketchpad. But the American lady beckoned me over. 'Aren't you going to show the Maestro your portrait?' she asked with a saccharine smile.

'To be honest, I'd rather not,' I muttered with embarrassment. The thought of letting Picasso see my tentative efforts appalled me, but he leaned over and talked to the bejewelled matron.

She turned back to me with a self-righteous expression and declared: 'The Maestro says he wants to see your drawing.' Realizing now that there was no alternative, I handed it over apprehensively.

To my astonishment and relief, Picasso did not snigger at the faltering image on the page. Nor did he dismiss it with a polite, impatient wave. Instead, he appraised my drawing with his voracious black eyes and gave it a generous nod of approval. Then he said something to our interpreter. She beamed at me before triumphantly announcing: 'The Maestro says he wants to do *your* portrait!'

I couldn't believe it. The whole event took on a weird, dreamlike quality as I passed over my Conté crayon to Picasso. How long would he need to do the drawing, and might he take outrageous liberties by asking me to pose upside down or take all my clothes off? I should not have worried. Within a few seconds, Picasso made some deft and incisive lines below the portrait I had made of him. It happened so swiftly that I could not imagine the outcome would be anything more than a doodle. But when he handed it back, I discovered a fully realized face delineated on the paper with crisp, exhilarating finality.

Since one eye had shifted to the middle of my nose, I looked slightly manic. Picasso must have sensed my mental confusion when I attempted to draw him, and he had the wit to reflect my bewilderment in his portrait. He also gave me a beard, as if to suggest that I reminded him of a shaggy satyr who had stumbled into his life from one of the mythological woodland scenes he often liked to depict. Above all, though, he gave me an excitable smile, summarized in a single vivacious line. Perhaps he saw me as an intruder from another world, peering in at him with the gauche inquisitiveness of a young man astounded to find himself face to face with such a legendary countenance.

At the time, Picasso was increasingly preoccupied with the absurd and painful difference between youth and old age. In March that year, during a sustained bout of inventiveness, he had painted some thirty canvases, obsessively revisiting the theme of the ageing painter and his model. So he may have derived wry amusement from placing my face beneath his on the same page, and aimed at highlighting the disparity between my wide-eyed jauntiness and his ruminative, vigilant features.

I thanked Picasso, and asked him if he would be kind enough to sign the portrait. After he'd had another discussion with the American lady, she reported, 'The Maestro says you already have his signature.' He probably did not want to sign a sheet of paper that also contained my drawing of him. But his reluctance was understandable, and in no sense detracted from the kindness he had shown me. Even now, over fifty years later, I look back and wonder at my good fortune. Meeting Picasso and, more importantly, receiving his attention meant an enormous amount at a formative stage in my life. It made me realize that this most protean and ungraspable of modern artists remained, at heart, a man fired by an exuberant love of mark-making. Today, when I view the sheet with the two portraits, I am impressed by the salutary contrast between my stumbling draughtsmanship and the joyful, effortless virtuosity of the face outlined below. Its high spirits sum up the exhilaration I felt when Picasso bestowed on me this unexpected, miraculous gift.

Henry Moore

May 1981

After catching the train from London to Bishop's Stortford station, I asked a taxi driver to take me to Perry Green. 'Henry Moore?' he said immediately, as if nobody else existed in the entire area. The sculptor was clearly as much of a landmark as Stonehenge. And when we arrived, after a brief run through remarkably green countryside, the driver told me to walk straight in through Moore's porch door without even bothering to knock. I was met by an elderly lady who led me to a large conservatory extension at the back. It looked out over fields where unusually white sheep were grazing. The interminable rain that month meant the grass and foliage everywhere had taken on an intensified depth and richness of colour.

When Moore came in, I was surprised by how small he seemed. His photographs, often showing him in monumental poses beside even more immense sculpture, deceptively suggested an imposing figure. But old age had clearly taken its toll on his physique. Supported by a stick and wearing glasses that appeared slightly too large for his face, he looked shrunken and quite frail. He wore a cardigan with a prominent blue tie: an odd combination of informality and dressing up for visitors.

The sheer extent of Henry Moore's international fame could easily make him seem over-celebrated and impossibly grand. Only first-hand contact with the man himself might dispel such a view, so I was glad that he had now given me the opportunity to visit him. Researching my book *Art Beyond the Gallery*, I had written to Moore about a large, breakthrough carving he had made as a young man in the late 1920s for the Underground Electric Railways headquarters at Westminster. To my astonishment, he had phoned early the next day and, with disarming friendliness, offered to show me some preparatory drawings for the sculpture at his Hertfordshire home.

Now, sure enough, he proved true to his word. Another grey-haired and hospitable secretary, whom Moore called Mrs Tinsley, bustled in with his substantial 1928 sketchbook and we sat down to talk. I had been expecting a brief session with a man who would regard my visit merely as a routine exercise. After all, how many curators, writers and collectors must he have received here over the years? But throughout our surprisingly lengthy conversation, Moore expressed himself with tremendous gusto and conviction. Almost without my bidding, he started to reminisce about how little sculpture he had been able to see during his youth in Yorkshire: before moving to London, a few stone heads in a Gothic church near his home were almost the only good carvings he had come across. What a treasure-house the metropolis must have seemed, and how avidly he would have seized on sculpture of all eras in its museums!

While Moore was talking, his arms and hands never stopped moving. Everything he said to me was backed up by restless physical gestures – not bombastic but unexpectedly gentle, even feminine. He clearly felt his thoughts very directly within his own body. And once, when emphasizing how 'central' the umbilical area was in his own work, he clutched at the protruding flesh around his stomach to drive the point home. I was impressed by the sense that everything he said *mattered* a great deal to him. When I asked why the umbilical area was so important, he answered simply and directly: 'Because that's where we were attached to our mothers.'

By the time we got around to looking at his sketchbook, I found myself utterly absorbed. Ten years earlier, I would have resisted the whole notion of visiting such a venerated figure, let alone being impressed by him. He would have seemed too much of a predictable, overbearing inevitability. But now I found that, despite all the hyperbole surrounding his name, it was possible to discover Moore all over again. He turned out to be delightfully straightforward, still the no-nonsense Northerner who would abhor any pretentious talk about his art.

He became especially animated and eloquent when I asked him whether the many sketches of reclining women in his 1928 sketchbook had marked the beginning of his obsession with this motif. He replied that it might have done, but then launched into a vigorous explanation of how all his work was wholly involved with the human figure, how that was the basis of all our experience, our sense of scale and touch, and how the reclining body in particular offered a sculptor so many inexhaustible possibilities and variations – far more than, say, a seated figure. I warmed to the passion in this stubborn octogenarian, so eager and animated despite his obvious fragility.

I mentioned Jacob Epstein's Strand statues as the kind of architectural sculpture Moore would have known when starting his own carving for the Underground Electric Railways building. In response to this he became very vehement about the Royal Academy's refusal to back Epstein in his attempt to stop the mutilation of the Strand figures during the 1930s. 'I'll never forgive them for that,' he said, so many decades after the event, 'nor for the things that Alfred Munnings said about my work. He used to carry a photograph of my Northampton *Madonna and Child* around in his pocket, and show it to people in order to mock it. That's why I'll never exhibit at the Academy. Hugh Casson, the current president, is far more enlightened, but would one ever forgive Hitler in view of what he once did? Fascism may have disappeared on the surface, but what brought it into being will never go away.'

Concentrating on the sketchbook, he stared carefully at each page before I turned it over. The commission for his *West Wind* carving – far and away the finest of all the flying figures on the building – had nearly been given to someone else, for when thirty-year-old Moore was approached by the architect Charles Holden (apparently at the urging of Epstein, who produced two powerful seated images of *Night* and *Day* lower down the facade), he viewed the invitation with considerable scepticism. He was gratified by it, of course, and naturally challenged by the prospect of carving a figure eight feet in length, a great deal larger than anything he had tackled before. And he also appreciated that fact that 'Epstein was very good to me: I'd already been round to his studio a few times.' But the drawback, as he explained to me during the interview, had been that 'I resented the idea that architecture was "the mother of all the arts". In the Renaissance period it was very different, because the sculptors were also the architects.' Moore instinctively reacted against any proposal that threatened to put sculpture in a subordinate relationship to architecture, especially when Holden told him that the carving would be placed all the way up on the seventh floor. Holden presumably imagined that positioning *West Wind* so high above the street would intensify its airborne character. The completed building, a white monolith in Portland stone rearing proudly above the jumble of narrow streets nearby, was hailed by one reviewer as 'A Cathedral of Modernity'. But most passers-by have probably never noticed *West Wind* and the other flying figures positioned about 80 feet from the pavement.

Looking back on the project, Moore wryly told me, 'Architects work things out from plans, and the idea may well look good on the drawing board.' He also recalled that the thought of carving a panel in relief had held no great pleasure for him. In this respect he differed greatly from Eric Gill, who was commissioned to carve three other flying figures on the same facade. 'Gill enjoyed making reliefs, you know,' Moore said. 'He was a great craftsman, and so far as I could tell, he liked doing carvings for buildings.' But Holden, sensing Moore's doubts, eventually won him round. 'He talked to me like a father,' Moore remembered, 'and he was very nice to me. He said: "You're just frightened of doing a carving bigger than anything you've done before!" So I had to accept the challenge.' This direct, friendly contact, so different from the usual strained and mistrustful relationship between architect and sculptor in the 20th century, helped to allay Moore's fears. He realized that Holden had also been the architect of the Strand building, where Epstein's damaged figures had once played such an outstanding role. And after

Moore made up his mind to do the Underground Electric Railways carving, he went about his task with accelerating enthusiasm and dedication. The exceptional abundance of preparatory drawings in the 1928 sketchbook reflects the eagerness with which he eventually approached the commission: the dozens of figures testify to his excitement at having found a theme that yielded such limitless possibilities.

Since Moore's first idea had been a recumbent figure, the Holden commission precipitated him into a profound exploration of a subject that would remain supremely important for the rest of his life. He recalled, 'Holden didn't in any way specify how the figure should be done, beyond giving me the "wind" theme, the carving's size and direction, and telling me it would be seen from below.' There was no precedent in Moore's work for the sudden proliferation of recumbent figure sketches he produced in 1928, when the theme finally began to dominate his imagination. It was extraordinary to leaf through the pages of this fifty-three-year-old volume with the man who had made the drawings sitting beside me, explaining how the female body gradually became more airborne and assumed the position seen in the carving. When the moment came, Moore felt free to abandon the reclining pose; he was, after all, supposed to be carving a personification of the west wind and, as he pointed out to me with a grin, 'a reclining figure might look as if the wind had dropped'.

His passion for monumental solidity was surely the principal reason why these sketches had clung to the notion of repose for so long. To depict a figure in flight was to run the risk of losing the massive, earthbound bulk Moore favoured, and at this stage he had felt no particular compunction to interpret *West Wind* as a body in motion. 'I didn't bother very much about which particular wind it was,' he admitted. 'After all, how can you tell what a north or a south wind should look like?'

Only once in the sketchbook was there a sign that he was concerned with the specific mythological identity of the subject Holden had given him. At the top of one page, Moore had noted that the north and east winds were male and the other two female. A couple of sheets showed how he had drawn swift ink studies of a woman in repose and then covered them with loosely applied green chalk marks, playing around the limbs and rising above her like gusts of air. But this was essentially a pictorial device, and he knew only too well that it could not be translated into convincing sculptural terms. Recalling his dilemma, he explained: 'In my drawings for the relief I was terrified of going too far towards movement, because I don't think that carving is much good at motion – it's best at static, weighty, monumental repose. If you model in clay, movement is far more feasible.'

In the end, as Moore reminded me, it was Michelangelo who had helped him to define a wholly airborne woman with conviction. During a trip to Italy in 1924, 'I had been very impressed by the flying figures in *The Last Judgment*, on the end wall of the Sistine Chapel.' But he also emphasized that he was indebted to a great Toltec-Maya Chacmool figure, executed in Mexico during the 11th and 12th centuries, which he had first encountered in early 1920s London. As the drawings reveal, nothing could have been more hard-fought than Moore's struggle to resolve the opposition between his need to give *West Wind* sufficient buoyancy and his equally strong desire to retain the plastic significance he favoured in all his sculpture.

Nor were his troubles at an end when he eventually felt ready to tackle the carving itself. The enormous three-part slab of Portland stone was delivered to his studio at the Royal College of Art. 'I did the roughing-out there,' he recalled, 'and it looked so vast that when my future wife, Irina, came in to see my works it was one of the things which bowled her over. Then, when it was nearly finished, we put it up on the building. I completed the carving on a scaffolding platform where there was a space of only about three feet to stand on, and at first I was alarmed. It was so high up. But when I got back down and looked at it from the ground, I realized that the figure's navel couldn't be seen properly. This was terrible, because the umbilical cord is absolutely central to me. By this time the scaffolding had been dismantled so I went up again in a cradle, winching it up myself from side to side until I reached the carving. But once there, I found I couldn't carve properly: every time I struck a blow, the cradle shot back from the figure. So in the end I got out some charcoal and shaded the navel in. I knew that it would wash off eventually, and that the navel would by then have darkened with London grime and become prominent enough. The cradle zig-zagged all over the place on the return journey as well. Epstein watched me, and after I'd come down he said: "I wouldn't have done that for all the money in the world."'

Epstein's far more prominent carvings for the building were positioned directly above two doorways – a privileged position that aroused bitterness among the other sculptors. Moore remembered 'meeting Gill at the building one day, and he nudged me as we walked side by side past Epstein's hut and said: "There's the *great artist*." He was a bit jealous, I think.' For his part, Moore thought at the time of our conversation that producing the *West Wind* relief had, in the end, been a 'valuable experience' despite the understandable misgivings he had felt at the outset. Working on an unprecedently large scale, he had pushed his own fast-developing abilities to a new extreme. The certainty he gained from working on the Underground project contributed to the resounding finality of his great Leeds *Reclining Figure* a year later, and helped give him the confidence to work on major public schemes.

Determined never again to supply reliefs for buildings, he turned down Holden's later invitation to carve eight seated stone figures on the facade of his Senate House for London University. But Moore remained ready, time and again, to execute work in the round for sites positioned near buildings as various as Serge Chermayeff's house in Sussex and the UNESCO headquarters in Paris. They all, in their distinctive ways, satisfied the requirements of a man who told me, 'When an architect simply wants to fill a space he thinks is too empty, the sculpture becomes a decorative thing. I think you've got to have the sense of meeting a sculpture face to face.'

Moore's memory seemed very clear. He took particular pleasure in the faithfulness of a newly published facsimile edition of the 1928 sketchbook; he even gave me a copy of it, 'as a souvenir of your visit'. Although our session had come to an end, he asked me if there was anything else I needed to enquire about. I was tempted to say that I would be happy to talk all day, but Moore had already made clear that he intended to work that afternoon, so it seemed wrong to presume any further. After all, he had told me earlier that he hadn't travelled to the recent opening of his Madrid exhibition 'because my back is bad, and besides, doing my own work is the important thing'. Maybe he suspected that time, for him, was fast running out. Although he still appeared so alert and energetic in spirit, his body did seem to be giving up on him.

Travelling home, I thought appreciatively about the hours Moore had set aside and the close attention he had paid to our conversation. I also wondered, looking through the cab window, why he had chosen to live in a place with such notably flat terrain when his sculpture implied that he favoured swollen, craggy forms. Maybe he found the low-lying landscape around Perry Green a relief, after giving shape to all that mountainous abundance.

Ian Hamilton Finlay

October 1984

On 4 February 1983, one of the most bizarre events in the history of Scottish culture was acted out in a remote and beautiful Lanarkshire garden called Stonypath. Sheriff Officer Sandy Walker of Strathclyde Regional Council drove his way up a bumpy farm track to claim the unpaid rates on an outbuilding he regarded as a commercial art gallery. But its owner and creator, the internationally respected artist and poet Ian Hamilton Finlay, had other ideas. He argued that the outbuilding was a temple – an integral part of a four-acre garden also known as Little Sparta, which had been transformed into an elaborate work of art by the carvings, plants, flowers and lakes he and his wife had carefully installed there.

Finlay was a fiercely independent man who admired the French Revolution and the rebellious example of Louis de Saint-Just. So when Sheriff Walker arrived, Finlay felt ready for him. Accompanied by a trusty group of 'Saint-Just Vigilantes', he thwarted all the Sheriff's attempts to seize carvings from the Temple. Outflanked by Finlay's ingenious minefields, hooded lookouts and a mock Panzer tank with its gun barrel trained on 'Checkpoint Sandy', the Sheriff beat a bewildered retreat.

Even so, when I talked to Finlay the following year in the kitchen of the ramshackle Stonypath farmhouse, he was under no illusion about the power of his opponent. 'Terror, a main ingredient of the French Revolution, was also a very real ingredient on this day,' he said with quiet defiance, 'and I don't think there was a Saint-Just Vigilante present who didn't expect to be in prison by evening. I hoped that the art would prevail, as it were, and it wouldn't come to that. But it was very, very possible, throughout the day, that things would go badly wrong.'

When I asked him why, Finlay wrapped a tartan rug around himself and became even more intense: 'At the moment when the Sheriff Officer left Little Sparta, and then found his car blocked so that he had to set off to walk to the region – six miles or whatever it was – nobody knew whether he would come back with a few police or five hundred armed police. And there was a very real feeling that if it had been armed police, nobody would have minded going into that other dimension – it really was a quite extraordinary sort of day. I feel that only those who were there, and who obviously still have very, very vivid memories of it, realize just how extraordinary it was.'

Since the epic events of that freezing February day, Finlay's battle with the philistines of Strathclyde had become even more bitter. Officers of the council did eventually seize artworks from the Temple at the centre of the dispute, intending to sell them to raise enough money to pay the outstanding rates demand. But the month before we met, the Scottish Arts Council had intervened in the struggle, announcing that they had accepted Finlay's side of the argument. Accordingly, they asked Strathclyde Region to delay any further action, asserting that Finlay had been quite right to describe the outbuilding as a garden temple.

Because the tussle between Finlay and Strathclyde started several years earlier, it had by this point assumed the proportions of a legend. Finlay's sturdy defence of an artist's rights and his outspoken condemnation of bureaucratic intolerance had made him a heroic figure. He had come to personify the individual's need to defend cultural freedom against the faceless forces of oppression. And his achievement took on an even greater significance in light of the fact that Stonypath had been created by Finlay and his wife, Sue, with minimal resources. Although the southern slopes of the

Pentland Hills are exposed to near-glacial weather in winter, the garden has flourished and developed enormously since the Finlays settled there in 1966.

What was it about Stonypath that appealed to them when they first moved in? 'Nothing attracted us to it,' Finlay told me wryly, 'except the fact that we were given it and it had a running cold-water tap.' He laughs. 'That was the basic attraction, and we began the garden really just because the ground was there and represented a possibility. But we didn't begin with any idea at all of having a garden that anybody would visit, or that it would become in any way known or a sort of serious enterprise of any kind. We knew nothing whatever about plants or gardening or anything. I suppose it began about twelve or fifteen years ago. Gardening was much less widely known about in those days and there were far fewer books on gardens of the past. It was very, very difficult to find out how things should be done. If you take for instance the question of siting inscriptions – which seems in a way quite simple – I didn't know how to do it. I thought the letter carvers would know, but they knew nothing about it at all. No one knew anything about it. I had the feeling that there must be someone I could write a letter to, you know, saying how do you do it?' More laughter. 'But it had been completely forgotten about, and this is one of the strange facts about gardening, that virtually the whole basis of the Western tradition has been forgotten.' Suddenly, Finlay grew vehement. 'The outcome is that there are these monstrosities called sculpture parks, which got plonked down on the landscape. And nobody remembers *anything* about the great English 18th-century gardens, which knew *perfectly* how to put art in relation to nature in the most exquisite manner. All that is *totally* forgotten about, as if it had never existed.'

Although Finlay continued to develop his garden, it was already offering visitors a rich and complex experience as they explored its different areas. At the front of the house, an 'English garden' contained a profusion of flowers, a walk paved with slabs inscribed with the names of types of sailing vessels, and a sunken garden featuring a one-word poem. As I walked round the house to the outbuildings, the scale changed from intimacy to grandeur. A small loch appeared, created by the Finlays when they dammed a tiny stream, and on the water were glass fishing floats inscribed with poems. Finlay was fond of using artists' names to evoke the classical images of Arcadia that fed his imagination; by the loch, called the Upper Pool, I found a stone tablet bearing the words '*See* Poussin, *Hear* Lorrain'. As the inscription suggested, the surrounding landscape had been shaped to recall the paintings of both Nicolas Poussin and his contemporary Claude Lorrain.

But perhaps the heart of Stonypath's meaning was located in the Garden Temple itself. As requested, I took off my shoes and put on soft slippers before entering, and once inside a spirit of stern dedication soon became apparent. Carvings on plinths referred to the French Revolution in general and Saint-Just in particular.

I asked Finlay why the revolutionary spirit was given such focal importance in the Temple, and his reply was unequivocal: 'In the French Revolution, one has the spectacle of men who believed that there was a direct connection between thought and action, that thought led to action, and that thought had implicit in it the capacity to become actualized. And that is crucial to my whole way of thinking and to the extraordinary problems in our own culture, where all faith in action has been lost and thought is therefore completely academic. What we see in our own culture is men who are completely given over to irony, which is a kind of wasting disease leading rapidly to satire and then to absolute nullity. In the French Revolution, there's this marvellous absence of irony. There are people absolutely committed to thought and thence to action. Part of the point of this is to make it impossible for visitors to come here merely as an afternoon's outing. I wanted to make a situation where the garden couldn't be treated as just an idle destination of a car drive – a fate to which gardens are only too obviously open. And I wanted through the whole Temple to have a kind of extremism manifest, so that there is no mistake about what is going on and no evasion. People would really have to face the fact that culture is not just a matter of aesthetics.'

Did Finlay therefore see the Temple, and indeed the whole garden, as a kind of challenge to the viewer? 'Yes,' he replied without hesitation. 'In terms of our present-day culture it couldn't be other than a challenge to the viewer. But it would also have to be said, in fairness, that while people may feel it's a challenge, they don't usually react in a hostile way. Most of the visitors who come to the garden and the Temple enjoy it, in whatever sense one would understand the word *enjoy*.'

All over the garden, Finlay proved adept at suddenly concentrating my attention on objects fused with the surroundings they inhabited. One ornamental stone bore the phrase 'Bring Back the Birch', and I realized that Finlay had wittily transformed an angry slogan about corporal punishment into a gentle plea for ecological renewal. Standing by the stone in his windswept garden, he laconically described visitors' reactions to this admirably subversive inscription: 'When people first see it, if they're familiar with Tory party policy so to speak, they immediately identify it as a party catchphrase and usually they laugh. But then an interesting thing happens. When they've come to the garden several times, because of the setting and the way the work is realized in pure Roman form, it gradually changes for them. It ends up becoming a completely serious, elegiac inscription, from which the humour has all gone. And I think for these people, if they encountered it in a newspaper, they would really feel: "Goodness me, they're quoting one of Finlay's garden poems."' He smiled, mischievously and infectiously.

As we continued to explore, I noticed further references to artists Finlay particularly admired. In particular I was impressed by the letters 'AD' – the initials of Albrecht Dürer. They rested within an almost uncannily accurate reconstruction of Dürer's celebrated watercolour *The Great Piece of Turf*. Why, I asked Finlay, had he and Sue used artists' names so much throughout Stonypath? 'I just want to make, in terms of our culture, something explicit that is overlooked,' he explained. 'One does not see landscape or a garden as an individual, but in terms of a culture, and it's just a question of whether one sees it in terms of a broad culture, a wide culture, or in terms of a minimized fashionable culture. But certainly the idea that one sees nature in some pure way as an individual is just nonsense.'

Finlay's latest addition to the garden was a grotto dedicated to the legend of Dido and Aeneas. A single stroke of lightning carved outside the circular building signified the storm that drove Dido and her companion to take shelter. Finlay had constructed niches inside, containing busts of both the lovers. Pausing in the grotto, he mused on Little Sparta. 'As a poet, I believe in action as a mode of the lyrical,' he said. 'Saint-Just is my great hero, and Saint-Just is to me the neoclassical politician but also the neoclassical poet. But he is the poet of action, who believed in the possibilities of action: doing things, actualizing, changing. And this is what our culture has lost, because it's ceased to be serious. Culture is just an aspect of entertainment, and there's also the fact that I continually harp on, in a rather hopeless way, that everything has become completely secularized.'

How, I wondered, would he sum up the overall significance of the garden? 'It does show that one can actually change a part of the world,' he said, 'that one gets this actual experience and that this is therefore a model of revolution. I feel that the garden is a very important political manifestation, and that it easily passes over into being politics. Of course, this has happened with a lot of the great gardens of the past. In the case of our own garden, the funny thing is that all this came about in the war with the region. And what had seemed merely sort of whimsical concepts became actualized. It was clear that the garden really did represent a challenge to the surrounding culture. And it's very important to see that actualizing the thing is *far* different from having it just as a concept in a notebook.'

Helen Frankenthaler

June 1986

The Savoy Hotel is no stranger to artists: Claude Monet stayed in a fifth-floor room there for three substantial periods between 1899 and 1901, while painting his fog-bound views of dissolving London. But when I visited Helen Frankenthaler there, she at first seemed preoccupied and withdrawn. Perhaps she was distracted by the river revealed through her window. After all, it had captivated Monet when he embarked on his extended series of Thames paintings. And water had likewise played an important part in the picture that established Frankenthaler's own precocious reputation.

In 1952, at the age of only twenty-three, she had exhibited a large, freely handled canvas called *Mountains and Sea*. Evoking the Nova Scotia countryside she had been visiting that summer, the painting's radiant washes of thinly applied colour float in veils of salmon pink, sky blue and pale green. It is a rapturous composition, conveying a passionate identification with the natural scenes that inspired her. 'I know the landscapes were in my arms when I did it,' she said afterwards, equating her own body with the terrain in terms that recalled another 20th-century woman, Barbara Hepworth, who summed up her experience of St Ives by declaring, 'I myself am cradled in the anatomy of the landscape.'

All the same, *Mountains and Sea* seemed such an audacious painting that its debt to Nova Scotia was overlooked by those who viewed the canvas back in 1952. And when I asked her about its initial reception, Frankenthaler suddenly became animated. 'When I first showed *Mountains and Sea*,' she recalled, 'I think there were about five people who were very excited and puzzled by it and said: "Do more like that." And this, besides myself alone, was the only support. When I did show the picture about a year or two later, one of my best-known and beloved former teachers saw it and said: "My God, she's using a giant paint-rag!"'

Frankenthaler, who had studied at Bennington College in Vermont before briefly attending Hans Hofmann's classes, needed both courage and confidence to ignore such insults and develop the vision defined by *Mountains and Sea*. 'I just plugged along because there was nothing else for me to do,' she said modestly. 'I had to follow what I had to do. And I was very puzzled, in a way, when I first saw it myself. Yes. But I think one evolves, and one's work evolves, and one's dreams evolve, and you become what you become.' Why, I asked, had she been so puzzled by the painting? 'Well, I had made it,' she emphasized with a sense of wonder, 'and aesthetically, historically now when I look back into the 1940s, this picture was clearly the next thing that had to emerge. But when I first did it, the painting was such a breakthrough that I myself had never seen anything quite like what my own right wrist had made. But something else stronger said: "Don't touch it – leave it alone – it's good."' Did it worry her at the time? 'No, it didn't worry me. I just thought, well, what'll I do next?'

It was not long before Frankenthaler found herself widely hailed as a leading exponent of avant-garde American painting. The 'giant paint-rag' accusation was forgotten when Clement Greenberg, the most influential US art critic of his day, placed this daughter of a New York judge at the very forefront of her generation. A champion of the abstract expressionist movement that was making Manhattan painters the focus of international attention, Greenberg saw Frankenthaler's work as an exciting development of ideas pioneered by older artists like Jackson Pollock and Arshile Gorky. Greenberg was impressed, above all, by the sheer visual presence of the flowing, melting expanses of stained acrylic paint that she employed, getting down on her hands and knees to pour it across her canvases and flood them with colour.

These delectable stained washes seemed more or less autonomous in Greenberg's eyes, and his formalist viewpoint discouraged any speculation about possible real-world sources for Frankenthaler's imagery. For many years the critical orthodoxy of modernism continued to stress the abstract character of her work, pointing out that Pollock had influenced her painting and that she, in turn, had inspired Morris Louis to develop the stained colour technique still further. Since that time, however, the references to nature in her work and her ongoing love affair with landscape imagery have become more clearly understood.

Even when she decided, in one of her most exuberant early paintings, to take as a springboard an Eighth Street jukebox bar in New York called Ed Winston's, the result looked more like a tropical garden. Frankenthaler had been attracted to what she called 'the celluloid palm trees and five-and-ten-cent-store Hawaiian decor' at Ed Winston's, rather than the sight of drinkers ensconced in a Manhattan bar.

At the time of our meeting, needing the constant stimulus of the countryside, she was dividing her time between a brownstone in New York and a shingled waterfront house in Fairfield County, Connecticut. It was only thirty miles from the city, and the presence of other houses nearby meant that Frankenthaler did not feel isolated, but her surroundings were sufficiently removed from the metropolitan context to generate in her work a feeling which could be described as arcadian.

Even so, I pointed out in conversation with Frankenthaler that the places stimulating her work were hardly ever acknowledged in the titles she chose for her paintings. Names as particularized as *Sunshapes*, *Hilltown* and *Autumn Farm* were quite rare, and she didn't generally use them to stress her starting point. 'My titles really have several reasons for being there,' she explained. 'Some are desperate moments: somebody will be walking out the door and I say: "This picture's going some place this afternoon – help me!" I'm calling it something because I don't believe in numbers, because I'm not that good at numbers and if I numbered all my work it would be into the hundreds of thousands by now. I think all titles are meaningful and meaningless. But sometimes I think, goodness, that would be a good title for a picture! I have something called a Title List, and if I have a body of work I will search through this list of titles and just apply them. Sometimes it's more specific. I have a general feeling in mind, and it has to do with a scene I've recently experienced, or a place I'm at, or a bridge, literally or symbolically, that I have crossed.'

Did she, I asked, ever paint straight from the motif? 'Oh yes,' she said, 'I have all my life. Yes.' But, I said, what she had just been saying suggested that she preferred to work at one remove. 'Well, I'm essentially an abstract painter, yes, and the subject matter is one of many things that might come after it – including the title.' Which was more important to her as an environment: New York or the Connecticut landscape? 'I think it depends on mood and need. Like anyone else there are times when I long for water and the horizon line, and to be alone in a certain way. There are other moments when I feel I want to experience reality in a different setting, and I need people and sights and another familiar longed-for sensation.'

Frankenthaler's use of the term 'longed-for' seemed revealing and, I thought, surely provided an insight into the nature of her art. Many of her paintings appear to convey a yearning for a golden age, an era of innocence and primal freshness, as if she wanted to make the world new again. Sometimes the feeling of evanescence, of fleeting happiness, is reminiscent of the mood in a *fête champêtre* by Watteau. But Frankenthaler seemed determined, time and again, to make this sense of impermanence into something ordered, lasting and visually incontrovertible. There is a perpetual tug-of-war between the yearning in her work and a hard-headed insistence that the painting is a painting and that's all there is to it. This latter quality must have served her well in the male-dominated world of abstract expressionism. She would have encountered a great deal of patriarchal prejudice at the beginning of her career, especially from painters who regarded women artists primarily as potential girlfriends.

So I suggested to Frankenthaler that the whole question of her achievement as a woman, in an art world presided over by male practitioners, deserved to be discussed. Feminist historians had drawn attention to the difficulties women often experienced in their attempts to be taken seriously as artists, and Frankenthaler's success in overcoming these barriers had been as rare as it was remarkable. Perhaps because her own rise to professional distinction had been so swift, she adopted a notably unsentimental stance whenever anyone asked her about issues of gender. 'It's never been a concern of mine,' she said to me firmly. 'Painting has been a concern. And when people say how brave or unique I was in the early fifties to have the courage to go against or defend or do what I did, I'm always taken aback and feel that I didn't think about it. I am for beautiful painting. If I go to a group show and I see paintings by men, women, Londoners, New Yorkers or whatever, and they really move me, that's the point.' She smiled. 'After that, I might say: "Who did it?" and find out that it's Jane Somebody, or Sir Somebody.'

Did she, I wondered, think there was anything specifically feminine about her work? 'I don't, but I think one's work reflects what one is *in toto*, and that part of what I am is a woman. But I don't think it's any more or less lyrical or soft or hard or anything else than any other good or bad picture.' Pursuing my theme, I put it to Frankenthaler that most of her work seemed to deal with lyrical, even ecstatic emotions, often hedonistic and life-enhancing. I didn't see any great evidence of negative emotions – of fear, for instance, or violence. 'I think it depends on one's aesthetic and one's aesthetic reading of it,' she replied, 'and you probably haven't seen all my work, either. But I know generally what you're referring to.'

Would she, I asked, therefore say that she was concerned, more than anything else, with celebrating her response to the world? 'I don't think about it,' she said. 'And I think a great deal of art that looks a certain way is loaded with perhaps very hard or ugly or depressed or whatever feelings, and might manifest itself as looking like a heavenly spring garden. And it's irrelevant.'

What remained relevant, though, was the inspiration Frankenthaler had provided. When she first decided to make painting her career, there were few women practitioners to whom she could point as convincing proof that art need not remain a male preserve for ever. By the time of our interview, the position was very different. I felt we needed a major retrospective to find out precisely what she had been up to, and only then would her achievement be possible to assess in full. But her stubborn determination to ignore fashion and remain true to an independent course compared very well with all those artists who repeatedly changed styles in a feverish attempt to stay in favour. Frankenthaler disdained that kind of manoeuvring, and her ability to pursue very personal preoccupations was a laudable one.

There will always be room for the single-minded voice, resisting fashionable conventions of the day. And an arcadian vision will continue to seduce us, even if its attainment seems so far beyond our reach in an era haunted by the shadow of *Paradise Lost*.

Jasper Johns

November 1990

His laugh, when it arrived, was surprisingly eruptive. The austere, silver-haired man in the all-grey shirt and suit suddenly became transformed with mirth. His face flushed and the eyes took on an unexpected impishness. It gave the lie to the legend that Jasper Johns was above all aloof – an elusive artist who shied away from interviews.

The first guffaw of our meeting came when his attention was caught by the poster for his 'Drawings Retrospective' at the Hayward Gallery. After scanning the reproduction of his classic 1957 pastel of the American flag – the image with which he is still most closely associated – Johns's gaze came to rest on the sponsor's prominently printed name and logo. 'I see Texaco appears on the poster twice, but I'm only mentioned once,' he said in mock consternation. 'Maybe I should get myself a logo, too.'

Part of Johns's good humour might have derived from seeing how well his exhibits were displayed both at the Hayward and at Anthony d'Offay, where more recent drawings were on show. Unlike so many artists, who only feel close to their current work and wince at the thought of a retrospective, he seemed to survey the past thirty-five years' output with ease. 'Everything looks as you remember it,' he said equably, 'and there are very few surprises. Most of the work exists in my mind as a template, which fits the thing itself when I see it on the gallery wall.'

Total recall was, I suppose, to be expected from an artist who consistently feeds off his previous work. He was still, at sixty, preoccupied with many of the images that had established his reputation in late-1950s New York. Over the previous couple of decades he had deliberately withheld major examples of his work from sale: 'I'd sort of like to keep everything,' he told me, 'although I know it's impossible.'

There would certainly have been an outcry from museums and collectors throughout the world if the availability of Johns's work was suddenly curtailed. His pre-eminent stature had been resoundingly reinforced two years earlier, when a celebrated early painting fetched $17.1 million – an auction record for a living artist. After that, his American dealer Leo Castelli was able to ask $1.5 million for a new painting, but the artist himself viewed these dizzying figures with conflicting emotions. 'What does it really mean?' he asked hesitantly. 'It's weird and questionable and distasteful on some level, but the fact that I've been able to live comfortably from my work has helped me a great deal.'

Before Castelli mounted Johns's first, immensely well-received show in 1958, the artist had been obliged to work in bookshops and then collaborate with his one-time close friend Robert Rauschenberg on designing department-store displays for Bonwit Teller. Since then, accelerating financial success has enabled him to concentrate solely on his work, either in a Manhattan town house that once belonged to Gypsy Rose Lee, or in an idyllic retreat on a Caribbean island. Although he acknowledged that his millionaire status might 'have an inhibiting effect on my work', he also saw it as a liberation. 'It's made me more willing to take chances, to question the possibilities of my thought and what might or might not be considered interesting,' he explained. 'It throws finished work into the past tense more quickly, and provides me with a trigger for the new.'

Perhaps the greatest change occurred a few years before our meeting, when Johns started basing some of his work on paintings by Grünewald, Munch and Picasso. Drawing upon these images was a significant departure for him. The flags, targets, maps, numbers and ale cans that had inspired his early pictures were all ordinary, familiar, numbingly standardized objects; whereas the plague-stricken figure from Grünewald's Isenheim Altarpiece, and Munch's elderly self-portrait *Between the Clock and the Bed*, are outstanding works of European art.

Johns did not pretend to understand why the change had happened. He was refreshingly honest about the aspects of his work that mystified him, and was quite prepared to say 'I don't know' whenever a question defeated him. But he thought these two kinds of imagery might be linked after all. 'In both cases,' he said, 'the initial image ends up accommodating my own play of form. The first flag came to me in a dream one night. I simply got up and began it. A gift of that kind bypasses the need to decide what to paint, and it set the model for other, equally ordinary objects. Before I used it, the flag was somehow invisible: everyone knew it, but nobody ever looked at it. The seeing that people did with the flag wasn't really what I would call *seeing*.'

In Johns's infinitely resourceful and subtle art, those ubiquitous stars and stripes became a source of extraordinary richness and mystery. As for the suffering figure in Grünewald's painting, Johns grew involved with him after receiving a large portfolio of the Isenheim Altarpiece 'with a lot of very beautiful details. Looking at them, I thought how moving it would be to extract the abstract quality of the work, its patterning, from the figurative meaning. So I started making these tracings. Some became illegible in terms of the figuration, while in others I couldn't get rid of the figure. But in all of them I was trying to uncover something else in the work, some other kind of meaning.'

Whether the springboard was a flag or Grünewald, therefore, Johns aimed to make us look, as if for the very first time, at an image we might otherwise take for granted. The metamorphosis it undergoes is bound up with his unusually protracted working method, too. The densely worked surfaces of these drawings, often carried out in a complex mixture of media, testify to the time they took to finish. Johns thought of himself as lazy, and said, 'I would be delighted if I could do a quick drawing. A long time ago my old friend John Cage said to me: "You should have a way of working that doesn't take such a long time." So I made a drawing called *Broken Target* in half an hour. I was very happy, but I've since relapsed.'

Although his regret was genuine enough, I could not imagine Johns ever remaining satisfied with a less cumulative, steadily meditated procedure. While working, he thrived on the ability to 'look away and then look back', incessantly revising and deciding that a void needed filling, or that lightness should become dark. Perhaps a stern work ethic impelled him as well, for he commented, 'I may have inherited something from my Protestant farming background in South Carolina.'

Johns had an insecure childhood, moving between different relatives' homes after his mother left the family. But one new drawing at the d'Offay show contained an affectionate reference to early memories. 'I think of it as a portrait of my grandmother,' he said, describing with relish how 'she used to sit at the piano and sing "Red Sails in the Sunset"'. His laugh exploded all over again, filling the dull November morning with infectious, puckish delight.

Howard Hodgkin

December 1990

When he won the Turner Prize at the Tate in 1985, Howard Hodgkin surprised many visitors by representing his work there with a diminutive painting called *A Small Thing but My Own*. It looked defiantly out of place among the far larger, more declamatory exhibits displayed by the other shortlisted artists in the vast central gallery. But the intensity of its fiery colours, blazing within a coal-black painted frame, went a long way towards explaining why he had won the award. The dimensions of the painting belied its potent ability to ignite the viewer's imagination, and its unfashionably modest size ended up reinforcing Hodgkin's stubborn individuality.

Having been dismissed in the early phase of his career as an idiosyncratic artist, puzzlingly outside the abstract mainstream, Hodgkin at fifty-eight deserved to be ranked among the most outstanding painters of his generation. But this reputation, substantiated at the time we met by a one-man show in New York and a touring exhibition about to open in Edinburgh, had not bred a sense of complacency. 'Winning the Turner Prize didn't cure my feelings of paranoia about being an artist in this country,' he said. 'You have no social identity here – it's like being a non-person. When people ask me what I do, and I tell them, they usually look slightly nervous.'

Hodgkin had no illusions about the status of the modern painter in Britain. The literary bias of our culture still held sway, and philistinism was always eager to mock artists who challenged predictable ways of seeing. As a result, they tended to retreat into themselves. Even the gregarious Hodgkin maintained that 'the worst problem for most artists here is being lonely. It must have an effect on their art. I've never managed to completely solve the loneliness problem.'

This remark sounded paradoxical coming from a man who had left the countryside a decade earlier to settle in the centre of his native London. Having lived in a Wiltshire valley for some while, he had discovered a flat for sale in a 19th-century house bordering the British Museum. 'I went to the estate agent's office and said: "This is what I've been looking for all my life,"' he recalled. 'Although that's not exactly the cleverest thing for a prospective buyer to say, it was true. I'd wanted to live in Bloomsbury ever since I was a young man, when I had a map of it on the cupboard door in my Shepherd's Bush flat.' Eventually Hodgkin was able to acquire the whole house, and to have the British Museum on his doorstep was ideal for a painter unusually well versed in the art of the past. For many years he amassed a distinguished collection of Indian art, which he then loaned to a museum in Washington. It became an obsession, achieving a level of quality that testified to the learning and discernment behind its creation.

No sign of that voracious activity was discernible in his house, with its deep green woodwork and flesh-pink walls. A painting by his old friend Patrick Caulfield hung in the kitchen, and there was a Japanese screen next door. But nothing appeared to be deliberately on display. Indeed, the disrepair noticeable on several walls implied a disdain for the whole notion of interior decoration. Another friend, Bruce Chatwin, remembering 'the crumbling plaster, the peeling shreds of wallpaper' in an earlier Hodgkin home, decided that 'Howard kept his house "untouched" for fear that any effort to improve it would detract from the energies he was pouring into his art and his collection.'

Since Chatwin wrote his witty and affectionate pen portrait of Hodgkin in 1982, the collecting had virtually ceased. In the end,

Hodgkin had come to the conclusion that 'collecting is a disease – my Indian thing was a hobby which got out of hand'. He had also removed himself from his previous involvement with the stewardship of our great public collections. Once a trustee of the National Gallery and the Tate, he no longer immersed himself in the world of committee meetings. Everything was more focused than ever before on his own work. He started accepting commissions for architectural projects, executing a panoramic mural, redolent of underwater rhythms, on one whole side of the swimming pool at Broadgate, the 'city within a city' near Liverpool Street Station. And the eminent Indian architect Charles Correa had invited him to contribute to the new British Council offices in Delhi; Hodgkin was designing an inlaid marble wall, which would be set into the building's facade. It sounded like a promising manifestation of the collaborative spirit increasingly being explored by artists and architects alike.

'Most artists enjoy doing commissions of any sort, whether public or private,' Hodgkin said, 'because they are a way of getting out of the studio.' He had also been invited by Katherine and Keith Sachs, collectors of contemporary art in Philadelphia, to paint their portrait, commemorating the twenty-fifth anniversary of their marriage. 'It would have been impossible to do if I didn't know them,' he explained, 'so we've been meeting for several years now and the painting is almost complete. Although they have sat still for me to look at them, I wouldn't draw them from life. The picture may not look like a portrait at all by the time I've finished.'

On the whole, though, Hodgkin still preferred to concentrate on uncommissioned work. His newly restored studio bore witness to the all-consuming importance of painting in his life. Approached from the back of the house via a courtyard containing a palm tree from Weymouth, this turn-of-the-century building had a superb all-white interior. The entire ceiling was transparent, giving the room an exceptional radiance even on a dull day. 'It's the best studio I've ever had,' Hodgkin said, 'and it gives me tremendous freedom. I feel as if I'm working in an envelope of light.'

No paintings were visible in this bright chamber. He never liked anyone to see his work in progress, and a dozen large stretchers were propped against the walls to hide the unfinished pictures behind. Hodgkin was a famously slow painter, sometimes taking years to bring an image to fruition. 'If I did show them to you,' he said, 'they wouldn't mean a great deal yet. They're keeping each other company in here, and at best you can say they're in an interesting condition. Slowness is something I can't help, but it's extremely frustrating. My dream is to paint quickly.'

Only once had he been able to break the habit. It happened at Ahmedebad in India, where the Sarabhai family had invited him to stay and produce a body of work with great rapidity. Twice a day Hodgkin was supplied with several sheets of handmade paper; during the couple of hours they took to dry, he painted pictures in pairs. At the end of this extraordinarily prolific period, the 'Indian Leaves' amounted to a corpus almost as large as a decade's worth of the paintings he produces in normal conditions. But he did not feel very happy about the Ahmedebad pictures in retrospect, and the truth is that slowness chimed with the unhurried, meditative way he took memories as his starting point for art.

The experiences that generated Hodgkin's work invariably occurred a long time beforehand. They had to undergo a period of marination before he could give them pictorial life on the surface of his sturdy wooden panels. Looking at the completed pictures, we become keenly aware of the accumulated deposits of pigment they contain. Passages executed early in the painting process are often allowed to remain, yet they coexist with other areas that have obliterated the previous set of marks. He used the word 'generalized' to describe how his pictures removed themselves from private experience and took on an autonomous existence. The titles he gave them often referred to specific events – *Waking up in Naples*, *Fire in Venice*, or, more erotically, *In the Honeymoon Suite*. But the images themselves were far from explicit in their representation of the people and places that inspired him. Although Hodgkin's art was attached by an umbilical cord to the life he had led, his mark-making enjoyed an effervescent freedom. It encompassed fierce, impetuous stabs and swipes of the brush as well as the most caressing and melting of strokes. If he took a long time to complete a picture, there was never any feeling of staleness or over-deliberation in the final work. On the contrary: freshness of touch remained one of Hodgkin's greatest virtues as a painter, even though he was constantly building on what had gone before.

'The only technical thing I'm proud of,' he said, 'is that I can continue a stroke from a year ago. To be able to take up from where I left off is something I've learned over the years – one more string to my bow.' Vivacity of handling therefore became fused with the layered complexity of the image itself. And the outcome gained in immediacy from the unfettered colours Hodgkin deployed.

He remembered his astonishment, as a student at Camberwell School of Art, when he came across 'a girl painting a copy of Poussin's exuberant *Bacchanalian Revel* in shades of beige, khaki, dull green and dirt. When I asked her why, she replied: "I'm painting it as part of a scheme to cheer up the inmates of Holloway."' Hodgkin was never in favour of insipid art. Even when his work conveyed anguish, it evaded the danger of dreariness with aplomb. The regaining of time, which lay at the centre of his ambitions as a painter, was a fundamentally affirmative idea. His most characteristic pictures brought back the past with a vigour that deserved to be seen as celebratory.

It showed no sign of diminishing on the day we met. Hodgkin was preoccupied with painting much larger pictures than before, and talking about them brought an additional excitement into his voice. A passionate admirer of Degas's monumental portrait of Hélène Rouart in the National Gallery, he pointed out, 'It couldn't have been done on a small canvas. Sometimes pictures get so small they become epigrammatic, like one-liners. I've long wanted to see what I can do on a bigger scale, and some subjects require largeness – like a painting I'm doing at the moment of a Moroccan room. It would be wonderful to do big pictures: you can put much more in.' And indeed, by the time his retrospective exhibition toured America and Europe in 1994, the painter of *A Small Thing but My Own* had metamorphosed into a master manipulator of memories on the grandest surfaces imaginable.

Gerhard Richter

February 1991

Gerhard Richter's Cologne neighbourhood looked unexceptional enough; like so much of the city, it had been devastated by Allied bombs and then rebuilt with haste rather than flair. But the size of the former fabric factory housing his studio and home surprised me. Travelling up to Richter's studio floor in the lift, I found a space very unlike the cramped intimacy of Francis Bacon's rudimentary London mews. The carefully marshalled rooms Richter had converted inside the factory were high, white and immaculate. They had an almost laboratorial air, and the artist himself seemed very composed as he opened the door to greet me.

Richter was to be given a Tate retrospective later in the year, and with true Teutonic precision he had decided many months earlier exactly how it would be hung. After building an impeccable scale model of the rooms at his disposal, he had placed his own tiny colour photographs of the selected paintings on its white walls. The possibility of improvisation or doubt was thereby eliminated, and Richter could look forward to the landmark exhibition without any agonizing hesitation.

'I always make these models before my shows,' he explained, 'because I can't bear to stand in the museum and make up my mind when I'm there. Some artists enjoy the challenge: it's like a performance. But I would be very afraid to come to a gallery unprepared. For me, making a model is like finishing the paintings. They aren't complete until hung properly together.'

This compulsive need to systematize his working process reflected the complex character of a man who, at fifty-nine, was widely regarded as Germany's most outstanding senior painter. 'I like being methodical,' he said, 'and I'm afraid of chaos. I would die if I didn't organize. I like discipline.' Quiet, deep-voiced and almost professorial in bearing, Richter certainly seemed calm enough to bear out his own words.

But he soon made it clear, as we surveyed the array of paintings in progress on the studio walls, that his passion for order and preparedness was accompanied by an equally nourishing need for destruction. 'Each learns from the others,' he said of the freely handled abstractions ranged round the warehouse-like space. 'I start with a brush and make a cloudy ground, and then comes a more abstract construction of strokes. To begin with it always seems beautiful, but then I have to become aggressive, because everything I do is stupid and I must destroy what I have done.'

Although Richter spoke gently enough, the tall plastic spatula hanging near the window silently testified to the devastation he wreaked on his canvases. He typically used the spatula in a variety of ways to drag successive layers of pigment across the paintings. A series of dramatic, irregular striations would be left behind – as he put it: 'They heal the wound, make everything harmonious.' But the drastic action of the spatula could not entirely hide the layers of paint accumulated during earlier phases of the work. 'I still show the terror behind,' said Richter, 'and I sometimes make scratch-marks with a knife. But I don't like to do it very often, because it might become a trick.'

This last remark offered some insight into how Richter, during his long and prolific career, had encompassed such an extraordinary variety of approaches to the act of painting. He first became noticed in the early 1960s, when he was producing images based on photographs culled from mass media sources. His 1964 *Woman with Umbrella*, a painting of Jacqueline Kennedy soon after her husband's assassination, was to be included in the Tate show. Warhol used the same subject, but Richter had always stayed at a remove from the more sensationalist and commercial concerns of pop art, pulling a brush over the wet surface of his photo-based pictures in order to blur and at times obliterate the image with which he began. Already at this early stage in his development, he was questioning photographic representation and making clear his fascination with the element of chance. In a subsequent series of townscapes he used paint to bombard the aerial photographs employed as his starting point; he then began to analyse the process of painting in his *Colour Chart* pictures as well as a prolonged series of all-grey canvases.

At that point, in 1976, Richter experienced what he now described to me as 'a crisis. I couldn't take these monochrome grey pictures any further. I'm not like a holy man devoted to one pure style only, and I had the feeling that I must change my life. I had reached a cul-de-sac, and started blowing up.' In this eruptive mood, he began experimenting with the scraping device that subsequently came to dominate much of his output. At first, he thought the results were 'funny things, to do with arbitrariness and breaking all the laws of modern painting'. Too shy to exhibit them in Germany, he displayed the first rough studies in Halifax, Nova Scotia. But then, encouraged by the enthusiasm of Joseph Beuys, he began dragging the spatula across large canvases. 'I felt better once I had scraped,' he recalled. 'It was like saying: "Look, leave all the stupid problems you previously had with painting behind and start fresh." But of course, this was a dream.'

Richter's innate scepticism had always prevented him from believing in the possibility of an ideal solution, either in art or life. Even as a child, growing up in a small East German village where his father was a schoolteacher, he could never bring himself to accept the notion of a Soviet-style utopia. 'My parents were Christians, and the remoteness of the village meant that I was brought up in a non-communist atmosphere,' he explained. Once he moved to Dresden and studied at art college, however, he encountered increasing doctrinal rigidity. 'It was very strict, and I had to learn Russian for five years. I liked impressionism, but the teachers didn't allow it. As the cold war developed, their disapproval of anything modern became worse and worse.'

Studying the German expressionist movement was forbidden: his teachers were as hostile towards it as the Nazis had been when the infamous 'Degenerate Art' exhibitions were organized back in the 1930s. So Richter lost little time in moving to Düsseldorf, where he settled in 1961 and lived for the next couple of decades. 'I had a big shock coming to West Germany and finding that every intelligent person was on the Left,' he recalled. 'I have been afraid all my life of fanaticism. I know we cannot exist without a belief, but the Germans are more in danger of believing in extremes – whether fascism or Marxism.'

Over lunch, which Richter served from an elegant chrome trolley laden with frankfurters, cold meats, celery and cans of Beck's Bier, I asked him about his response to the recent reunification of his tragically sundered nation. Far from welcoming it with delight, he gave a guarded reply. 'We'll need thirty years to come together properly. East Germany is a different country. Although I lived in Dresden for so long and still have a sister in the city, it is terrible there after all those decades of nothing – dead, *kaput*. I have more in common now with people in London than with the East Germans. Their fear of money and success is as remote as Islam, so I have no real feelings about reunification. It is a historical necessity.'

All the more surprising, then, that the disaffected Richter put aside his obsession with abstraction in 1987 to paint an extended series of pictures about the Baader–Meinhof gang. By producing a melancholy sequence of blurred, photo-based images of Andreas Baader, Gudrun Ensslin and Jan-Carl Raspe, who probably committed suicide in their prison cells, he testified to his own involvement with their fate. But despite the paintings' elegiac power, they proved enormously controversial in Germany. 'Some critics thought I should have condemned Baader–Meinhof,' he recalled, 'and some maintained that I should have declared my support. English-speaking critics understood [the paintings] better.'

When the ICA showed the entire Baader–Meinhof series in 1989, I was at once moved and impressed. In earlier decades, though,

Britain had been oddly oblivious to Richter's merits. As he recalled during our conversation, no dealer had ever asked him for a London show before 1988, when he began exhibiting at the Anthony d'Offay Gallery. So a large part of his achievement was still, in 1991, unknown to British viewers, and the Tate retrospective seemed likely to prove a revelation to many. 'I was out of fashion for a long time after the early 1960s work,' he said, 'and painting itself was unfashionable, too.' During the past decade, though, he had benefited hugely from the resurgence of interest in paint on canvas. His reputation was now higher than ever, and yet he remained a quietly independent figure, eluding any facile attempt to pigeonhole his multifaceted work.

Apart from continuing to develop his grand abstractions, Richter had recently produced some fascinating mirror paintings saturated with grey, blood red, umber or blue. He also retained his old preoccupation with the tension between painting and photography, using pigment to alter images taken with his own camera. The original photograph was often transformed beyond recognition, yet he still occasionally enjoyed reasserting his former involvement with painting in a photographic manner: *Betty*, an enigmatic painting of his daughter turning away to stare at a grey Richter abstraction behind her, is carried out with consummate skill.

All the same, by juxtaposing two wholly different ways of painting – the figurative and the abstract – *Betty* implied that Richter would never be content to settle for one at the expense of the other. He believed that a retrospective could, at best, 'be for me like a confirmation. It makes me more certain. But the important thing is work in progress, where I remain unsure.'

Francis Bacon

March 1991

Entering Francis Bacon's surprisingly spartan bed-sitting room was an uncanny experience, rather like finding myself inside one of his paintings. The walls were bare, and dangling from the ceiling were the same naked light bulbs that swing like demented pendulums in his pictures or bear down glaringly on a nude sprawled across a bed. The preoccupation with reflections evident in many of his paintings was also echoed, with a startling dash of the macabre, by an enormous wall-sized mirror. Its surface had been partially riven by a spectacular crack, as if someone had picked up the small electric fire perched on a nearby chair and hurled it straight at the glass. Rather than replacing the mirror, Bacon had simply taped up the largest slivers to prevent them from falling off. So the crack's explosive power was preserved, almost as disturbingly as one of the convulsive figures writhing in the immensity of a Bacon canvas.

When I remarked on the austerity of the room, with its single bed flanked by an anglepoise lamp at the far end, Bacon replied: 'My surroundings simply don't interest me very much.' In one sense, this comment was understandable enough. The studiously neutral colour of the walls implied an utter lack of concern for the niceties of decoration. Two sofas, half-obscured by rows of fresh shirts and other clothes, likewise suggested that their owner had no time for wardrobes. The entire interior looked like a student's digs, inhabited by someone who disdains bourgeois propriety and feels impatient with the whole notion of possessions.

'I once had a very early Frank Auerbach,' Bacon said, when I mentioned the absence of pictures on the walls. 'At one stage I also bought a Sickert of a woman lying on a bed with a man seated next to her. But like a fool, I gave it to Lucian Freud. I wish I had it now.' He spoke like a man who lacked the financial resources to remedy his loss, and Bacon's home certainly seemed untouched by his ability to command millions of pounds for a single painting. 'Earning vast amounts of money doesn't affect me one bit,' he said. 'I'd be quite happy going back to the income I had as a young man, when I worked as a cook and general servant for someone in Mecklenburgh Square.'

Looking round the room, I could see what he meant. There was nothing fixed or settled about the interior, no hint of any expenditure having been lavished on it since Bacon had moved in thirty years earlier. It resembled the room of a man in transit, someone unshackled by the conventional ties that bind most people to their houses. Perhaps because Bacon tended to become so absorbed in thinking about his art, and in reading the books which festooned every available surface, he simply had no time left to worry about the details of domestic life.

In another sense, though, the parallels between this strange environment and his work indicated that it nourished him as powerfully as the life-mask of William Blake once did. He still kept it, sitting on a cupboard next to an electric fan – a very Baconian juxtaposition. Blake's blanched and enigmatic face had inspired a mesmerizing sequence of paintings in the mid-1950s. It had also prompted Bacon, more recently, to have his own life-mask taken, an experience he regretted undergoing as soon as they started smothering his face with plaster. At the time of my visit Blake's life-mask presided over the room as loftily as a mysterious spirit from the past, eyes closed like a seer meditating with stoicism on the inevitability of his own eventual demise.

What, I wondered, did Bacon himself feel about the prospect of death?

He stirred restlessly in his chair while considering a reply. 'Well, Picasso abhorred the thought of death: he loathed being reminded of mortality so much that he didn't even want anyone to mention his seventy-fifth birthday when it arrived.' Bacon, who referred to Picasso a great deal and regarded him as by far the greatest artist of our century, understood exactly why he'd felt that way. 'I hate the thought of death,' he said. 'I hate the thought of it all coming to an end.' He paused, stared ruminatively out of the window for a moment, then brightened with a defiant rallying cry: 'Shall we have some champagne?'

He leapt up with astonishing agility and, betraying no sign of a typical eighty-one-year-old's stiffness, disappeared into the kitchen. While he was away, I reflected that anyone who retained so much energy and savoured his pleasures with such undiminished eagerness was bound to regard the whole notion of extinction as anathema. Within seconds he was back, bearing a bottle which he uncorked with seasoned aplomb. The two stemmed glasses he placed on the table were elegantly inscribed with the initials 'FB' in flowing script. They had been the gift, apparently, of an admirer in Germany, where his work was regarded with almost as much veneration as it enjoyed in France.

Did he, I asked, think that his paintings were appreciated more warmly over there than in Britain? 'Oh, they don't like my work here at all,' he said bluntly. 'Maybe it's the savagery they find in it, or maybe it's the homosexuality which I suppose is in the work. I don't go about shouting that I'm gay, but AIDS has made it all much worse, you know. People are very, very odd about it. The other day a telephone engineer came round, so I offered him a drink. He looked at me strangely and said: "You're gay, aren't you?"'

With characteristic honesty, Bacon never made any attempt to hide his homosexuality. Some of his finest and most erotic paintings depict male figures embracing or making love. Moreover, he was intrigued by the fact that his distant ancestor, the celebrated Elizabethan Lord Chancellor Francis Bacon, was gay as well. 'It comes up in Aubrey's *Brief Lives*,' he said, bounding up from the table again and moving swiftly over to a pile of books on a cupboard near the bed. The search proved fruitless: 'Where *is* it? What *have* I done with it? I've thrown all my books away, you know, because I've got no room for them.'

I challenged him about the British perception of his work. He was, after all, widely and in my view justly regarded as our most outstanding living painter at that time, and over the previous thirty years the Tate Gallery had paid him the unique honour of staging two great retrospectives within his lifetime. In the Tate's latest rehang he had been given the accolade of a large room devoted to his work. It was immensely powerful, and prompted me to phone him on impulse after I'd visited the gallery. Bacon's line had been engaged for almost an hour before it started ringing; he answered at once, and I told him that I had been particularly impressed at the Tate by his loan of a grand triptych painted only three years earlier, in 1988.

Bacon had conceived this as a second version of a smaller and far more rasping triptych called *Three Studies for Figures at the Base of a Crucifixion*. Painted in 1944, that work seemed at the time to encapsulate the horror of war by showing three monstrously deformed hybrids, half human and half beast, yelling their despair against a vehement orange ground. This thoroughly disconcerting trio reappears in the later version. But the two figures on the sides now point inwards rather than outwards, seeming to direct their anguish towards a blindfolded form with bared, vicious teeth in the centre. This time, moreover, the extra space around each figure intensifies their isolation, and Bacon exchanges the parched, angry orange of the earlier triptych for a sumptuous deep crimson.

Having mentioned on the phone my fascination with these two versions, I had asked Bacon if we might meet – with little hope of a positive reply, for he was rarely inclined to give interviews. But to my surprise he had agreed immediately, warning that the entrance to his South Kensington mews had no name-plate to identify it. Nor, he added, did his bell work. 'I'll leave the front door open,' he said rashly, 'so that you can make your own way in.'

I went round the very next morning, slightly alarmed by the risk Bacon seemed to be taking with his security. Although the anonymous grey door pushed open at a touch, there was hardly any space between it and the narrow staircase beyond. I almost bumped into the first step and, hearing my host speaking animatedly on the phone somewhere above, started to climb. The stairs rose at a precipitous angle, more reminiscent of something on a boat than living quarters in an exclusive part of London. This nautical air was reinforced by the rope slung through hooks attached to the left wall. It helped me to haul my way upwards, yet I could not stop myself wondering why an eighty-one-year-old living alone should have to negotiate such a vertiginous hazard each time he left or entered his home. Bacon's legendary appetite for alcohol must have made the stairs even more unpredictable. Maybe he relished the danger involved, I thought, just as he savoured the action of chance in painting itself.

My worries about his safety subsided as I reached the summit. For there, standing next to the cooker in a small kitchen area, was a man who looked far fitter and more agile than his age had led me to expect. While he finished his phone call (centring on his anxiety about the welfare of a much-loved young friend who had vanished in Bangkok and might have been arrested for drug-carrying), I found my bearings. To one side, near a chest of drawers half-obscured by a heaped miscellany of clothes, was a door festooned with paint splashes of every imaginable colour: the entrance to his studio. But it was shut tight, and having heard of his reluctance ever to be seen at work, I assumed – wrongly, as it turned out – that it would remain private territory throughout my visit.

His greeting after the phone conversation was very cordial. Although his work might suggest that Bacon was a reclusive and difficult man, he could not have been more convivial. Unusually for an artist, he was also very frank in his criticism of the work he had produced.

'I did that second triptych because I'd always wanted to do a large version of the earlier one,' he explained. 'I thought it might work, but I think the first one is the best. I should have reiterated the orange to give it a kick, because the red dissolves. But I may have been dissuaded by the boredom of putting it on, because mixing that orange paint with pastel and then spraying it was a terrible lot of work.' Why, I enquired, had he remained so obsessed with the crucifixion theme? 'Well, I'm not in the least religious,' he said, 'even though I was brought up in the Protestant faith and went to church as a child. At my age, I've known many people die or commit suicide and I've never thought they were anything other than dead. I'm certain there's nothing after that, and I like the finality of the American expression "drop dead". But I am fascinated by the great Crucifixions which have been painted in the past by Cimabue and Grünewald.'

Lying on the table beside us, next to an assortment of bottles and a linguaphone course, was W. B. Stanford's book *Greek Tragedy and the Emotions*. Seeing it reminded me that Bacon's gruelling interpretation of the Crucifixion had been profoundly affected by his love of Aeschylus. One of his most haunting late triptychs was 'suggested by' the *Oresteia* plays, and although he can only read Aeschylus in translation, 'the whole of surrealism is there'. Picasso's paintings of bathers from the surrealist period likewise influenced Bacon profoundly, to the extent of inspiring him to start painting. 'But I've been influenced by everything, really,' he insisted, 'even the extraordinary colour photographs in medical textbooks from a bookshop in Gower Street. I got one there recently on small wounds.'

He rose again and returned this time with a well-thumbed, paint-smeared copy of *A Colour Atlas of Nursing Procedures in Accidents and Emergencies*. I flinched from the pictures of syphilitic sores and other excruciatingly painful afflictions inside, all reproduced with glistening vividness. But Bacon seemed captivated rather than appalled as he leafed through the pages. How was it, I asked, that he didn't shudder at them? 'I suppose when I look at these photographs, I think, my God, I'm lucky I don't have *that*,' he replied, pointing at a particularly gruesome wound. 'But they don't alarm me in the way that they do other people. Once I was driving through France with a friend, and we came across a terribly bad motor accident. There was blood and glass all over the road. But I remember thinking that there was a beauty about it. I didn't feel the horror of it, because it was part of life.'

Sensing that we were approaching the central reason why some viewers recoil from Bacon's art, I pressed him to speculate on the origins of his preoccupation with the normality of violence. 'Well, you mustn't forget that I was born in Ireland,' he said, 'where my English father trained racehorses very unsuccessfully. I grew up there at a time when the Sinn Féin was going around. All the houses in our neighbourhood were being attacked, and I'll always remember my father saying: "If they come tonight, say nothing." He expected to be attacked, and on all the trees you'd see the green, white and gold of the Sinn Féin flags.' Although Bacon's family moved to London at the beginning of the First World War, when he was nearly five, the atmosphere of fear did not abate. 'We lived near Hyde Park, in Westbourne Terrace, and after the bombing started they sprayed the park with a phosphorescent substance from watering cans. The idea was that the Zeppelins would identify this glow as the lights of the city, and drop their bombs there. Then we went back to Ireland again, so I was brought up to think of life having this violence.'

Even at the time of our interview, this remained a powerful motor force driving Bacon's work. At an age when most men have mellowed and lost some, at least, of their youthful fire, Bacon stayed close to his old obsessions. 'I was planning this year to do a series of paintings about places where murder has been committed,' he told me, describing how there would have been 'one in a field, one on a pavement, and one in a room. But I'm going to abandon the idea.' One of the canvases sat half-finished on an easel in his studio, a modestly proportioned room where we had now arrived after passing through a narrow kitchen lined with colour reproductions of his work. A grey upper area in the painting led down to a central section spattered with blood. It had the rudiments of an authentically chilling image. But Bacon, an inveterate and ruthless destroyer of pictures he considered to be failures, said it was no good.

He seemed reluctant to show me any of the other works in progress stacked against the wall. Responding to my interest, though, he did allow me to explore the rest of the studio. It was cold, probably because his anxiety about the risk of fire prompted him to leave unheated the rooms he was not currently using. The walls, like the door, were gaudily covered with paint splashes of every conceivable colour. As for the floor, it was heaped to the point of outright congestion with books, paint pots, squeezed-out tubes of pigment and smeared rags. How Bacon moved around in such a cluttered space remained unfathomable, but I did manage to bend down and retrieve a small, discarded canvas from the wreckage. The painted face it once contained had been cut out with a few swift slashes of the knife, leaving behind only the tantalizing vestige of a head.

In this cramped interior, illuminated by a skylight window he had installed for the purpose, Bacon managed to work on even the largest of his triptychs. When assembled, they must have stretched across virtually the full width of the room, but he found this constriction oddly stimulating. 'The best exhibition I've ever had', he said, 'was in 1977 at the Galerie Claude Bernard in Paris, where the spaces are all small and the paintings looked more intense.' So here, hemmed in by detritus and a studio which most artists would find claustrophobic, the indefatigable octogenarian repaired every morning. Unlike Lucian Freud, who had painted a masterly little portrait of Bacon from the life during nocturnal sittings almost forty years earlier, he preferred working in daylight. 'I get up very early and paint in here until one o'clock. Then I'm finished, I've had it. I hate afternoons, I think they're absolutely revolting, they're a wash-out. But I feel better again in the evening.'

He looked spry enough as we talked, and while walking to a nearby Italian restaurant for lunch his gait seemed positively jaunty. His laced-up gym shoes, fawn pullover and corduroy slacks only accentuated the inner vitality of a man whose enthusiasm for work, and eagerness to talk about the artists and writers he admired most keenly, remained undimmed. During our time together we touched on Constable (he cherished the oil sketches at the Victoria & Albert Museum just up the road), T. S. Eliot, Velázquez, Picasso's Boisgeloup sculpture, Stanley Spencer ('the best English painter since Turner, but his pictures don't really touch me'), Buñuel, Soutine, W. B. Yeats (Bacon was intrigued by my recent realization that 'The Second Coming' was first published in the very same year as Ernst painted *Celebes*) and Proust, who 'produced the last great analysis of human behaviour, with extraordinarily refined and subtle insights into the psyche'.

But the man who seemed most on his mind over lunch was Eric Hall, the donor to the Tate of the great 1944 triptych. Bacon felt that he owed Hall an enormous amount, above all perhaps as the man who had helped and encouraged him when young to overcome his early inhibitions and become a serious painter. I got the impression, from the untypically wistful way he discussed Hall, that Bacon still missed him.

In the end, though, Bacon's conversation always returned to his own work. 'People think I must have learned a lot from the German expressionists when I was in Berlin as a young man,' he said, 'but I don't really like them. If I allowed an entire painting to become convulsive, it would be like one of those splashy romantic things.' Hence his determination to contrast the wildly handled figures with large areas of flat, immaculately applied colour and strong structural lines, giving his pictures an aura of magisterial finality. Extreme anxiety and isolation are pitched against outright grandeur, and I was not surprised to hear Bacon saying, 'I really prefer artists like Seurat – I'm drawn to broken classicism, where disorder enters the classical framework and makes violence impinge all the more forcefully.'

Before I took my leave back at the mews, Bacon insisted on lending me the complete three-volume edition of the letters of Van Gogh, who inspired him to produce a marvellously fiery sequence of paintings back in 1957. I thanked him and mentioned that the first time we met, twenty years earlier, he had outlined an ambitious plan to embark on an extended series of autobiographical pictures that would 'crystallize time in the way that Proust did with his novels'. What had happened to that plan, I wondered? In particular I recalled his idea of basing a painting on his memory, aged four, of 'walking up and down a pathway lined with cypresses at my Irish home dressed in a bicycling cape which I used to borrow from my brother'.

Bacon smiled, then shrugged. 'I've thought of doing dozens of things which I've never finally done,' he said, with an old man's acute awareness of the role played by temporality and chance. 'One's energy fluctuates, and there's never enough time. With life passing so quickly, you can never talk in ultimate terms, never plan for the future. It just happens.'

James Turrell

September 1991

If James Turrell could raise $6 million over the coming five years, he explained to me, he would be able to complete his visionary transformation of an extinct volcano in Arizona's Painted Desert. The Roden Crater Project had been at the centre of the Californian artist's ambitions for well over a decade. The complex task of shaping the cone was already finished, after some 200,000 cubic yards of earth had been bulldozed from the rim. And he now planned to build an intricate sequence of pathways, chambers, stairs and corridors within the 400,000-year-old crater.

It was a formidable task, but Turrell himself talked about the venture with an assurance bordering on serenity. In London for his first ever British exhibition at the Anthony d'Offay Gallery, he explained: 'I want to make space there which will perform the music of the spheres in light. I'm interested in creating a place where you become involved with geologic time, making you feel as if you really are on the surface of the planet. The series of spaces will be a combination of bunker and observatory, with the different orientations adding up to a full work covering all aspects of the sky.' In order to ensure that the positioning of the spaces accorded with the stars and planets visible through the volcano, he had used his expertise as a pilot and aerial surveyor to map the crater's celestial location with impressive precision.

How had Turrell come to dedicate himself to such a daunting, almost superhuman enterprise? The fundamental answer lay in a formative experience he had relished during his boyhood – for this articulate, white-bearded man, now in his late forties, had been fascinated by the mysteries of light and cosmos since an early age. Growing up in Pasadena, he inhabited a bedroom which his father, an aeronautical engineer and amateur ornithologist, had earlier peppered with little windows to let birds fly in and out. Wartime blackouts meant that each window was supplied with a dark blind, and the young Turrell would use these to shut out all sunlight. Then, in the darkness, he would get to work. 'I made pinholes in the blinds to represent a constellation of stars,' he recalled, 'making visible the things that were in the sky but normally invisible during the day.'

Although his fascination with light grew from that point onwards, he had for a while no idea what to do with it. After graduating from Pasadena High School in 1961, he studied psychology and mathematics for a BA at Pomona College in Claremont. Only then, at the age of twenty-two, did he begin graduate art studies at the University of California. His ambition at that stage was to become a painter. 'I looked at the artists who had painted with light, especially Monet, Rothko, Reinhardt and Newman,' he said. 'But with my American directness and naiveté, I decided in the end to dispense with painting and take light itself as my working material.'

The outcome, so far as his early work was concerned, could be seen in one section of the d'Offay show. Descending to a darkened, empty basement room, I found myself confronted by *Decker*, a dazzling rectangle of light projected onto an end wall. Turrell had made this taut, economical piece back in 1967, when the minimal movement was at its height. All his work of this period was very spare, a quality he related in part to his Quaker upbringing. 'They thoroughly disapprove of art and don't even believe in decoration,' he remembered with a smile, 'but the whole Quaker thing is to do with going inside yourself to meet the light. Consciously or not, the Quakers do in fact relish a kind of lush severity: their meeting-houses of plaster and wood are very beautiful.'

So was the most spectacular installation in Turrell's show, a monumental work from 1982 called *Rayzor* which occupied half of the main gallery. The room had been transformed into a wide, white box, and at the far end a colossal oblong hovered in space with intense blue-green light pulsating around its edges. Using a blend of natural and fluorescent light, Turrell managed to flood the entire space with a soft, hazy radiance. Within this highly charged chamber, the oblong seemed to float with ease, changing colour from near-silhouetted blackness to a deep, rich purple. It was a magisterial work, at once severe and sensuous. The light pressed itself forcibly upon the viewer, helping to explain why Turrell wanted to 'move consciousness out through the eyes to feel the space. The eyes are the most exposed part of the brain, and we have this great capacity to feel through them.' He regarded his gallery work as 'chamber music, which helps me learn how to handle the symphony'.

But the volcano remained 'the thing I most want to do', and he flew all over the western states in his own aeroplane looking for the site before he found it near Flagstaff. It would allow him to use the sky 'as my arena, my canvas if you like'. Here, with luck and the requisite amount of sponsorship, Turrell would be able to generate 'the sense of awe I find in Egyptian art, Maya culture and the great cathedrals. If you're taken away from the city lights, you'd be surprised how much you can really see.'

Turrell used the word 'odyssey' to describe his path towards this enormously ambitious goal. At a formative stage he had found the writings of Antoine de Saint-Exupéry and Sir Francis Chichester inspiring in their dedication to epic journeying. A similar commitment sustained his own belief in the feasibility of the volcano scheme. Ultimately, he regarded art as 'a long-distance race, and only when you've gone way down the road do you see art as it really is'. He quoted with approval a remark Fats Waller once made: 'People never change, they just stand more revealed.' If everything went according to plan, the unveiling of the Roden Crater Project in the late 1990s would be the moment when Turrell's life's work was finally defined, in all its single-minded tenacity, dedication and sense of wonder.

Anthony Caro

October 1991

After driving through the narrow archway leading to Anthony Caro's studio, a former piano factory in Camden Town, I found his ample parking space almost filled with colossal sheets and cylinders of rusted steel. Stacked alongside a mighty ship's anchor culled from a maritime scrapyard in Chatham, they all looked ready to be incorporated into new Caro sculpture. But they had endured a long wait, for Caro had spent most of the previous six months labouring on by far his tallest and most ambitious work to date: the 25-ton *Octagon Tower*, spiralling 22 feet into the air.

Poised halfway between sculpture and architecture, this walk-in cluster of twisting stairways and secret chambers formed the spectacular centrepiece of a Tate exhibition of Caro's work due to open soon after our meeting. 'It's taken up our lives this year,' Caro told me, half rueful and half excited. 'We've had seventeen people working on it, and the noise has been unbelievable at times. Because this is a very residential area, I tried to minimize the disturbance and wrote letters to all the neighbours. But when we moved the tower outside, somebody started throwing eggs at us.'

A white-bearded, spry sixty-seven, Caro remained undaunted by this outburst of local resentment. Since Henry Moore's death in 1986, he had been regularly trumpeted by publicists as Britain's most eminent living sculptor. All the same, neither international fame nor a knighthood prevented him from regarding the Tate show with apprehensiveness. Part of his concern centred on practical considerations. 'The tower contains six separate flights of steps and a number of rooms on different levels,' he explained. 'I like the idea of people entering it, climbing up and walking round inside. The work can't be experienced properly otherwise. But I feel totally inhibited by the problem of public safety. Nick Serota said to me: "Don't worry, you're making a sculpture, so concentrate on that." But if somebody falls, the steel will hurt them and it'd be awful. The Tate would have to close the tower at once.'

Despite his immense productivity and the panache with which his sculpture was cut and welded into flamboyant form, Caro sounded surprisingly anxious. 'I'm very insecure, always worried,' he confessed. 'When I'm working, I don't have the confidence to say "That's it." I need a lot of confirmation from people whose opinions I respect, like the critic Clement Greenberg or my wife, Sheila. She's an artist herself, and since her studio is above mine, we talk about each other's work the whole time.'

Commissions made him particularly anxious, and he did his best to avoid them. But the Tate invitation – to display work throughout the building's central spine – had proved an irresistible opportunity to work on a grand scale. Increasingly fascinated by the relationship between sculpture and architecture, Caro had realized that the Tate's high octagon space would enable him to install a full-size example of what he described as 'sculptitecture'.

Even so, the immensely complex task of assembling the tower's sixty-one individual pieces, in a studio too low to let him make and appraise the whole structure with ease, proved an arduous experience. 'With commissions, I'm inclined not to leave them alone,' he said. 'I fuss about whether I'll get it done in time, and whether some idiot will buy it. I've already been asked to show it again at the Seville Expo next summer, where they want to rename it *The Tower of Discovery* to fit in with the 500th anniversary of Columbus's arrival in America. But I don't know who would ever want to acquire such a thing. Sheila said I should paint it white, and call it the white elephant.'

Caro's jaunty, engaging sense of humour prevented him from falling into a Grand Old Man persona. The very opposite of stuffy or remote, he became instantly concerned when I happened to mention that my back had been strained the previous day. 'Oh, God,' he cried, 'is it terribly painful? All sculptors suffer from back problems, you know, so let me give you the card of a marvellous osteopath I went to recently.'

Then, without any warning, he asked me to take off my jacket. I complied, wondering what on earth he had in mind, and found Sir Anthony advancing on me with an elaborate electrical appliance in his hand. 'Where does it hurt?' he asked, pressing the humming instrument against my back and letting it vibrate around the top of my trousers. 'Is that any better?' he enquired after a while, continuing to deploy his massaging device with admirable vim and conviction. There was a distinct sculptor's relish about the way he manipulated my aching body, and it responded well to his unexpected ministrations.

Although it astonished me at the time, Caro's spontaneous gesture seems in retrospect to have been wholly typical of his attitude to art. He thrived on unpredictability, and in recent years had never hesitated to push himself in fresh directions. When he first revolutionized British sculpture in the early 1960s, welding steel into brilliantly coloured abstractions and dispensing with the customary plinth, his flouting of convention had appeared radical indeed. An entire generation of emergent sculptors was nourished by his controversial initiative, and he seemed at that stage to have broken decisively with the classical tradition espoused by his teachers at the Royal Academy Schools. Charles Wheeler, now almost forgotten but then a celebrated sculptor of public monuments who later became the Academy's president, had told the student Caro: 'Look at the Greeks, you'll get a lot of ideas about style from them.'

Caro recalled Wheeler's remark with disdain. His audacious leap into abstraction was inspired above all by the welded sculpture of David Smith, which he encountered during a decisive trip to America in 1960. The move was bitterly denounced by many British critics but Caro was unrepentant, and later in life there was still a subversive streak in him – an innate rebelliousness that, at the time we met, had recently prompted him to rebuff an invitation to join the Royal Academy. A visit to the 'bloody awful' Summer Exhibition persuaded him to say no, 'but if the RA could treat sculpture and painting with the same seriousness it gives architecture, the show wouldn't be the crowded mess it is today. There's no point in pouring a bucket of clean water into a dirty river.'

In the mid-1980s, the arch-modernist finally made a trip to Greece. The Hellenic experience impressed him far more than he would ever have thought possible, and another of his exhibits for the Tate was a 77-foot-long homage to the Temple of Zeus at Olympia. The pediment carvings preserved in the museum there had stimulated him hugely, even if he noticed that the curators 'keep changing the pieces around because they're still not sure which order the different lapiths and centaurs should go in'.

As the Tate show would disclose, *After Olympia* was in no sense merely imitative of its august source. But Caro, like Picasso before him, was engrossed in a fruitful series of dialogues with great artists of the past. Manet's *Déjeuner sur l'herbe* and Rubens's *Deposition* had also generated freely inventive Caro variations over the previous few years. They showed the supposedly diehard abstractionist prepared to tackle complex figurative compositions, and his former obsession with steel giving way to a more open-minded use of other materials.

The previous year, on a visit to Japan, he had made a series of sculptures with washi paper: 'You can't tear the stuff, and it's so strong that the Japanese even make armour out of it.' None of these pieces had yet been exhibited. Caro still wanted to work on them, and he also harboured ideas for cardboard sculpture as well as carvings in concrete. 'I've had no time so far this year,' he explained, 'but when the dust settles at the Tate I'll get down to making them.'

Did he expect his work to continue changing so dramatically in the future? 'Oh, I hope so,' he replied without hesitation. 'If I see a path and want to go down there, I've *got* to do it. Otherwise, you see, I'd be bored.'

Roy Lichtenstein

October 1997

Just inside Roy Lichtenstein's New York studio, a window-barred brick building on the west side of Greenwich Village, a scowling guard dog confronted me. But he was only a comic-book animal, safely mounted on the wall, and the 'GRRR!' erupting in bold capitals from the base of the image made him endearing rather than ferocious.

Nor was Lichtenstein himself at all intimidating. In his early seventies, the grand old man of American pop art turned out to be the very opposite of self-important. His paintings of the early 1960s may have seemed brash in their brazen reliance on strip-cartoon imagery, but Lichtenstein the man was understated, soft-spoken and disarmingly modest. Spry, with unusually large eyes and white hair tied back into a neat pigtail, he paced swiftly around the ground floor of his wide, barn-like studio in T-shirt, jeans and trainers. An inviting sofa stood near the centre, strewn with evidence of his continuing interest in visual culture at its highest and lowest: big books on Cézanne and Matisse, as well as a copy of *Falling in Love* magazine subtitled 'Yesterday's Sweetheart'. But Lichtenstein did not sit down once; he remained energetically on the move throughout my visit. And the big new paintings ranged on easels around the studio proved that he had no intention of slowing up as an artist.

Most of them were interiors where young women ruminated among plants, furniture and bookshelves or lingered mysteriously at one side, sliced off by the canvas edge. They were clearly related to the flaxen-haired, full-lipped beauties who throng Lichtenstein's early pop pictures. The dots, diagonal stripes and thick contours deployed in these new paintings were consistent with the style he had developed thirty-five years earlier. But the colours now were lighter, cooler, more airy than before. No speech bubbles floated in space, and the women all appeared to be alone.

These limpid, distilled images offered impressive proof of Lichtenstein's continuing prowess. He was much in demand that summer, with a roomful of clangorous, brilliantly coloured sculpture at the Venice Biennale and a one-man show of paintings in Boston. An exhibition of new work was also coming up in the autumn, at the Anthony d'Offay Gallery – his first show with a London dealer for a surprisingly long time.

The pop art label, however, still hung round his neck like a noose. Did he ever find himself resenting it? 'I don't mind,' he said with a faintly rueful smile, 'although it's a bit like someone continuing to call Matisse a fauve throughout his life.' What had dramatically changed, though, was the public response to his work. In 1964, after his first notorious show at the Leo Castelli Gallery in New York, *Life* magazine had published a feature headlined 'Is He the Worst Artist in America?'

Although the Tate Gallery and the Stedelijk Museum in Amsterdam were quick to buy substantial examples of his most provocative work, he found himself shunned at home: 'The US museums weren't looking at my paintings at all – they hated them, irredeemably. People metaphorically threw up when they saw my work. They thought I was enlarging comics, or just copying them.' His stance was anathema to a generation reared on Jackson Pollock and the abstract expressionist movement, with its heroic emphasis on a wholehearted, instinctive, muscular interaction between the canvas and the paint-splattered artist. Lichtenstein's deliberately 'vulgar' reliance on cheap commercial images seemed like an appalling, sensationalist rejection of everything that had made post-war American art so extravagantly admired across the Western world.

His radical change of style around 1961 even alarmed the artist himself for a while. The new work contrasted greatly with what he had been producing throughout the previous decade, quietly exhibited at low-profile galleries and politely reviewed. Looking back on this sudden metamorphosis, Lichtenstein told me, 'I felt my change from the 1950s work was a rupture, a huge shock – like the one Picasso delivered to everyone who saw his new work in 1906. For me, it started with the idea of painting cliches, jotting down little drawings of Mickey Mouse and Donald Duck. The cliche gave my work a certain power. It was brave, risky and so far from anything I'd been taught in art schools. It was saying something about real life, and it wasn't done as a joke. But I knew that it couldn't be taken seriously.'

Even at that perilous stage in his career, though, Lichtenstein appears to have remained unshakeably assured. In another part of his studio, on a pinboard festooned with family snapshots, I noticed a black-and-white photograph of the young, newly famous Lichtenstein on a visit to Andy Warhol's Factory. Standing in a group including the model Jean Shrimpton as well as fellow pop artists Claes Oldenburg, James Rosenquist and the enigmatic Andy, he looks calm and contained. The extraordinary controversy generated by pop art was at its height and the media exposure of Warhol and his friends utterly relentless. But Lichtenstein kept his composure throughout the hysteria.

In a celebrated 1963 *Art News* interview called 'What Is Pop Art?', he was at pains to stress that 'I think the formal statement in my work will become clearer in time.' I asked him what he had meant by this prediction and his answer was unequivocal: 'I think what distinguishes good from bad painting is the formal statement, the position of marks and contrasts. If you forget that I'm trying to depict a table, a window or some flowers, abstract qualities to do with size and positioning become important. That's what Mondrian was doing.'

So maybe the outcry over Lichtenstein's popular sources obscured the paradoxical fact that he was a rigorous and highly refined artist, less concerned with subject matter than his most vociferous critics might imagine. In some of the newer pictures, I noticed that a single passage of looser, freer paint had been brushed in. But it could almost have been in quotation marks, a deliberate exception to the rigid marshalling of lines and colours around it. I also saw that one of his new paintings was tilted at a diagonal on the easel; Lichtenstein told me that he often liked working on them upside down. The easels were specially built, enabling him to swivel his canvases to whatever angle he wished. This provided closer access to every area of the painting, helping him to arrive at a more exact way of working.

The studio was immaculate, a former ironworks that Lichtenstein had converted eight years earlier into a superb working environment. With a smooth wooden floor and generous skylights in the raftered ceiling, it provided an ideal setting for paintings and sculpture alike. Trolleys abounded, carrying paint pots with brushes carefully taped on top of them. Even though paint-smeared assistants wandered in and out, the entire tranquil space testified to Lichtenstein's overriding need for precision and control.

'Order and unity are the whole point,' he explained with a characteristic wave of the arm towards one recent canvas. 'I don't know what the girl and the plant are doing there. Even in my cartoon-based work of the 1960s, I only chose one frame from a story, thwarting people's desire to find out what happened to the characters.' Some of those paintings were deliberately melodramatic, like the much-reproduced *Drowning Girl* of 1963 who weeps as her thought bubble exclaims: 'I don't care! I'd rather sink...than call Brad for help!' But the painting as a whole was so deadpan that it did not offer a distressing experience.

Lichtenstein was never a tragic artist. He remarked to me that 'nothing ever happened that was untoward' in his cartoon paintings, and laughingly insisted that the sinking girl 'didn't drown. I've always felt optimistic, I don't know why. I know it would be much more interesting if I wasn't. I've never done an anguished painting. I don't think about how I feel: I'm very even. Something terrible can happen in my life, but I wouldn't put it in my art. Is that the right yellow – that's all I'm thinking.'

He certainly appeared very serene and in harmony with himself. There was an almost philosophical aura about him, doubtless enhanced by his decision to spend only a couple of days each week in Manhattan. The rest of the time he preferred working in the country, 'right near the ocean, too seductive to believe'. But he continued to think of himself essentially as a New Yorker, someone who had grown up in the city and still relished living there. He loved the life of the streets, and even confessed, 'I nearly killed myself roller-booting round here the other day.' But he insisted that his work stayed the same wherever he painted, in town or country. 'My studios are my playpens, it's fun being in them. I'm there seven days a week.'

Lichtenstein struck me as one of the least puffed-up artists I had ever encountered. Genuinely appreciative when I complimented him on his new work, he did not appear at all complacent. I asked him what kind of art he expected to be making in his old age, and his reply sounded restless enough to bode well for his future development. 'I'd love to find an opening, I'd like to have an enormous change, to show that I had an additional vision. But I can't imagine what it would be.'

Damien Hirst

May 1998

After catching my train at Paddington and travelling south-west to Tiverton Parkway station, I found Damien Hirst waiting for me in his car. He drove us through the sunlit and verdant Devon countryside towards his spacious, recently acquired farmhouse near Combe Martin, and as we approached our destination I became aware of just how excited he felt. Having bought the house 'and its surrounding acres for £160,000', Hirst told me he had 'spent £400,000 on it already'. He explained with great enthusiasm, 'I'm building a house for my mum in the grounds, which are next door to a dinosaur park.' Then, walking towards his front entrance, he described ambitious plans for 'a snooker room, a conservatory and a circular library in the barns'.

While Hirst cooked me a delicious pasta lunch with the help of 'garlic from the woods', I was intrigued to notice a very vigorously handled painting in the next room, reminiscent of David Bomberg. Hirst explained, 'It's a picture of Leeds I painted years ago, during my teenage student days there at the Jacob Kramer School of Art.' But his most crucial college days were spent at Goldsmiths in London, where he responded to his teacher Michael Craig-Martin's helpful emphasis on professionalism. 'There were a lot of good artists at Goldsmiths, and the stuff produced in college was better than the stuff we saw in galleries,' Hirst said. 'I was working at Anthony d'Offay's three days a week, constantly going from Gerhard Richter's paintings back to Goldsmiths. Our art seemed a fuck of a lot more exciting than Richter. The level of work we made there was in desperate need of an audience. We had already been exhibiting at Goldsmiths from day one: the students had a gallery space, bookable in advance. We were making art for people to look at. But after building and photographing the work, we often had to destroy everything. It seemed a shame, and I thought there was no way we could get into the art system *en masse*. That's why we did "Freeze".' Invited to participate in a modest Goldsmiths exhibition organized at the Institute of Education gallery in 1988 by his fellow student Angus Fairhurst, Hirst helped to put on the show and 'it hooked me'. So he decided to mount a far larger, more ambitious event. He borrowed the venue from the London Docklands Development Corporation, who also sponsored the show.

So far as the young Hirst was concerned, painting proved as stimulating as sculpture. When he painted the Bomberg-like *View of Leeds* back in 1981, at the age of sixteen, his ambitions centred on brush, pigment and canvas. He felt as a student that 'Francis Bacon was definitely important to me. He blew my mind, and I still think about him a lot. I was completely, one hundred per cent interested in painting, but didn't have the guts to take it on.' That did not prevent him from admiring the neo-geo movement when Charles Saatchi exhibited young American artists at his newly opened gallery in North London. 'My tutors at Goldsmiths said neo-geo was shit, but I was interested in it.' He also found the radiant interior of the Saatchi Gallery an inspiration in itself. 'Charles did the best thing, opening that space,' Hirst told me. 'Those white walls and floors gave me snow-blindness. I thought, if Saatchi can do it, I'm not fucking waiting for anyone. I had no time for anything less than that.' So when Hirst coordinated the cleaning up of the Docklands building for 'Freeze' – even smashing up the cast-iron radiators in order to get them out and create an uncluttered arena for art – the brilliant clarity of Saatchi's remodelled paint factory in Boundary Road must have spurred him on.

In one sense, then, 'Freeze' provided a positive experience for Hirst. 'It made me realize that it was possible to get a big space and a catalogue – it was easy. Ian Jeffrey did the essay, arguing that although the artists were part of a group, each one was isolated within it.' The catalogue, sponsored by 'Olympia and York Canary Wharf Ltd', was handsomely produced and looked confident. Jeffrey called his essay 'Platonic Tropics', and admitted that 'even among artists who know each other, as is the case here, there seems to be little in common'. But he caught the mood of the venture by emphasizing that 'FREEZE is NOW, as the title implies,' and explained that the show's name came 'from Mat Collishaw's light box, dedicated to a moment of impact, a preserved now, a freeze-frame'. Jeffrey omitted to point out that Collishaw had used a photograph of a bullet hole in a human head, a monumental and openly gruesome image reproduced as the first illustration in the catalogue. Its obsession with mortality would prove prophetic of the concerns explored by many young British artists over the decade ahead.

'Freeze' opened at the worst time of year, when most potential visitors were away on summer holidays. Few saw the exhibition and it was scarcely reviewed. Hirst reacted with typical persistence, collecting Norman Rosenthal from Central London and driving him down to Docklands. According to Rosenthal, Hirst arrived on his doorstep 'very early one morning in a rickety old car', but Hirst himself insisted: 'It was a black cab – Norman's memories are so romantic.' Once Rosenthal had seen the show, he said to Hirst: '"Don't let guys like Nick Serota and me get hold of it and ruin it." That wasn't what I wanted to hear. I guess that's what made me hold back afterwards and be awkward. When Nick came, he said: "I'll be seeing more of you," and that was it.'

After lunch, Hirst made me some ham and mustard sandwiches 'for your train journey home', and then took me out into his extensive gardens. 'I'm going to spend £10 million out here, and fill a field with magnolia trees.' Gesturing excitedly, he said, 'I also want a flock of sheep in formaldehyde, for my Devon field over there.' He spontaneously played me a very loud and crazy Fat Les song called 'Vindaloo'. He was clearly enjoying the freedom of deciding what to do here without consulting anyone else. But once we sat down outdoors, he frowned when I asked him what it had been like emerging into the art world after Goldsmiths and 'Freeze'. Hirst had a combative attitude towards dealers who professed an interest in his work.

'I was a totally horrible human being,' he said. 'The demands I made were a nightmare, and I turned into a monster. After I had lunch with Karsten [Schubert] and his partner Helen Windsor, he said: "Great, go back to your studio for six months and if there's anything interesting then I'll come and see it." I said: "Fuck you." I had a *have you any idea who I am, kiss my arse* attitude. I freaked out all my friends as well. I'd tell them not to go to dealers. "They're all shit," I said. They thought maybe I wanted to run my own gallery.'

For a while, at least, he was indeed interested in the notion of controlling his own space. 'Anthony d'Offay tried to get me to run a gallery opposite his on Dering Street, and he paid me to go to Cologne Art Fair. Anthony wanted Charles [Saatchi] in on the project. I was going to call it Pharmacy, and the first show would have been "Pharmacy Installation".' But the venture came to nothing, and in 1991 Hirst ended up making a highly impressive installation with Malaysian butterflies at empty premises in nearby Woodstock Street. *In and Out of Love* was one of his most memorable early achievements. Hirst was probably wise to let Tamara Chodzko and Thomas Dane organize it while he concentrated on making the art. 'It was completely mad, putting it on right next to d'Offay's,' he said, 'but I hadn't even thought "this won't fail". I don't feel like that now!'

Eventually, though, Hirst found the dealer he needed in Jay Jopling. 'I wanted to make the shark piece, and Karsten said: "Damien, you're mad, there's a recession on." But Jay said: "Let's do it." He head-hunted me. He was working with Marc Quinn, and came along to my studio. Jay was the first one who made sense. He said: "I'll take forty per cent," but I said: "You'll take fifty."' When Saatchi bought the tiger shark suspended in a tank of formaldehyde and exhibited it in his gallery, Hirst became the most notorious artist of his generation. *The Physical Impossibility of Death in the Mind of Someone Living* soon began to be regarded as one of the defining works of the decade, but the artist who produced it found that he was himself more celebrated than anything he had made. Almost alone among his contemporaries, Hirst achieved the rare feat of establishing a name far outside the limits of the art world.

In this respect, he matched the reputation David Hockney had acquired in the early 1960s after leaving the Royal College of Art. The desire to be noticed by others had manifested itself on Hirst's very first day at Goldsmiths, when, according to Richard Patterson, 'Damien grabbed a hammer, got his nob out on the floor and pretended he was bashing it.' When I asked Hirst about this, he maintained, 'I've always wanted to be famous. I never wanted to be the best draughtsman in the class. I went kamikaze-style into art. I've doubted everyone, including myself, but the only thing I've never doubted is art. It all boils down to the desire to live for ever. This is what art's all about. If life was perfect, you wouldn't need art.'

After wandering off to urinate under a nearby tree, Hirst came back, his conversation buzzing with ideas for future projects. 'I'd like to open Pharmacies in Berlin and Delhi,' he said, 'and I want to do a really old one, like Schwitters. I'm thinking about outdoor sculpture: galleries are the most boring shops in the world. After the shark, I just imagined a zoo of dead animals. I want to do a trussed-up chicken in formaldehyde – an unlimited edition, so that you'd fight over it in supermarkets. I prefer Sainsbury's to art galleries.' He had, nevertheless, enjoyed showing at the Royal Academy in 1997: 'I was so proud of "Sensation", I thought it was really fantastic. The RA's fucking superb. Ant, Steve and Jarvis Cocker from Pulp thought it was the only show where they felt the work was part of our generation. I love Norman, and the Academy works because it's got him there. Over eighty per cent of the visitors were under thirty. I think it would be a great shame if the "group" broke up now, if it was all just individuals. I feel attached to the people in my year at Goldsmiths.'

All the same, it was clearly going to become increasingly hard for the old feeling of London cohesion to survive. Hirst himself was not only busy transforming the 24 acres of fields and woodlands around his West Country house and neighbouring barns; he would also shortly be transferring the contents of his three studios in the metropolis to a large building in Gloucestershire. 'I'm more isolated now,' he confessed, 'but not in a bad way.' Above all, he seemed preoccupied with painting rather than sculpture. When I went back into his house, the only recent work of his on display there was a large spot painting. 'Jay once said: "I love your work, but I hate the spot paintings." Now he says: "Do some more spots." I really do think they move, that's why I'll never stop doing them. They won't fucking keep still.'

Nor would Hirst. Hostile critics, who still derided him and his fellow students in 'Sensation' at every opportunity, were quite wrong to regard them as the arch-enemies of painting. Nobody could have been more committed to the possibilities of brush and paint than Gary Hume, Richard Patterson or Jenny Saville. And Hirst himself claimed, 'I'm an artist who wants to be a painter. It's a hell of a lot more seductive than being a sculptor. The infinite possibilities in painting just kill me. Sculpture collapses under the weight of gravity, and "installation" is an Airfix word. There are lots of things you can't do in sculpture – if you want a rainbow in a room, you can do it with a hell of a lot more magic in painting. The history of it is daunting, but my favourite paintings in the whole world are *Ghost of a Flea* by Blake and *The Snail* by Matisse. I go and look at them in the Tate. They appeal to different sides of me.'

In the next breath, though, Hirst said, 'Even my paintings are sculpture – I'm now producing spot paintings made of marble.' I was left with the sense that nothing about his future development could be predicted. Apart, perhaps, from one thing: 'I like blurring the boundaries,' he insisted, with a subversive smile.

Jenny Saville

May 1998

Next to a vintage London pub called the Narrow Boat, I went through a small orange door and climbed the back stairs to the third floor. There, in Jenny Saville's studio, her courageous preoccupation with disease and corpses became evident at once. 'I've got lots of medical books,' she said with great intensity, showing me copies of *Foetal Pathology* as well as Julia Kristeva's *Powers of Horror: An Essay on Abjection*. According to Saville, Kristeva 'sees the corpse as the ultimate abjection, something beyond the pale of art'. Saville, by contrast, told me: 'I'm part of a pathology group at the Hunterian Museum. I go there quite a lot – down to the vault parts, because I was interested in strange mutated births and I'm painting hybrids with all these broken parts. Man-made pollutions mean that there are far more monstrous embryos nowadays. I have an interest in plastic surgery – mix and match – ideal parts of the human body as opposed to those who have not. My mum says I've always had a morbid fascination with people who had cut themselves in accidents.'

When Saville herself was only 'about twelve years old', her grandfather 'suddenly had a heart attack. Everybody collapsed in our house, feeling sick, and for the next three or four days there was all this grief around me. I wondered at such incredible intensity of feeling, because my family are not very emotional. I felt fascinated by the way he had died, collapsing in the bathroom. But I was accused of being selfish.' Since then, her fundamental attitude has not changed. 'If someone had a scar in hospital and I visited them, I'd just stare at it. Pharmaceutical drugs and genetic engineering and facial creams seem so futile. What are we all worrying about? We'll eventually be dead anyway.'

Saville passed me another book. Called *Death Scenes*, it contained pictures of corpses taken by a detective in the morgue. This time, I was reminded of Francis Bacon, who had invited me to look at similar books in his studio. I mentioned this, and Saville said, 'Bacon has a huge influence on our generation.' She much preferred his work to that of Lucian Freud: 'I don't like his stagey surroundings, whereas in Bacon it seems to work because of the flat background and furious energy in the figure.'

Showing me a work in progress, she remarked, 'I'm stubborn with my paintings, and this new one is driving me crazy!' No less than 18 feet wide, it had the impact of a cinema screen. It showed three female figures: 'I'm there at the top,' she explained, 'but we're all overlapping and bits of us are in each other. I'm trying to loosen up and avoid being too academic-looking. I want the bodies to intermingle. I've also just done composite heads of my family because we are all quite similar, and I've mixed in some diseased flesh.' When I mentioned my thoughts about the cinema screen, she said that she was 'a massive filmgoer and I know filmmakers – I'm really good friends with a documentary maker.' In Glasgow, where she went to art school, 'you could see films for a pound at the Glasgow Film Theatre! I go to the London Film Festival now and watch lots of good movies in the middle of night. I can work until four a.m., so I'm a night person.'

Although Saville was aware that people tended to assume she worked from life, she explained: 'I've always used photography. It has been far more influential for me in terms of subjects than paintings.' She had also 'worked on a computer with my photographs – shifting colours on a computer, I think, is so like painting. I'm attracted to the time element in painting, the layers. It can have a sculptural nature to it. Film has sound and speed, whereas the sense of time is in painting and the body of paint and my body.' Rather than having people pose in her studio: 'I love working on my own, I like the solitude. I work for an eight-hour stretch, so I'd find a model distracting. I like listening to football on the radio.' During her childhood, she moved around frequently. 'I've been to fourteen schools. My bedroom became hugely important to me, I made things all the time. Today my studio is an extension of all that.'

Saville went to Glasgow School of Art in 1988, so she experienced 'Freeze' and the work of young London artists largely at one remove. 'There were a limited number of books on contemporary international art in the library at Glasgow,' she recalled, remembering how 'our painting tutors seemed largely dismissive of the British Art Show when it opened in the city'. Needless to say, she disagreed and saw there, for the first time, work by Mona Hatoum, Gary Hume and Rachel Whiteread, the three artists who most excited her in the exhibition. But at Glasgow, 'the painting school had only one female tutor, and issues such as gender and representation were rarely discussed. If they thought you were too cocky and self-assured they'd put you down as a woman.' All the talk at Glasgow was of male artists: Georg Baselitz, Anselm Kiefer and the neo-expressionist heroes of the 'New Spirit' in painting. Saville and her fellow students 'thought we'd only achieve something in our late thirties or early forties. The idea then was that you had to wait patiently for a curator or dealer to spot you, and put you in a show.'

Having found her first two years at art school so frustrating, Saville went to Cincinatti University on a scholarship in 1990. 'It completely changed my work,' she said. 'I had my first contact with feminism in theoretical classes on literature and philosophy. I saw a big Polke show, and so many alternative ways of making something, with different materials. In the USA I got a different perspective on what contemporary artists were doing and embraced feminism in a way that, in retrospect, verged on evangelism. I made cabinets with corsets inside and decided that, historically, painting was too much a male territory.'

Only after returning to Glasgow did she embark on the large, powerful paintings of the female nude that would make her reputation.

'Since I realized that women had so often been seen as models rather than painters, I eventually decided to use myself as both painter and model. I felt starved of painting, but had to make it work around the things I'd been thinking about. Taking up brush and canvas again was like realizing that you're physically attracted to a particular kind of person.' Her degree show at Glasgow in 1992 included pictures as assured as *Branded* and *Propped*, extraordinary achievements for an artist who was still only twenty-two. 'I sold some pieces, and *The Times*'s Saturday magazine published an interview with a colour reproduction on the front cover. Charles Saatchi may have noticed that, and then he saw my work in a London show at the Cooling Gallery. I didn't see the exhibition – I couldn't afford to travel down from Glasgow.'

As a result, Saatchi became her patron in a uniquely all-encompassing way. 'Charles bought the paintings I'd sold to people in Glasgow,' Saville remembered, 'and then he said: "I'll give you an advance." He effectively bought me time to paint, from August 1992 until January 1994. I worked absolutely like I'd never worked before, and produced seven large pictures. I never realized quite how much it all meant at the time, which was just as well.' The paintings were shown at the Saatchi Gallery in 1994, arousing widespread interest. 'Charles was vital, providing institutional-like space for me when I was so young. He was very encouraging. I was never part of the Freeze group, but much of their work does seem to overlap with my concerns. I'm especially interested in Sarah Lucas's view of femininity, Damien Hirst's interest in death and Marc Quinn's exploration of the self.'

By the time Saville was included in the immensely controversial 'Sensation' show at the Royal Academy in 1997, her paintings were displayed there with great prominence. She recalled 'walking towards the entrance surrounded by people with protesting placards, and I thought, this is astonishing, it's what controversial exhibitions must have been like at the end of the last century. I suppose "Sensation" might be seen in the future as the moment when certain young artists joined the establishment, and became blue-chip. But you could see the energy and motivation in the work. And in Charles, too. We didn't have anything like "Sensation" when we were at art school. It wasn't a particularly radical show in terms of the art world, since much of the work had been seen previously. But it was essential for Britain. The Royal Academy Summer Exhibition represents everything that's horrible about British art – like members of your family who would like you to paint nice flowers and cats. But things are changing, and now there are women in the landscape of art, and they're major players like Rachel Whiteread. I thought her *Ghost* was breathtaking, one of the most beautiful things I'd ever seen.'

Saville admitted, 'I don't know if London will continue to be the fashionable, cutting-edge place it is at the moment. But there's an infrastructure of galleries here, and an energy about making and viewing art. It looks positive for the future. You wonder if other wealthy people will be as enthusiastic as Charles. It has tended to pivot on collectors, because our institutions are more cautious about collecting British artists. So it's fitting that Tate Bankside is happening after this decade of art-making: it'll reflect what's going on here. I think it's great that video art and found objects are on an equal footing now with painting. But painting's very resilient, considering that photography has been knocking on its door for over a century. People still want to make marks, one way or another. Working with a camera myself recently has made me more confident of painting. You realize there are certain things that photography and computers can't do.'

Steve McQueen

February 1999

Steve McQueen was building a 70-foot brick wall when I met him at the ICA in London, where his keenly awaited one-man show had just opened. Spanning the entire length of the narrow Concourse Gallery, always an awkward place to display art, the wall transformed the space with its forbidding bulk. McQueen mounted a ladder and began placing pieces of smashed glass into fresh cement along the top. Beside him, a large bucket was heaped with fragments of beer bottles jagged enough to lacerate anyone attempting to scale the bricks. 'I'm hoping that the wall will be scribbled on,' he said with a subversive smile. 'If it's not covered in graffiti by the end of the show, I'll be disappointed.'

McQueen's light-heartedness could not entirely mask the inevitable tension he felt, staging his first major British exhibition of films, sculpture and photography. Shown extensively abroad since his debut in a mixed ICA survey in 1995, the ebullient twenty-nine-year-old was already widely regarded as an outstanding young artist. So far, however, McQueen had enjoyed greater acclaim abroad than in his native London. 'I get a better response in the US,' he said, 'maybe because Black artists are more noticeable over there and gain a broader acceptance.'

Talking about his student years, McQueen soon made it clear that they had not been easy. At Chelsea School of Art, he painted and 'did a lot of drawing, but they didn't have any equipment for film'. Even at pace-setting Goldsmiths College, where he went on to study in the early 1990s, he had to 'beg, steal or borrow from the film department. Goldsmiths was a tricky time: you had to find your own way. It was only when I saw a contemporary show at the Whitney during a visit to New York in 1993 that the wide variety of possibilities in art really blew me away – like an explosion with fragments flying off in different directions.' It was a revelation compared with his experience at Goldsmiths, 'where I had no tutorials in my last year. Then, after leaving, a friend and fellow student who was Black committed suicide.'

Already, though, McQueen was fascinated by the potential of film as an artist's medium. 'I was a zombie for foreign films,' he said, remembering in particular the impact of 'a John Cassavetes season in 1992. I loved the intimacy of his films, their changing moods, and the feeling that you never knew what was coming next.' This fluidity and unpredictable excitement characterized the two films he showed at the ICA's 'Mirage: Enigma of Race, Difference and Desire' in 1995. Both were silent and black and white, like so many of the early movies he admires. They stood out with impressive conviction in this large international exhibition, which took its cue from the writings of the Martinique-born Frantz Fanon, whose 1952 book *Black Skin, White Masks* proved a widely influential study of colonialism and its traumatic psychological legacy.

McQueen's highly precocious 1993 film *Bear* plays with the notion of a threatening Black aggressor, yet soon replaces it with a far more stimulating alternative. The promised struggle between two naked Black men never really takes place. They grin at each other and even embrace. When eventually their bodies lock in a bout of wrestling, it soon gives way to a slow-motion, lyrical dance that banishes all thought of war. By this stage, McQueen seems to rejoice in his film's provocative and defiantly joyful escape from racist cliches.

'I didn't want to do "Mirage" at first,' he confessed. 'It was an all-Black show, but that's never been an issue for me and I said no. But I didn't have a dealer, and nobody else was interested in showing my work. So I had to go back to the ICA.' His decision paid off. I was sufficiently impressed by *Bear* and McQueen's other work to put his name forward for the British Art Show, the large touring exhibition of young artists that I co-selected in 1995. After it was exhibited there alongside his *Five Easy Pieces*, another impressive early film where a female tightrope-walker is intercut with hula-hooping men, *Bear* was bought by Tate. At once threatening and playful, this Bacon-like confrontation between the two men has a dramatic, improvised flow that still typifies some of McQueen's recent work. '*Bear* is constantly changing, it's aggressive, tender and gay,' he said. 'But you can't put your finger on it – the two men seem to be passing through.'

The principal film in his new show at the ICA was just as enigmatic, even though McQueen had now moved on to colour, a triple screen and – for the first time – sound. Called *Drum Roll*, it recorded the giddy journey of an oil barrel pushed by a pink-coated McQueen through the streets of New York. Different viewpoints from the drum were projected alongside each other, with dizzying glimpses of pedestrians, traffic, skyscrapers and the artist himself. The soundtrack added to this onslaught, with its cacophonous fragments of drum rattle, car din, startled comments from passers-by and McQueen's reiterated 'Excuse me, please,' as he hurtles along. 'It's uptown, posh Manhattan,' he told me, 'and the location was the nearest to the Marian Goodman Gallery, my New York dealer. The drum goes through a very interesting piece of real estate, so damn expensive. But the film is more to do with economy of movement, the wheel, oil, and taking the city – anyone can do it.'

McQueen first went to New York when he was six years old. 'Most of my family live in the US, either in Brooklyn or Miami, and I've considered moving to New York myself. But I didn't think I'd survive there. For artists, it's like an elephants' graveyard.' *Drum Roll* was filmed there a year ago, and he sat on it afterwards. 'Thelonious Monk wrote "Straight, No Chaser" in his head during the 1930s, but he didn't write it down until the 1950s. I like keeping things in my head, too, and then releasing them. With film, it's worth the wait: you have to learn how to slow the heart right down.'

Not that McQueen is averse to surprising the viewer. His other new film at the ICA, *Deadpan*, paid a highly dramatic homage to a celebrated slapstick moment from Buster Keaton's movie *Steamboat Bill, Jr.* Commissioned by the Museum of Modern Art in New York, where McQueen held a solo exhibition in 1997, it centres on the collapse of a newly built house. McQueen himself stands beside it, looking as if he will be fatally injured. Instead, an open window in the facade descends directly on him, leaving the artist uncannily upright and untouched. We see the miraculous event several times over, from various vantages and at different speeds. McQueen, the very image of the defiant survivor, remains extraordinarily still and impassive throughout, even though he must have dreaded filming such a potentially lethal sequence. '*Deadpan* is all about that wait, about passing through the body,' he said. 'I'm framed by the window frame and by the institution where my work is shown.'

Perhaps that was why McQueen seemed like such a restless individual, whose sculpture at the ICA took the form of a chrome funfair roundabout where visitors could spin themselves into queasiness. Aware of the dangers besetting artists, he was a loner who liked moving on. Two years earlier, he had decided to decamp with his Dutch partner to Amsterdam. Their child had recently been born there, and he told me he could not imagine ever returning to London. 'I don't like it here any more,' he explained. 'I was getting into a routine, and I love the idea that nobody knows me in Amsterdam. The living conditions are great, especially for kids.'

Didn't he, I asked, find Amsterdam a bit quiet compared with London, which is regarded as a Mecca by so many young artists today? 'Don't forget that I grew up in Ealing,' he said with a wry grin. 'Anyway, it's not important to me to live in an artists' milieu. I've never liked groups – they remind me too much of joining the Boy Scouts. Even though I'm a Catholic, and definitely an English guy, I'm open and changing, not stuck in a particular identity.' The key, for McQueen, lay in his art. 'It enables you to work things out in public, creating your own world. Otherwise you're powerless: it would be terrible.'

Louise Bourgeois
May 1999

Many artists would feel daunted by the prospect of making a sculpture for the colossal Turbine Hall at London's Tate Modern. Running the entire width of the old Bankside Power Station, designed by Sir Giles Gilbert Scott in 1947, this immense space surges to the height of a secular cathedral. Prior to the opening of Tate Modern in 2000, the Turbine Hall was stripped of its original machinery, restored and hugely enhanced as a great public concourse, capable of housing even the most titanic-sized artworks with aplomb. But its sheer monumentality can easily crush the work displayed there, reducing exhibits to utter insignificance.

Louise Bourgeois was feisty enough to savour the risk involved in tackling the first special commission for the Turbine Hall. The resulting work was, after all, the largest she had ever made. Details of the sculpture, subsidized by the first instalment of a £1.25 million sponsorship deal with Unilever, were kept secret. But it was rumoured that it would reflect the artist's preoccupation with walk-in cells, and take the form of three separate installations made from sheet steel. At the time, Bourgeois herself had never laid eyes on the Turbine Hall; aged eighty-seven, she was too frail to travel from her home in Manhattan. Even so, the space was revealed to her in plans, videos and photographs, as well as detailed descriptions by her assistant, Jerry Gorovoy, who flew to London and scrutinized the location with great care.

It was Jerry who answered when I phoned Bourgeois in her New York studio in May 1999, a year before the opening of Tate Modern. Normally averse to giving interviews, she had nevertheless agreed to talk to me if I rang her from London at a pre-arranged time. And she had no intention of reneging on her promise. 'Louise says she's coming at top speed,' said Jerry, and before long Bourgeois was on the line. Speaking fast and very clearly, with a sharp sense of humour and an accent still distinctively French even after sixty years in America, she responded with relish when I asked her how she felt about the Tate venture. 'It's very exciting and a great pleasure,' Bourgeois declared with evident vigour. 'I'm not foreign to this type of project – there is one I am involved with at the moment in Pittsburgh, where they are organizing the rehabilitation of old architecture for the sake of tourism. But I enjoy it. I think you are very lucky in London that the government lets you do it, and the Tate has not fallen into the hands of private people.'

Could she, I wondered, tell me anything more about the work planned for the Turbine Hall? 'I'm ready for it but I don't want to tell,' she said with a laugh. 'If I did, it would take away from the surprise element at the last minute. That's important: if you receive a gift of candy, and there's a red ribbon round it, you want to attack it quickly. It's a sudden thing.' So did she always think a great deal about how the viewer would respond to her work? 'I care very much about the viewer,' she replied without hesitation. 'Everything I do goes towards you the spectator, not myself.'

Bourgeois emphasized how grateful she was to Nicholas Serota and Lars Nittve, directors of the Tate and Tate Modern respectively, for giving her 'the chance to realize a work bigger than anything I've ever done before: it'll be fifteen metres high, that's forty-five feet. I've done a maquette, and little by little it will multiply.' Was there enough time to complete and install such a complex and elaborate work before the Turbine Hall opened the following May? 'I usually am not late,' she said firmly. 'I'm a very steady worker, and I don't let myself get distracted by other things. I'm never late if I promise something for a date. You can't predict accidents, but it'll be ready one year from now.'

To my surprise, Bourgeois was prepared to reveal how she planned to cope with the challenge posed by the vastness of the site. 'You need something dramatic for such a big space,' she insisted. 'The sculpture is made of steel, so the cleaning of it is something very special. You clean it like the way you clean pots and pans on the stove. So if you swing lights above the work, it creates shadows and points of brilliance.'

Who, I asked, would carry out this crucial act of cleaning? 'In the studio we have different people doing different things,' she explained. 'It's something very special, this studio. It's an old industrial building in Brooklyn. There was a labour dispute history and a slump in the market, so from one day to the next all these hundreds of sewing machines were packed up. The work was all transferred to Indochina instead. So the building remained empty, but artists came and saved it. Artists are the saviours of the things nobody wants.'

Bourgeois moved to her studio in 1980, and its epic dimensions 'encouraged me to work on a bigger scale. There's a solid cement floor all across the building, fifteen inches thick, and I have to communicate between the first floor and the basement. So we have spiral staircases, like a submarine.' Suddenly, without any prompting on my part, she disclosed that 'in the Turbine Hall you will see circular staircases. The metaphor is three elements representing a working family relationship. A happy metaphor, a happy relationship, which is very unusual for me.'

It certainly was. Most of Bourgeois's work is riddled with anxiety. Death, loneliness and paternal disloyalty give her sculpture its haunting power, and at the time of the Tate commission she was still obsessed by intense feelings about her father's shameless philandering with the family governess during her childhood in France. Paris-born, she grew up in a family dedicated to restoring antique textiles. Her mother worked as a weaver repairing tapestries. Bourgeois, who thought of her mother as a benevolent spider and 'my best friend', remembered wrapping herself in these heavy fabrics to play hide-and-seek. But game-playing gave way to a deep-seated feeling of betrayal when her father, who ran the textile business, indulged in a protracted affair with a young Englishwoman called Sadie.

In this respect, I suggested, the Tate's invitation must have brought back melancholy memories with renewed force. 'England is very, very important to me,' she said with irony audible in her voice, 'because in my family the English could do no wrong. When my father picked a mistress, it was always an English girl: if he made her pregnant, she could be shipped back to England and he would not be held responsible. It never happened. But since then I've made a lot of work called *The English Can Do No Wrong*.'

Once Bourgeois had discovered her father's liaison, the pain was almost unbearable. As a girl, she fantasized about exacting revenge. After moving to New York in 1938 with her husband, the distinguished American art historian Robert Goldwater, she learned how to place this formative trauma at the turbulent centre of her work. One major installation was brazenly entitled *The Destruction of the Father*. The urge to kill and devour gave Bourgeois's sculpture much of its outspoken, macabre energy. And in 1982 she published a memoir called *Child Abuse*, revealing how her father's ten-year infatuation with Sadie the governess had profoundly affected her imaginative life.

Did the wound still fester inside her, I wondered? Bourgeois sighed. 'My memories still bother me,' she confessed. 'All this should have been cleared away by analysis, but I never had it. Only making art really works for me: my friends were worse after analysis than before. All the art I make comes from my childhood and adolescence.' Then her mood lightened. 'But I am in a forgiving mood at the moment, because you are happier if you are on good terms with people who live around you. I forgive their boo-boos, and I'm more relaxed now.' Was this, I asked, to do with the mellowing of age? 'No, I won't tell you how old I am,' she said with a laugh. 'But I'm old enough to know better than to answer such a question.'

Looking back, did she feel fortunate that America had become her home at the age of twenty-seven? 'If I'd stayed in France, I'd not have become an artist,' she declared flatly. 'I'd have been earning my living in other ways. I am a runaway child, because I was absolutely delighted to leave the old country. And I never feel at ease when I return there.' But she still found it a struggle to win a substantial reputation in her adopted land. The United States was slow to recognize her, and the Museum of Modern Art in New York only staged a large survey of her work as late as 1982.

In the years that followed, Bourgeois won widening international acclaim, and her outstanding achievements made me wonder if she had been a victim, earlier on, of the widespread male prejudice against women artists. 'It's not that the men were against us,' she explained. 'They simply didn't know we existed. They could not be bothered to look at little women. I was an insider, but men had tremendous power as gallery owners and taste-makers. It doesn't bring much butter to the spinach to be an artist, so women tended to have other jobs.'

At the time of our conversation, by contrast, Bourgeois was basking in the accolade of exhibitions across the world, and I wondered if she regretted her inability to visit England for the opening of her Turbine Hall installation. 'I will be there in spirit,' she said stoically, before revealing in a mischievous voice, 'I lived in Putney for several periods during the 1930s. In England it rains all the time, the food is very strange, and people drive on the wrong side of the street.' Besides, she was far too busy to waste time travelling across the Atlantic: 'I have a dozen projects at the moment, and almost too much to do. I only manage because of a very rigid work programme. But I have lots of energy, perseverance and curiosity.'

June 2007

Visiting Louise Bourgeois's New York house was like embarking on a mysterious journey into her imagination. Then in her ninety-sixth year, she was enjoying immense international acclaim as one of the most outstanding artists at work anywhere. Frances Morris, who was curating the eagerly awaited Bourgeois retrospective at Tate Modern, due to open that October, felt sure that 'she ranks among the major sculptors of the 20th century. Like a surfer, she rides lots of waves, and even now she's incredibly hungry for new challenges.' But as I approached my destination along a quiet Chelsea street near the Hudson River, the modest simplicity of her narrow brownstone building did not even hint at its owner's titanic reputation. Standing opposite an old Episcopal church, the four-storey house showed absolutely no sign of ostentation or the wealth her highly priced art must have given her. The house number had been painted, very quickly, on the wall. Ironwork railings flanked the steep steps leading up to the door. Directly in front of it was a plain metal outer door designed by Bourgeois herself in a sequence of purged, curving lines reminiscent of burgeoning leaves or hillsides swollen with fertility. But they were very discreet when compared with the damaged bodies, cruel cages and torn dolls that so often erupt in the rest of her work, unnerving us with their angry memories of childhood trauma.

I rang the bell. Within seconds, Jerry Gorovoy emerged to greet me. Tall, slim and soft-voiced, with long hair and a full, dark beard just starting to go grey, he had been Bourgeois's assistant for many years. When she created her three monumental towers for Tate Modern's immense Turbine Hall to mark its momentous opening in 2000, it was Jerry who had travelled to London and installed them; quite understandably, the octogenarian Bourgeois did not feel like undertaking the long journey herself. And besides, she trusted him completely to oversee the erection of a work developed with such obsessive audacity in her studio.

He led me along a narrow corridor into the shadowy heart of the house. Its floor and walls immediately suggested that the owner had no need to rely on smart, streamlined decor. Fashionably designed interiors clearly did not matter to Bourgeois at all. Unashamedly bohemian, this looked like the home of someone who lived entirely inside her own head and had not bothered to change her surroundings since moving in nearly half a century earlier. Jerry explained that the house, erected in the 1860s, had originally been occupied by sailors. The basement floor was built with rocks, because the Hudson used to flow much closer to the house than it did now. If the basement ever flooded, the stubborn old rocks would refuse to rot.

This toughness seemed wholly appropriate to me, for the woman living there was nothing if not resilient. She insisted on continuing to work with great single-mindedness. Most of us would be either dead or decrepit well before reaching her advanced age. But Bourgeois defied all thought of senility as she devoted herself, as ever, to work in progress. Mostly producing prints on unusual materials like sackcloth, linen or banana paper, she was fascinated with the process of making images on a flat surface. Although she had by this time sold her enormous studio in Brooklyn, where her sculpture had been made in the vastness of a converted industrial building, Bourgeois still retained a large portion of a foundry in Queens. Her strong sense of continuity was proclaimed by a painting that invaded my vision as I entered the house. It depicted flowers exploding with convulsive energy from a tiny vase, and Bourgeois had made it as long ago as 1945. It hung on a bare brick wall just outside the room in which she worked, affirming the vitality that still drove her forward with an obstinate sense of determination.

Jerry admitted he was astonished that Bourgeois had agreed to see me. She no longer gave interviews, and had been suffering from chronic insomnia. Yet he led me into a fascinatingly cluttered room at the back of the house, where the artist herself was sitting at one end of a large, well-worn sofa and leaning against a wrap-around royal-blue cushion. Smaller than I remembered from my previous visit several years earlier, Bourgeois was nevertheless very upright. Sipping water from an old enamel cup, she clutched a plain white handkerchief in her pale hand. Although she wore small gold hoop earrings, not a trace of make-up could be detected on her face. She appeared very self-contained. After taking my seat on a spindly folding chair, I noticed that an ample red velour dressing-gown covered her legs.

Directly in front of her, taking up a lot of space, stood a sturdy revolving table with thick wooden legs and a circular piece of metal set into the top. It had been custom-built for making sculpture, but at the moment the only new work visible in the room was a soft-ground etching propped on the floor. Its bare contours and pale salmon colours testified to Bourgeois's eloquence as a draughtswoman. Looking through the window, I remarked that the forms in the etching reminded me of the trees visible in her back yard. She responded very simply, with an accent still distinctively French: 'I see. Right.' I gathered from this notably clipped response that she wanted to conserve her energy by keeping conversation to a minimum. Although I felt a little frustrated by this new reticence, I could understand it. I asked if her art had altered recently. 'No,' she replied firmly, 'it is not changing at all.' Her recently completed maquette of a five-legged dog had surely issued from the same imagination that produced her celebrated sculpture of a spider. So did she, I wondered, want to carry on working and live to a hundred? Her response was immediate. 'Yes, right,' she said crisply, 'we are all doing that.' She smiled, as if confident of her ability to achieve that goal.

The strength of her will to survive was abundantly clear, and at one point she showed just how vibrant her mind really was. After I explained that my New York visit was largely devoted to presenting a BBC programme on Picasso's revolutionary painting *Les Demoiselles d'Avignon*, there was a pause. Bourgeois went silent. She appeared to be meditating and preparing herself for an utterance. Then, quite out of the blue, the atmosphere in the room was transformed by the sound of her high, clear voice singing the old French song 'Sur le Pont d'Avignon'. Perfectly in tune, very fast and word-perfect, it was a magical performance. Bourgeois must have been remembering it from her early days in Paris, where she was born on Christmas Day 1911. The song's sudden resurfacing had a haunting power, testifying to the extraordinary spirit of the woman who was so unexpectedly singing it to me.

The shelves lining the walls opposite her sofa were heavy with an abundance of books and files. They reflected a lifetime of indomitable commitment to work, and wherever I looked in the room my eyes were invaded by heaps of accumulated documents. On the cracked wall above her, a vast noticeboard was likewise festooned with old posters, cards and other material fixed to its surface. They were all evidence of the enormous international admiration for her work, and the upcoming Tate retrospective promised to be a revelation. The hugely potent art she had produced in the 1940s and 1950s was then barely known in Britain, so the show was bound to transform all our ideas about the extent of her overall achievement. I left Bourgeois's house with the feeling that this intense, highly focused woman was reserving her energy almost entirely for the overriding priority of art.

Frank Stella

October 1999

According to the breathless posters outside the Victoria Palace Theatre in London, *The Pajama Game* was 'Hot, Sexy, Fresh Dance Fun'. The saucy words made me wonder if this vintage Broadway musical of the 1950s was about to be given a dire dumbing-down – but I need not have worried. Inside the theatre, the director, Simon Callow, issued some last-minute instructions with evident intelligence; sitting nearby, Frank Stella toyed with an unlit cigar while assessing the impact of his exuberant set designs.

How, I wondered, did a seasoned Manhattan abstractionist make sense of such an unlikely commission? Spreading his jeans-clad legs over the chair in front, the sixty-three-year-old Stella admitted that he 'couldn't have done this project when I was younger. Abstract art was a totally different world, and I wouldn't have had the confidence to design a kitchen, a factory, or Hernando's Hideaway.' When he first settled in New York, as a precociously daring young Princeton history graduate in the late 1950s, Stella pioneered the austerity of minimalism. But his later work broke free from monochromatic austerity, with shaped canvases, flamboyant colour and freewheeling excursions into sculpture.

These high spirits gave his *Pajama Game* sets their zest, especially in a spectacular picnic scene where boldly patterned hills surged in front of a backdrop splashed with vibrant colour – inspired, as Stella explained, by the painted dots of pointillism. Each set was utterly distinct. At one point, for the 'Steam Heat' dance number, a colossal sculpture shot upwards and writhed in space with invigorating dynamism. But the Sleep-Tite Pajama Factory, where so much of the industrial and amorous action occurs, was a more sober, monochrome affair dominated by a fiercely diagrammatic, spiralling clock. Here the stripped rigour of Stella's earlier paintings was detectable, the work of a man who still counted Malevich and Mondrian among his heroes.

Scene after scene in this revival was dominated by classic Stella images, all closely related to the art he made in his studio. Far from straining for a 1950s look, or referring in any way to the original Broadway production of *The Pajama Game*, Stella remained unashamedly himself throughout this fast-moving evening. That was, after all, why Simon Callow had invited him to design the show. 'Ironic, post-modern revivals have had their day,' Callow insisted. 'I wanted a painter who could use exuberant primary colours, and when I visited Frank's New York studio I knew he was the right choice. The moment you walk into that incredible space, you want to flush the Prozac right down the lavatory.'

Although Stella could remember seeing *Guys and Dolls* with his mother back in 1954, musicals held no special appeal for him. His only previous stage designs had been made many years earlier, on 'a tiny set for Merce Cunningham, with five minimalist bands of canvas'. But he needed little persuasion to take on *The Pajama Game*. 'Frank moved very fast,' said Callow, 'producing four huge models in four weeks flat.' The more he worked with Stella, the more fascinated Callow became: 'Frank isn't prepared to negotiate about his work, but he's quite happy to start all over again. He'd say: "I don't know what I'm doing, I'm only the designer." His mind works with astonishing speed, and the only difficulty is to hold him down for more than three minutes.'

After a while, Callow realized that he had found the ideal artist for the task. 'Most painters don't think three-dimensionally, but Frank does. He's made free-standing sculptures, and some wonderful architectural decorations in David Mirvish's Princess of Wales Theatre in Toronto. They convinced me that he would be ideal for *The Pajama Game*. Producers often used painters to design their revues in the 1920s and 1930s, and this musical is like a revue. It's a very young piece.' The youthful Bob Fosse worked on the original *Pajama Game*; it was his breakthrough as a choreographer. The same production also projected the young Shirley MacLaine into the limelight, and the 1957 film version became a vehicle for the talents of Doris Day.

Stella saw the movie while he was preparing his designs, and enjoyed it. 'But I felt that I didn't have to be so literal in my sets. Even in the kitchen scene, which can't be abstract, I took as my starting point the illustrations in a sales catalogue.' Reminiscent of Roy Lichtenstein's interiors derived from Yellow Pages drawings, these illustrations were already stylized enough to be one step away from banal realism. And Stella would ideally have liked his kitchen design to be even more simplified than it is. 'That's my only bone of contention with Simon,' he said. 'I'd prefer not to have props on any of the kitchen surfaces. If it were a propless play, that would be good.'

He also found the sewing machines in the Sleep-Tite Pajama Factory 'a nightmare – they were too static and cluttered up the stage'. His ideal was a set as spartan as the shallow office scene: 'Nice and clean, we don't need to have endless equipment filling the space.' Listening to the show's 'sweet music' by Richard Adler and Jerry Ross further convinced him that the designs should be as pared-down as possible: 'The music affected me in the sense that I had to keep everything moving, I didn't belabour any static ideas.'

Working at top speed, with 'some kids who came to help me set up models in the studio', he even found the constraints of a tight budget unexpectedly stimulating. 'It focused my mind on what was really necessary,' he explained, adding, 'People want realism to get into it, but Christopher Woods's costumes do that. They're very full and beautiful, and integrated with my sets as well.' The presence of the costumes seemed to have freed Stella, allowing his love of abstraction to thrive. As we talked in the auditorium, an astonishing drop curtain descended on stage. It was painted with an ecstatic design, filled to the point of congestion with exhilarating flourishes of colour and intricate geometrical structures.

Looking at this joyful explosion, I told Stella that it reminded me above all of a Kandinsky painting. He warmed to the comparison at once. 'If I have an ambition,' he said, 'it would be to make good on Kandinsky. I even defend the geometric paintings he made in the 1930s and 1940s. They're full of new ideas, and the potential is bursting out of them. I'm picking up on the late Kandinskys and trying to make them as good as the early ones. I love his feeling for the power of abstraction: he brings it from the real world into his rarefied art.'

The same could be said of Stella himself, in the way he applied himself to the demands of a London theatre without compromising his work in any way. He saw nothing strange in having attempted such an enterprise. 'Painting, sculpture and architecture, they're all the same,' he said. 'Artists used to design all the settings for royal and church ceremonies, so it's an old tradition.' But he did not intend to do any more stage work, still less branch out into film design. 'The last movie I saw in the cinema was *The Treasure of the Sierra Madre*,' he recalled, before telling me with a shudder, 'I don't like going to the cinema and being trapped in a dark room. The sound is so loud that you have to wear earplugs, so I won't ever go again. But I might go back to the stage one day, and do a one-off set for an avant-garde production. There's a kind of magic about the theatre – it seems to turn everyone on.'

Gilbert & George

May 2001

An unexpected heatwave hit the East End of London on the day I visited Gilbert and George. The doors of Hawksmoor's great Spitalfields church, rearing so doughtily at the end of their street, were open to let in some air. But when Gilbert and George answered my ring at their bell, they both seemed impervious to the weather. They were dressed in their customary matching suits, with crisp white collars and beautifully laundered ties.

After walking through to a small outdoor area at the back of their early 18th-century house, we paused for a moment under the sun's fierce impact. A handsome carved and painted bench by their favourite Victorian designer, Christopher Dresser, glittered in the light. Over the wall, Hawksmoor's Christ Church surged with even more startling force, and when I marvelled at it George murmured: 'It's rather terrifying, isn't it?'

But we soon disappeared into the coolness of a surprisingly extensive studio beyond, converted by the artists from a clothing factory built in the former back garden half a century earlier. Tea was promptly served in plain white mugs, and they remarked that 'we don't normally notice the weather. We're inside all the time working. In the winter months, we get up soon after six, go out for breakfast in Brick Lane and come back to start work before it even gets light.'

Despite their long-standing reputation as the bad boys of British art, Gilbert and George are formidably disciplined and prolific. Ever since I'd first visited them three decades before, when they were only renting two rooms on the ground floor of the same house and producing art in their kitchen, they had concentrated their energies on making a prodigiously inventive body of work. And now, in their late fifties, the indefatigable duo gave no sign of letting up. They showed me proofs of a gigantic, multi-volume and profusely illustrated publication surveying their thirty-four years of work, devised without a particular publisher in view. Ever mindful of reaching the widest conceivable audience, they explained, 'We'll go for the one who's prepared to sell it at the cheapest possible price.'

On a nearby table, I inspected careful scale models of two museum-sized galleries where Gilbert and George were holding large exhibitions later that year. One was the Factory at the School of Art in Athens, the other the enormous Centro Cultural de Belém in Lisbon. Judging by the miniature reproductions of their exhibits, already fixed neatly in place on the walls of the scale models, Gilbert and George would pull no punches in either Greece or Portugal. One colossal, multi-panelled work was called *Blood, Tears, Spunk and Piss*, while the word 'cock' was prominently displayed in another, equally provocative picture. But Gilbert and George had not experienced any resistance from their hosts. 'Both Athens and Portugal have recently come out of rather oppressive times, so they've gone to the other extreme now and haven't questioned any of our choices. Other galleries probably would.'

The last time Gilbert and George had staged a show at a public gallery in London, controversy had centred on the wording of advertisements for the exhibition. It was held at the South London Gallery in 1995, and formal complaints were made about the title: 'The Naked Shit Pictures'. 'But the judge found in our favour, because he said it was a truthful and accurate description of the work on view there.' Soon afterwards, Gilbert and George had finally fallen out with their London dealer, Anthony d'Offay. I was astonished when, on his birthday, they announced their decision to leave him. They had been close friends with d'Offay for many years and first held a show at his gallery in the early 1970s. But when the end came, it had been very bitter. Why did the relationship turn so sour? 'We just didn't feel that he had the time to look after us properly. And Anthony can't connect with young artists.'

Gilbert and George were widely admired among the generation collected by Charles Saatchi and promoted in the 'Sensation' exhibition at the Royal Academy. Although Saatchi had never bought Gilbert and George's work, they got on well with the YBAs (Young British Artists). Tracey Emin and Chris Ofili lived in their neighbourhood ('When we look out of our back window, we can see Ofili sunbathing'). And Jay Jopling, the influential young dealer who showed so many of the Sensation artists, had lost no time in asking Gilbert and George to join his White Cube gallery. 'Jay has always wanted us, ever since he was at Eton. He used to go through the school grounds walking very stiffly, in unison with another boy by his side. And when someone asked him what on earth he was doing, Jay said: "We're doing a Gilbert and George."'

Jopling's new gallery, White Cube 2, situated on a prominent site in nearby Hoxton Square, had played a key role in their decision to join his stable. Their new show, due to open there in June 2001, would include the largest single pictures they had ever made. And the severity of the images would be matched by the simplicity of their display. 'For us it's ideal, a new beginning. We're turning the space into a gallery in the classical way, so that the content of the art comes alive.' Nothing would be permitted to distract attention from the images themselves, and they were bound to provoke censure. Called *New Horny Pictures*, they juxtaposed images of Gilbert and George with rank upon rank of gay sex advertisements found in magazines.

The artists themselves were depicted looking very subdued, if not grim. In the biggest exhibits, stretching to an immense width, they either stood rigidly to attention or leaned unsteadily against each other for support, as if overwhelmed by the sheer number of personal, erotic details enclosed in the circular forms surrounding them. In one picture, each advert began with a name: Cain, Rudy, Nando, Chase, Leo, Tyrone, Ric, Jason, Bjorn. They seemed endless, testifying to the extraordinary proliferation of such printed matter in a country that, as Gilbert and George pointed out to me, 'leads the world in sex adverts'. Below the names were anatomical descriptions, ranging from the brazen to the lyrical and always boasting. They terminated in phone numbers, many with old dialling codes that showed just how long Gilbert and George had been collecting this mass of lewd ephemera. In another large picture, the adverts avoided names altogether. Instead, the headlines called our attention to 'Naughty Black Boy', 'God's Gift', 'Dead Cute', 'Huge Nipples' and 'Active Service'.

At first entertaining, the adverts gradually took on a cumulative melancholy, even desperation. In the smaller pictures, Gilbert and George presided over 'Lingerie David' or 'Let Me Be Your Fantasy' with far graver expressions, as if meditating on both the relentlessness and the transience of the commercialized erotic drive. After a while, I realized that the images even began to resemble war memorials – perhaps reflecting Gilbert and George's passionate admiration for Lutyens's great monument to the soldiers killed during the disastrous Somme campaign, and their keen awareness of precedents in art for their engagement with prostitution. They mentioned Augustus Egg and Holman Hunt, pioneers who courageously introduced 'fallen women' into Victorian painting. 'Turner used to draw people shagging for money, but after his death Ruskin destroyed most of these pictures. And then Picasso produces *Les Demoiselles d'Avignon*, basing it on a group of whores in a brothel.'

Gilbert and George were highly conscious of history. Remembering how they began, after meeting as fellow students at St Martin's School of Art in the late 1960s, they explained, 'We wanted to make pictures that would look well in the National Gallery. With our conservative use of form, we soon became far more weird than the so-called experimental artists with all their bananas and umbrellas. We'll never move away from using the camera, but we don't think of it as photography. They're Big Pictures.' Gilbert and George were also proudly conscious of the unifying themes running through their output. They show me a 1977 work called *Prostitute Poof Cock VD*, and seem pleased that it links up so clearly with their latest work. 'You can always trust us to do the worst – we're very consistent. And we'll never become part of the establishment. Unlike so many of the Young British Artists, we haven't been invited to tea at Downing Street.'

Even so, they have always resisted being confined to a 'gay artist' ghetto. 'We don't have a strong gay feeling – the sexual feelings we get are the ones everyone gets,' they told me. 'But we've always had a big following among women. They love the work. Men are often terrified of it, and male collectors have a big problem about displaying our work on their walls. But one man bought a picture without even realizing that there was shit in it. He thought the giant turd was a tree, until a dealer congratulated him on being brave enough to buy it. "What do you mean?" he said, then realized with horror and cancelled the sale.'

Having exhibited across the world, including major surveys in countries as immense as China and Russia, was there anywhere they would especially like to show in future? The answer was unexpected. 'London,' they said emphatically. 'It's fifteen years since we last had a really big show here, and the Tate has never done anything for us.' Hadn't they even been asked to make a Tate Christmas tree? Their reply was withering: 'We'd tell them exactly where to put it.'

More seriously, Gilbert and George deplored what they called the 'racist barriers' in the two new Tate galleries. 'There's very little English art in Tate Modern, and we'd never show our work in Tate Britain,' they said angrily. 'We wouldn't even visit it. We want to be shown as part of modern art, not just English modern.'

In the end, though, Gilbert and George felt no need of help from museums. They were bullishly confident about their work's ability to communicate with anyone who encountered it. 'We've managed to sidestep the museum professional who explains modern art to the public. The professional always condescends to the viewer, but the public don't need to rush to the information desk for an explanation leaflet with our work. We always try to make a picture we want them to remember. We talk to a lot of Bangladeshi young people round here, and they complain that, if it's just three buckets of water at the Whitechapel gallery, modern art is too simple. They want something complex, elaborate, and we believe in visual power.

We always say that the idea of art has to be sexual and religious. It must have a moral dimension.'

On our way out, George pointed to an old stone drinking fountain in the garden inscribed 'Jesus Said If Any Man Thirst Let Him Come Unto Me And Drink.' Looking at me with a smile, he observed: 'It could be a text from our work.' And just before I went back out into the heat-laden Spitalfields street, Gilbert darted forward and gave me a printed postcard. Signed by both of them with kisses, it read: 'We Are The *Most Disturbed* People We Ever Met'.

Rachel Whiteread

May 2001

After driving past gasometers punctuating bleak industrial terrain off the Old Kent Road, I entered the colossal workshop where Rachel Whiteread's Trafalgar Square sculpture was being made. At first, she was nowhere to be seen. Amplified rock music, combined with the sound of technicians' equipment screeching on metal, filled the entire shed-like interior with a fierce, echoing din.

Plenty of focused activity was occurring beneath the skylight of this former truck repair centre for British Gas, where Mike Smith now ran a centre for the construction of ambitious artworks. Mark Wallinger was there, discussing a major project for his show in the British Pavilion at the Venice Biennale. Over in another area I finally discovered Whiteread herself, wearing blue overalls spattered with white paint. She was standing inside half of an immense resin sculpture, intended for the empty plinth where Wallinger's poignant *Ecce Homo* had once stood. While a masked colleague used a machine to smooth out the base of Whiteread's work, she sprayed the sides with methylated spirits.

My instinct was to reach out and tap on the transparent resin wall before me, but 'Do Not Touch' notices were ranged all round the sculpture. And once Whiteread had used a ladder to climb out she explained, with a sigh, that a very sensitive stage in the sculpture's development had been reached. 'The main thing we're worried about is the material cracking,' she said, adding that the whole process was 'behind schedule'. With the inaugural deadline of 4 June approaching all too quickly, she seemed concerned about just how much remained to be done. The resin for the other half of the sculpture was still suspended in the air nearby, looming expectantly over a steel container.

The epic scale and complexity of the whole operation contrasted with the potent simplicity of Whiteread's idea for the work. It had begun 'roughly three and a half years ago, when James Lingwood called and asked me if I was interested'. Lingwood, a member of the Royal Society of Arts committee under the resolute leadership of Prue Leith, was determined to commission three bold new sculptures for a granite plinth that had been unoccupied ever since it was built 160 years earlier. But Whiteread's first reaction was scathing. 'Trafalgar Square?' she told Lingwood. 'This is ridiculous – I'm not interested at all.' Her feelings about Trafalgar Square had centred only on distant memories of 'going there on anti-racist marches when I was a kid'.

To her own surprise, however, Whiteread then 'made the mistake of going back there, as a kind of tourist, to find out what went on'. She realized at once that Trafalgar Square was 'not a naturally contemplative place'. But she also found that it was 'not so different from the Judenplatz' – the ancient Jewish Quarter in Vienna where her potent *Holocaust Memorial* had recently been installed, to justified acclaim. 'Roads run off both places in a similar way,' she said, 'and I found the plinth itself architecturally very beautiful, with extraordinary proportions.'

From that moment, Whiteread became absorbed in trying to 'figure out how to make a pause, a quiet moment in the middle of all that urban chaos'. And her typically bold, lucid solution was to propose an inverted plinth, cast in resin from the existing granite slab and placed on top of it. At the time, she had been making a cast of a water tower in New York before installing it on a rooftop in the SoHo district. 'So I'd figured out in some degree that you could cast large objects in resin,' she explained, 'but the water tower was easier and circular. The Trafalgar plinth is three times the size, and square, with much more difficult corners.'

After producing a one-tenth scale resin model in 1998, she realized that 'cracking was a big problem. So I got in touch with Mike, and a lot of head-scratching went on.' He tracked down a company in Germany capable of handling 17 tons of resin. 'They said "No problem," but it all went horribly wrong and cracked very badly.' So a Pennsylvania firm was approached instead. 'They developed a material specially for this project and, so far, it hasn't cracked.'

The inverted plinth, which now weighs a daunting 20 tons, is far and away the biggest piece of resin ever cast. 'So I'd like to get in the *Guinness Book of Records*,' Whiteread said with a smile. 'But at every level it's been very, very complicated to make – much more than we ever thought.'

Mike Smith, who had been listening to our conversation and nodding sympathetically, now pointed out that the real problem had been 'the indeterminate state of the resin, and the fact that the biggest piece we'd cast before was only half a ton'. But he had soon become aware that Whiteread was undaunted by these issues.

'Maybe if I wasn't so stubborn,' she agreed, 'the project wouldn't have gone on. But that's how I'm made. You have a vision of something, and you want it done. When I'm in my own studio, I use Stone Age technology and a bunch of people who know how I work. Here, you have to figure things out much more scientifically. But I've got an ambition for the work I produce. I want to cross boundaries, and make things happen that people say can't happen.'

At a fairly early stage, Whiteread discovered that she could not take a cast directly from the real plinth. 'English Heritage won't let you,' she explained, 'and actually I was quite relieved. So we've made a facsimile in a special material: heat will come out of it, but it'll also withstand the heat. Poor old Mike – I insisted that we did a leak test, to avoid the danger of tons of resin splashing all over everything. I've been very "hands on" with this project, probably much to Mike's irritation.'

How much was her sculpture – which had originally been meant for installation in Trafalgar Square in October 2000 – now going to cost? Whiteread preferred not to reveal the final figure, but acknowledged that it was probably far higher than the cost of its predecessor on the plinth: an 11-ton, £300,000 bronze by Bill Woodrow called *Regardless of History*. His sculpture, surging 27 feet into the air, had showed a titanic head supporting a heavily bound book surmounted, in turn, by a bare-branched tree whose roots held book, head and part of the plinth in a predatory grip. It had been funded by the Sculpture at Goodwood charitable trust, but Whiteread preferred to bear the cost herself – aided by contributions from her London dealer, Anthony d'Offay, as well as her dealer in New York. 'We're probably going to make an edition of two for sale afterwards, in order to cover the cost,' she explained. 'We'll remake the stone plinth in each case, so that they'll both look the same as the one in Trafalgar Square.'

But what about the historical context that her sculpture would initially inhabit – dominated by Nelson's looming column, the Landseer lions and sundry bronze effigies of obscure generals from Britain's imperial past? 'They're not an issue,' said Whiteread firmly. 'My relationship with Trafalgar Square has nothing to do with all the bombastic militarism, although Nelson's Column is quite wacky – I quite like that. And I actually hate pigeons, they're nothing more than flying rats. When I last went there, the Nelson Mandela concert was being prepared, and this ridiculous woman with a massive bag of grain and bread was feeding them. It was like Hitchcock's *The Birds* – the pigeons were all over my hair.' Instead, Whiteread responded to the people, the sky and, quite unpredictably, the traffic. 'I like the way the buses go round the plinth,' she said. 'You'll be able to look down on it from the top deck. But I also like the thought of pissed people encountering it around three o'clock at night.'

The most arresting quality of Whiteread's sculpture, which she had decided to call *Monument*, was its sense of enigmatic restraint. 'I hate public sculpture that's in your face – I absolutely loathe it,' she explained with a sudden burst of vehemence. 'This is my response to what I found in the square. I started off as a sculptor responding to humble places, and in its low-key way the plinth is like this.' Was it also, I asked, at all conscious of Lutyens's great

Cenotaph, that masterpiece of severity in stone positioned near the other end of Whitehall? Her reply was immediate and warm: 'The cenotaph's a beautiful, memorable, simple and poetic piece of architecture. It was just left alone, and became very moving.' It seemed as if Whiteread's *Monument* might well possess a similar air of austere understatement, although she told me with a grin, 'I'm quite looking forward to peering through my sculpture and seeing Nelson's Column tilted in the distance.'

The purged mystery of her sculpture would, Whiteread hoped, command the attention of 'an enormous number of people who are not interested in art. I'd really like to know what they think of it.' Like her previous public projects – above all the elegiac and much-lamented *House*, unforgivably demolished by a philistine East End council in 1994 – *Monument* would also, inevitably, attract hostility. How, I wondered, did she typically react to venomous criticism? 'After going to enormous efforts to do something that might change people's lives a bit, I do get irritated when the press says "What a load of old bollocks,"' she confessed. 'But I developed a thick skin after the loss of *House*, and now I'm covered in protective resin as well.'

She had been encouraged by the response to her Holocaust memorial in Vienna, initially treated with so much anger and scorn by certain sectors of Austrian political opinion. 'It hasn't been damaged, and people leave flowers there. It reminds me that *House* deeply affected some viewers, by making something present in the world that we usually ignore: the four walls we live in, placed on a green grass plinth. In all my work since then, whether it takes the form of a hot-water bottle or library shelves, I've tried to draw attention to something that wasn't there before.'

Unlike *Holocaust Memorial*, Whiteread's *Monument* only inhabited its location for a limited time. Would she, I asked, prefer to have it stay in Trafalgar Square on a permanent basis? 'I don't know,' she replied cautiously. 'I haven't seen it yet. It might look out of place there, but I'm hoping it'll have a presence – a ghostly, phantom presence.'

Anish Kapoor
September 2002

From the instant it opened in May 2000, the Turbine Hall at Tate Modern became one of the most commanding art spaces in Britain. The immense interior, 550 feet long and as impressive as a secular cathedral, possesses an intense air of drama. It looks expectant, and offers a formidable challenge to any artist brave enough to place a work there. Art could easily look dwarfed by such a daunting context. But that danger has not stopped Tate Modern commissioning, with the help of £1.25 million from Unilever over a five-year period, an ambitious series of special Turbine Hall installations.

Anish Kapoor, whom I interviewed shortly before his commission was due to be unveiled in late 2002, adopted a bolder approach than either of the artists who preceded him. Louise Bourgeois, the irrepressible octogenarian, had erected three towers in the second half of the Hall. Visitors could enter them, climb tortuous stairs and emerge at the top to survey the vastness around them. The following year, the Spanish sculptor Juan Muñoz had gone further, erecting a pair of empty lifts that rose silently through his network of enigmatic rooms and glided right up to the Hall's ceiling, 115 feet above the ground. But Kapoor wanted, from the outset, to work for the first time with the entire space. Everything, including the normally empty entrance ramp that slopes down towards the information counters, would be engulfed in his unashamedly overwhelming sculpture.

Not that Kapoor felt at all smug about his ability to perform such a colossal feat. When I visited his extensive South London studio during the summer, he admitted with a rueful smile, 'There are so many decisions to make, and so much pressure, it's driving me crazy.' He pointed out that the invitation had 'only arrived in December – a terribly short deadline'. But the unflappable Donna De Salvo, the Tate curator working with him on this titanic project, had responded very positively when he revealed the full temerity of his plan: 'She was able to go the whole hog with it, so I decided to take the entire Turbine Hall.'

Kapoor's innate assurance was beyond question: ever since I first met the engaging Bombay-born sculptor in the early 1980s, his energy, ambition and distinctive vision had been abundantly clear. But he realized that the Turbine Hall was 'an incredibly difficult space. It feels like a station, and seems to want to be something else. There's architectural unclarity there, as if it hasn't been fully redefined. It appears to be waiting, and I dare to say arrogantly that I'm going to use it properly, for the first time.'

Looking back on his predecessors' work there, he felt that Louise Bourgeois 'didn't animate it. Then Juan [Muñoz] claimed that he'd "found the ultimate solution to this space", and he was very clever. But he miniaturized it, turned it into a mise-en-scène. I don't want my work there to be theatrically staged. One can say "wow" to a sculpture without the "wow" being a matter of showmanship.' By using the whole Hall, and 'trying to persuade the Tate to get rid of all those information desks', Kapoor believed he could 'get hold of the fantastic horizontality, and this allows you to work vertically. You have to in such a space, but how do you do that without using towers?'

In order to answer this question, Kapoor drew in particular on the experience he had gained working at the BALTIC Centre for Contemporary Art three years earlier. At that stage, the gigantic former flour mills at Gateshead had been completely emptied. It was a shell, waiting to be transformed into an 'art factory', and its director, Sune Nordgren, asked Kapoor to fill it with a temporary installation. The result was spectacular. Its jubilant title, *Taratantara*, hinted at the experience to come. Kapoor used a blazing red, lightweight PVC membrane and stretched it over the open end wall. The aperture tempted you to enter the building. And there Kapoor delivered a flamboyant visual blow, comparable in impact with the mighty sound Joshua made when he brought down the walls of Jericho. Sprouting into the form of a double trumpet, *Taratantara* stretched right across the 170-foot void. The redness, combined with the swollen size, stunned everyone walking underneath. But its taut skin showed how rigorous Kapoor could be, giving his vaulting apparition a remarkable amount of tensile strength.

Anybody fortunate enough, as I was, to encounter *Taratantara* during its all too brief eight-week life in the summer of 1999 would have realized that Kapoor handled this behemoth of a building with masterly aplomb. The insights he gained there, at the edge of the River Tyne, must have proved invaluable when he came to tackle the Turbine Hall. Although BALTIC is only a third of the size of Tate Modern, the converted Bankside Power Station is similar in style and in the nature of its location. 'I learned about scale with *Taratantara*, and it surprised me,' Kapoor explained. 'The outside became the inside and vice versa. The formal properties of what we understand as the building were reversed. And there was something ungraspable: no way could you perceive the whole thing.'

Those words applied even more forcefully to the experience Kapoor aimed at offering in the Turbine Hall. He predicted that it would be 'very mysterious, even though walking round it will give you a definite experience. It's the not-holding of the full picture that makes the mystery. Like Bosch's amazing painting of the egg, in his *Garden of Earthly Delights*, it'll be a proposition on a different scale about the origins or the end of life. The fact that the work has been constructed from unknowable motives is a really important part of it.'

Even as he stressed the role played by enigma, Kapoor was also quite willing to show me how he had arrived at his Turbine Hall sculpture. Upstairs in his studio, a capacious building which used to house a shutter-making company, tea was provided in a room hung with preliminary drawings and photographs of the Tate project. Displayed on a wide, white wall, perspectival studies, side elevations and three-dimensional computer images from the engineers Ove Arup showed how tenaciously he had approached his formidable task. 'These are my beginnings,' he said, and I realized that a single, sensuous, swollen form would take over much of the vastness at his disposal. But it looked taut as well as biomorphic, making me appreciate how much discipline informed his exuberant yet pared-down vision.

Eager to show me the models he had subsequently made, Kapoor took me down to a far larger room on the ground floor. Assistants, some with masks attached to their faces, could be seen in even bigger spaces beyond, working on a monumental two-piece sculpture in which extremes of concavity and convexity were powerfully juxtaposed. Intense, concentrated activity was occurring here, with loud drilling and other noisy eruptions – not least in a closed-off section where a man was spray-painting an enormous deep-blue dish. Occasionally someone came into our room with a query about work in progress. It was clear that Kapoor had a great deal on his mind apart from the Turbine Hall project; but most of the time he was able to concentrate on the array of models and computer graphics, which yielded fascinating insights into the genesis of the work.

I noticed a white, insect-like creature stuck with pins, and then a red floating object, its yellow limbs outstretched and overtly erotic. Many possibilities were explored; at one stage Kapoor considered using silver fabric, before deciding that 'the quality of the material was not up to scratch'. He finally settled, as in *Taratantara*, on PVC. But unlike the BALTIC work, which he had attached to the building, his Tate sculpture would be 'a finite object with three steel rings. I started with the idea of three ovals, pulled them out and ended up with a Fallopian object, somewhat of a surprise to me.' This highly organic form, 'deep red and, I think, very dark', would bulge, dip and arch its way through the Turbine Hall. The first oval would confront visitors immediately as they walked through the west entrance, doubtless astounding them with its prodigious size. Another would be positioned at the far end, and the third was intended to hover over the bridge in the centre of this epic chamber, unsupported either from above or below.

At the outset, Kapoor had regarded the bridge as 'problematic. But since I couldn't get rid of it, I decided to use it as a resource. Now that Foster's Millennium Bridge is open, a lot of people come into Tate Modern through the middle entrance. I wanted to deal with that, enabling them to walk up the staircase of the Turbine Hall bridge and straight into the middle of the sculpture.' This promised to be a momentous, not to say unnerving experience. 'I want to make the oval above the bridge as frightening and oppressive as I can,' said Kapoor. Those words reminded me that his work had often delighted and disconcerted in equal measure. He had never been afraid of confronting and exploring the void at the heart of things, undermining the whole notion of sculptural solidity and bulk. 'Mantegna remains my star,' he said. 'His painting *The Descent into Limbo* shows Christ going down into a dark, cavernous opening within. What is it? We don't know. But the piece I want to make all the time is a hole in the ground, the entrance to a Dantean underworld.'

In order to give me a more visceral idea of what his work would be like on the bridge, Kapoor lifted up a model and held the central cavity directly over my head, so that I could look straight up into its darkness. 'The middle ring will envelop you when you move underneath,' he said. His words triggered a memory of the similar sensation I had experienced standing below his immense, deep crimson *At the Edge of the World II*, hovering like a spacecraft above my head in his 1998 Hayward Gallery retrospective exhibition. He also encouraged me to kneel in front of the final fibreglass model, covered with black felt-tip lines showing where the seams would be. Putting my head next to the floor, I was able to gauge the vastness and a sense of something suspended far above me, high in the Turbine Hall's upper reaches. 'Models tell you a certain amount, but by no means everything,' Kapoor warned. 'This final model is far too rational and explains too much. The horrible feeling I have in my stomach is that I honestly don't know what it'll be like.'

Six weeks before the opening, Kapoor and his team would be on site. 'We'll spend a month on the three steel rings, which weigh about fifty tons,' he said. 'But the PVC membrane is only one millimetre thick, so it's got the contradiction of a thin skin with a huge presence.' He was determined to ensure that the execution of the work had a flawless outcome: 'I want it to be wrinkle-free, like the most perfectly tailored suit.' But he was all too conscious of the problems involved. 'God help me, it's very difficult,' he said. 'We're pushing technology to the absolute limit here – it would have been impossible to achieve without the aid of computers.'

He was also relying on the expertise of Cecil Balmond, the structural engineer from Ove Arup. 'He has unbelievable skill, clarity and vision – he really gets it.' Balmond's advice would be invaluable, for, as Kapoor emphasized, 'The logistics are phenomenal.' When the sculpture was assembled in the Turbine Hall, 'huge cranes will have to lift it up without tearing the fabric or letting it go floppy. Whether it'll all be done on time I don't know yet.' The fierce deadline pressure was forcing him to abandon his usual ways of working. 'Normally I like not letting work out of the studio for six months after it's finished. I need to live with it and know it. But with this project, it all has to be done in public, which is exciting and terrifying as well.'

At least Kapoor had been able to study for some time a large stretch of the PVC material, pinned on an elaborate wooden structure in his ground-floor studio. Looking at it regularly helped him to think about and appraise its likely impact in situ, and it had made him very clear about one crucial priority. The immensity of the work was important to him: 'I'm interested in the sheer scale of that moment, that monochromatic moment, when colour will be translucent at the edges of the rings and then darken as it goes into the cavity.' At the same time, though, he wanted each viewer to be intimately involved with the encounter. 'Soutine is one of my favourite artists,' Kapoor said. 'There's an immediate emotionality and direct contact with his hand; it's a simple connection. So however many engineers are involved, one has to come to a simple moment of Soutine-like contact. Otherwise, it's not worth doing. It must be intimate, and engage each viewer singly and personally.'

Kapoor knows a lot about that kind of involvement. Although his reputation rests on his work as a sculptor, he liked at this point to spend as much time as possible on his own in a special room set aside for painting. He liked exploring colour with the immediacy of a brush, and contrasted it favourably with the frustration of knowing 'how long it takes to make big, technically demanding sculpture'. He had five assistants in the studio where we were talking, and two more at his stone-carving studio in Battersea. So the isolation of his painting room provided a refreshing, necessary alternative, and the discoveries he made there fed, in turn, his sculptural activities.

Walking round the studio with Kapoor, I was impressed all over again by the range and inventiveness of this prolific artist who had arrived at the fullness of maturity. Now forty-eight, with a worldwide reputation that had grown dramatically since he won the Premio Duemila prize at the 1990 Venice Biennale, he was in understandable demand. He was in the process of making a monumental piece in stainless steel for the city of Chicago: 'It's a gate, with a passage through to a big reflective chamber inside,' he said, explaining that it would be unveiled the following year in a 'huge new park where Frank Gehry is doing a new building and Renzo Piano an extension to the Art Institute'. Although the commission excited him, he also remarked, 'Public sculpture is very difficult: there is an absence of shared symbolic language. I'd like to return to some kind of engagement with symbolic meaning, and the gate and the house are very important.'

In another room, a gleaming model for a large sculpture in the British Museum's Great Court testified to Kapoor's lifelong, passionate interest in architectural possibilities. He had been very frustrated when his model for a colossal walk-in sculpture inside the Millennium Dome came to nothing; and he shook his head when I suggested that his Tate piece might be the largest he would ever produce. 'I dream of doing a sculpture as vast as a landscape, or a mountain range,' he said.

For the moment, though, his imagination was focused above all on the Turbine Hall commission. With accelerating excitement, he described how the sculpture should 'start by stopping people in their tracks at the west entrance, before leading them in to an all-enveloping presence that shortens the space, making it tight and small. Then it reveals the building and shrinks to a slender form before reaching the bridge. There's a wonderful Heidegger essay about the act of bridging, of leaping from different positions.'

Although Kapoor had not yet decided what to call the work, he acknowledged the importance of naming it and said, 'A title will condition how it looks.' All he did know, at this stage, was that the eventual title would be 'much more moody than *Taratantara*, which came from the idea of a trumpet sound. I do see the Tate sculpture as a much darker piece. Frightening, but not in a fairground way. *Awe* is perhaps a better word.'

Tracey Emin

November 2002

In the early 2000s, no living artist was more of a national celebrity than Tracey Emin. She had even outstripped Damien Hirst and David Hockney as a personality familiar to people who knew nothing about contemporary art. Everybody, it seemed, had heard of the ubiquitous 'Tracey'. They associated her name with the stained and crumpled bed she had displayed at the Turner Prize exhibition in 1999. The fact that Charles Saatchi had purchased it for a rumoured £150,000 only added to the notoriety of the work and its outspoken maker. Emin had launched a thousand brazen headlines, and I imagined that she would greet my request for an interview with the alacrity of a seasoned performer.

To my surprise, though, she told me, 'I've made up my mind to do as little publicity as possible.' And when I went round to her new studio in the East End, she wasted no time in emphasizing her unwillingness to see journalists. Why? 'People have no idea how "anti" most of my press coverage over the Turner Prize really was,' she explained. 'I don't mind serious art criticism, and writers saying that Rauschenberg's *Bed* is better than mine. Fine – okay. But you can't attack me and my work by accusing me of being a publicity-seeker. That really winds me up. A researcher for the Graham Norton programme rang recently, and I ended up saying if Graham asked me questions like that on the show, I'd just walk out.'

Her words reminded me of the now legendary moment when Emin announced that she was leaving a live TV discussion 'to see my mum'. I was a fellow panellist on that programme and I can vividly recall how drunk she appeared, and how she shouted abuse at the rest of us while we struggled to make ourselves heard above her din. I remember feeling annoyed when she walked out of the studio, then relieved that she wasn't there to interrupt us any more. But it was an act of supreme bravado on her part, and the outrageous 'bad girl' performance on the programme catapulted her to far greater notoriety than before.

Now, by contrast, a different mood prevailed. As she warily contemplated the prospect of her fortieth birthday the following year, Emin seemed to have lost her appetite for incessant media exposure. She was staging three important shows that autumn: *I Think It's in My Head*, an exhibition of recent work at Lehmann Maupin in New York; a ten-year retrospective at the Stedelijk Museum in Amsterdam; and, the month of our conversation, another show of new work at Modern Art Oxford. But she insisted on her lack of interest in talking to the press. 'It seems so soon after my last exhibition, and I don't have time.' The only exception she was prepared to make was for art magazines. 'It's brilliant that you're doing this,' she said, 'because most of the articles about me have appeared in newspapers – usually the tabloids. I've hardly ever had any reviews in art magazines.'

Emin was in no mood to resign herself passively to the drawbacks of celebrity status. 'It's important to me that I'm seen as an artist,' she insisted. 'But because I'm not "worthier than thou", most museums have avoided me up until now. Museums go for worthy. I haven't been included in "Documenta" or "Aperto" at the Venice Biennale. But I have got the work. Curators can go to Charles Saatchi's house and see that my stuff would hold up in a large space. A museum show has to cater for a wide sector of society, and be a visceral thing. Saatchi has got Paula Regos hanging next to the paintings I did at college: they look macabre and disconcerting.'

She took me upstairs to the main studio – a long, airy and well-lit space, dominated by an immense work surface strewn with appliqué fabrics next to a sewing machine and ironing board. 'I found this place two years ago,' she said. 'It was a sweatshop, bordering on nineteenth-century conditions, making coats. They kept building more and more partitions inside the room, so it was really warren-like.' Outside the large windows, I could see a neighbouring rooftop festooned with plants and flowers. Emin led me out there, pointing to the building below us, where Gary Hume had an equally capacious studio. While clearly relishing the explosion of colours on the roof, she explained, 'My dad does a lot of looking after the plants up here. We're frustrated because the weather's been so bad.'

I was eager to return to the studio and explore Emin's work in progress. In one area, a woman sat silently sewing the words and designs. But it was Emin who cut them out, and she had just arranged the letters of a grand new appliqué intended for her New York show. At its centre, one sentence leapt out: 'Every Moment of My Hole Existence'. I asked her if the spelling was deliberate. She nodded, grinning. 'I've kept the spelling of *hole*, but I had trouble with *existence*. When I first cut out the letters, I spelt it *exitsisence*. Then I looked at it and thought, this word seems wrong. I have a dictionary, but I don't always correct things. The biggest change I had to make was the word *tomartoes*, in a big appliqué blanket called *Garden of Horror*. I corrected it, but it looked stupid so I put it back. Doing that took me more than a day's work. But the worst one was a work called *Psycho Slut*. I spelt it *Pysco*, and left it like that.' Mat Collishaw, her boyfriend, approved. 'Mat says my spelling is an endearing thing to me, and it also looks like I don't give a fuck.'

Apart from complaining about an unwelcome attack of herpes, Emin seemed in buoyant spirits. With considerable satisfaction, she told me, 'I've just got funding from the BBC to make a feature film. It's low-budget, but far more money than I've ever been given before.' Although it was going to deal with Emin's familiar theme of growing up in Margate, she surprised me by declaring, 'Me being in it isn't necessary. The extras will all come from Margate, and I'll hire a church hall there to hold auditions for the part of a girl who's thirteen years old' – the age at which Emin herself was raped. 'I'll ask each of the girls: "What is it you really hate about your mum?"'

The question was reminiscent of Emin's own concerns, but she had no desire to make the film wholly autobiographical. 'I don't want it to be me,' she said. 'I'm bored to death of me, so it'll be like amalgamates of different girls.'

Although Emin had never been afraid to pinpoint the pain she suffered in her adolescent years, she explained that the film would also present Margate in a positive light. 'It's near the sea, and good for the soul,' she enthused, adding, 'Some people think I'm far too romantic.' So how did Emin cope with life in London, where she had recently bought a house near Hawksmoor's great baroque masterpiece Christ Church, Spitalfields? 'My house is only two minutes' walk from my studio,' she said, 'and I wouldn't ever want to travel across London to work.' She loved the depth of history in the area: 'I've cycled round all the Hawksmoor churches and sketched them.' She took particular delight in the fact that her house, built as early as 1729, had first been inhabited by Huguenot weavers. 'I've got a "family tree" of everyone who lived in the house, and I want to start collecting Egyptian artefacts for the interior. My great-great-great-grandfather came from the Nile, and I'm bowled over by the scale of everything in Egypt.'

As she talked, reinforcing everything with vivid hand gestures, my eyes strayed up to the image hanging on the wall above her: a 1995 colour photograph of Emin sitting on her nan's old armchair, very incongruously located in Monument Valley, Arizona, with immense rock formations rearing out of the parched land beyond. In the photo she was holding a copy of her book *Exploration of the Soul*. As we looked at this, she mentioned that she was aiming to write her long-promised memoir the following year. 'I want to make it short – a small, thick book with drawings. It'll be very frank, starting with my earliest memories.' Would members of her family be at all offended if she disclosed their secrets? 'My family are okay if it's the truth,' she said, before conceding, 'If it's not the truth, then it's not okay.' The book plan seemed to contradict her earlier insistence that she was 'bored to death' of herself, but she said she was fascinated by the whole idea of autobiography. 'I like reading about people and their lives. I've recently read biographies of Elizabeth I, Henry VIII, Barbara Windsor and Boy George. When I get going, I can write a hundred words a minute, but I'm profoundly tired at the moment.'

Perhaps she regarded her own memoir as a means of arriving at closure on her past life. Driven by an inner need to express herself in words, she said that she 'used to write furiously all the time'. And when her dealer, Jay Jopling, decided to give her a solo show at White Cube in 1993, he 'wanted me to spend one week in the gallery writing letters. He liked the way that I thought. He was totally bemused by my letters, and intrigued that they were so visual.' As the deadline for that show approached, 'Jay was fucking wetting himself, but with the utmost confidence.' As for Emin, she recalled feeling very self-critical. 'But if I don't struggle with my work, and have this mental kind of thing with it, I know I can't sort it out for myself.'

Her turmoil paid off. The success of the 1993 show was a turning point for Emin, helping to define her singular identity as an artist. Now, almost a decade later, she had grown enormously in assurance. But she still agonized about her work and, at the moment, was suffering misgivings about the sturdy Victorian bed intended as the centrepiece of her New York exhibition. Occupying a great deal of space in her studio, this redoubtable iron-frame structure had been strewn with highly emotional appliqué inscriptions. The words on one pillow, for instance, conveyed a strange warning to the bed's potential occupant: 'Don't Touch My Heart'. Other messages, on the blanket and sheet, gave vent to more violent, feverish or terrified emotions.

Emin acknowledged that the new bed explored painful areas of feeling, and said that in its early stages she had also harboured severe doubts about the work's effectiveness. 'I've been spending far too much time in Liberty's and John Lewis looking at curtain samples for my house,' she explained with a grimace. 'So I've had terrible traumas with this bed: it looked like I'd just done a course in home furnishings, as if I wanted to display it in some village craft show.' Now, however, she had injected a more disturbing level of emotion into the work. 'I'm petrified of the dark,' she confessed. 'I've always been intensely frightened of it, like a phobia. I still have terrible nightmares. Once, when I stayed in this Elizabethan house, I woke up and thought that a dog had gone to sleep on my leg. I was still dreaming, but I couldn't tell that I was. Sleep is somewhere I've always been afraid of. When I slept in my Turner Prize bed, I thought I'd die in it, never wake up.'

The dark, damaged side of Emin's imagination has always coexisted with the romantic side, giving her work much of its volatile, unsettling power. She showed me a plaster cast of her death mask, to be displayed in a gold version near the bed in her New York show. 'People have said they've never seen anything more alive,' she said with an ironic smile. But mortality was undoubtedly becoming an increasing preoccupation in her work. For her Oxford show, she was concentrating on her father. 'My dad is eighty-two, and I'm really scared about him dying. I made these films in Cyprus of him waving to me. So when my dad dies, I'll have all these films of him waving.' She was also making a major installation at Oxford based on her recent visits to northern Cyprus. 'There's a derelict copper mine, incredibly dried out, and a bridge to transport the copper to boats in the sea. I really like the bridge, which is going nowhere, so I'll make it for Oxford. I also saw barbed wire a lot in Cyprus, and I've always wanted to do a piece of work with it – barbed wire is rather like the lines in my drawings.'

Her Oxford show was going to be called *This Is Another Place*; I wondered whether the title referred to the different world she had found in Cyprus. Emin shook her head. 'It's like, if someone says: "You can't behave like that," I say: "But this is another place."' Bloody-minded defiance had always played a strong, self-defining role in her art and life alike. She used it to fight off her many demons, and much of the work she was producing could legitimately be seen as a stubborn attempt to achieve catharsis. 'One of my recurrent nightmares is biological warfare,' she told me. 'It's a constant thing on my mind. After September 11th, I had to make three aeroplane journeys. And on a floor somewhere, I found this paper selling "biological war suits". So I made this blanket repeating those three words as a headline, and then saying: "Don't try and sell me your fucking fear."'

Sarah Lucas

November 2002

Arriving at Sarah Lucas's house in a chilly autumnal downpour, I battled my way to her door past an orgy of overgrown flowers and bushes. They made a riotous contrast with the orderly, potted-plant neatness of the neighbouring front garden in this quiet North London street. Then, pausing on her doorstep, I was unable to find the bell, for Lucas had smothered her entire door in a blizzard of fast-food flyers. Exciteable headlines leapt out, urging me to order Free Chicken Wings, A Quarter Aromatic Duck, Summer Sizzlers and a concoction called Lamb Shish Pizza. They added up to a dizzying collage of instant gastronomic delirium and, like so much of the work Lucas had produced over the previous decade, the cumulative impact was both hilarious and disturbing.

I gave up on the bell and decided to knock. Lucas came to the door, talking on her mobile and protected against the cold by a thick blue polo-neck pullover. She gestured me inside with a smile; I edged my way past a smashed-up white urinal on the hall floor. The broken pieces reminded me of her long-term fascination with Marcel Duchamp and lavatorial images – most notoriously, a photograph of the naked Lucas sitting on a toilet cradling a disconnected cistern on her lap. She has never been afraid to explore the seediest, most taboo areas of modern life. Standing next to a fireplace was another example of Lucas at her most provocative:

a gigantic egg-shaped sculpture inscribed with the words 'FUCK THE EGG MAN' in yellow, red, black and blue capitals. It looked abandoned, unfinished and very, very bolshie – rather like Lucas herself in the early nineties, when she thought nothing of posing for the camera, legs wide apart, in jeans and a T-shirt with two fried eggs over her breasts.

Nothing was too subversive for the young Lucas, attracted by the most degrading aspects of our tawdry urban scene. After taking part in the seminal 'Freeze' exhibition in London's Docklands organized by her fellow Goldsmiths student Damien Hirst, she abandoned her involvement with minimal brick-wall sculpture and started all over again. It was painful at first; Lucas felt left out of the initial extraordinary rush of interest in young artists from her generation. But she stuck to her own emerging spirit of defiance. 'It started with that photograph of me eating a banana,' she recalled during our conversation, with a throaty, wicked laugh. 'I did want art to be very close to my own identity.'

Further photographs followed, each one flouting conventional decorum in order to present a direct and wryly humorous self-portrait of the artist as an unapologetic Bad Girl. But Lucas also began trawling the tabloid press for raw material. She gave her first solo show in 1992 the title 'Penis Nailed to a Board', after a sensational story unearthed in a newspaper. The following year, she joined Tracey Emin in a dilapidated little East End shop where they sold funny, sad and titillating T-shirts with hand-painted slogans like 'Love Comes', 'Complete Arsehole' or 'Sperm Counts' scrawled across them. The six bawdy months they spent there, brazenly offering customers 'Big Melons' or £5 ashtrays with a photograph of Hirst glued to the base, proved liberating for both artists.

'The Shop worked well because we're so different,' said Lucas. 'Tracey can be quite harsh and nasty, whereas I wasn't. It was very intense. Tracey is very moral but in a black-and-white way, and she loves melodrama. I hate melodrama: it's anathema to me.' Lucas also admitted, 'I can feel embarrassed by some of the stuff I've done.' And following those reckless days in the Bethnal Green shop, the differences between her and Emin widened so much that their friendship eventually broke down. 'Tracey's the perfect person to feed the media with the fame stuff,' said Lucas, 'but I want a normal life. Tracey's so recognizable that she can't even take the Tube any more. We had a row recently – we're not close. We're really not well suited.'

The longer I talked to Lucas on that rainy afternoon, the more I sensed that she was at a turning point. Tate Publishing had just produced a thoughtful and well-illustrated book by Matthew Collings surveying her career to date. Its arrival, combined with the stark fact of her fortieth birthday on the horizon, must have made her hungry to move on from the past and experiment with new directions.

Leading me across the back garden, she showed me round her newly constructed shed at the far end. Large and filled with light, it contained a painting of a girl's face in close-up. 'She looks like an alien,' Lucas remarked, 'and I thought the painting could be shown in my current Berlin exhibition, next to a coat I've made out of trainers. But I've decided there's no point in it being a painting – it'd be better off as a photograph.' Even so, Lucas looked forward to doing more paintings soon. Despite the preposterous 'concept art' label often applied to her work by ignorant critics, she has always been a hands-on artist who does not mind getting dirty. 'My shed's good for doing anything smelly,' she said with a grin, adding, 'One of the reasons I went to Goldsmiths College was that you didn't have to choose between painting and sculpture – you could do anything.'

Now she wanted that kind of freedom more than ever before. We went upstairs to her capacious bedroom, where she sat down in a black leather swivel chair and talked about the hunger for change. 'I've got really tired of doing photographic self-portraits and then realizing that they're not received as I intended,' she explained. 'They weren't really about me, but people in this country see them as a lewd celebrity statement. It made me feel depressed and pigeonholed.' That was why she had decided, for her upcoming show at Contemporary Fine Arts in Berlin, to focus on the legendary Arsenal footballer Charlie George. He served as a kind of surrogate for Lucas, enabling her to shift attention decisively away from her own image. 'I grew up round the corner from Charlie George, and he married a girl who lived two doors away from me,' she said, pointing out, 'I'm still only three-quarters of a mile from Arsenal in this house. I can hear the crowds roaring on Saturdays.'

An image of George's head and shoulders, with the team's symbolic gun emblazoned on his shirt, appeared on the invitation to her Berlin show. But his head was made from a collage of pizza adverts, menus and garish photographs of fast food congealing on plates. His features almost disappeared in a welter of melting cheese and tomato. 'I'm really interested in Saint George,' Lucas said, 'and the use of those flags goes back to something much earlier, filled with grittiness, violence and racism. I feel things are opening up a lot in my work.'

Along with football paraphernalia, she included references to Seventies rock music in her Berlin show. 'I've taken images from a Led Zeppelin album and turned them into sculpture,' she said. 'There are nine-foot-long concrete Zeppelins suspended on wires in the courtyard.' Along with the concrete footballs and boots that would be displayed elsewhere in the gallery, the new work seemed to her 'quite different. There are no overt sex things, although the Zeppelin seemed a logical step to take after my earlier phallic work.'

Looking round Lucas's bedroom, I noticed that the space was punctuated at every turn by bizarre or dramatically arresting objects. A lion's head snarled from a kitsch rug on the floor, as if warning anyone entering this sanctum not to abuse her hospitality. 'I found it in a rag-and-bone shop in Iceland,' she said, picking up a stray tooth and ramming it back expertly into the lion's mouth. The shelves behind contained equally unexpected items: a severed leg, a bunny sculpture, a ram's head sprouting a menacing pair of horns.

Several of these objects must have helped to inspire Lucas's own work. They certainly testified to her long-standing love of scavenging for junk. One of the self-portrait photographs shows her sitting in a beaten-up armchair outside a second-hand shop on the Holloway Road, where she grew up. 'I've always rummaged,' she said as we looked at the objects. 'I like to be out and about – it gets me going. I go to cafes, or sit in pubs and have a half. That's how I spend my time. I like to go to the market: I love the accents and the banter. I like the feeling of being connected to it all – I feel full.'

As she talked, Lucas shifted restlessly in her chair. She rubbed her face with both hands and twisted her trainer-clad foot around, or folded both legs together tightly on the seat. But she is capable of settling down for an avid read as well: a book called *The Life of the Cosmos* lay open on the floor beside her. 'I've just finished *Breaking Open the Head*, a book about psychedelic drugs and shamanism,' she said, fascinated in particular by the fact that 'if you're American Indian, you're not separate from nature'. To my surprise, this quintessentially urban artist confessed, 'I'd like to live more in the country: I love walking and sailing. I'll end up as Richard Long.'

A wide-format photograph of a glistening waterfall on one wall reinforced her claim to be 'a romantic'. But leaning against the opposite wall was a blatant reminder of the earlier, in-your-face work Lucas used to do. Jokily called *Got a Salmon On (Prawn)*, this shameless colour photograph shows her naked former boyfriend, Gary Hume, pulling open a drinks can. With typical effrontery, Lucas trains her lens on his groin, where he holds the can. The foamy drink explodes in orgasmic profusion, threatening to drench the onlooker. And behind the photograph stood one of Hume's own paintings from the same mid-nineties period, showing a hermaphroditic figure revelling in an outrageously camp pose. Different kinds of raunchiness are explored by both images, and Lucas planned to 'hang the two Garys on the wall next to each other, as a kind of collage'. She regarded them with amusement and affection, her expression conveying no hint of rejecting the outspoken art she had made in those days.

She still smoked as much as ever, filling the ashtray on the floorboards with stub after stub. 'I do intend to give up, but I've smoked since I was nine,' she said, adding, 'I never thought I'd be smoking beyond the age of thirty.' In a small study leading off the stairs, I had previously noticed a monumental self-portrait made entirely from filter cigarettes: an ironic admission of Lucas's dependence on nicotine. On one level it was a light-hearted work, but a darker layer of meaning could surely be detected there as well. When I suggested as much, she agreed, 'There's a sense of death in my work. The early things are quite dejected, and I do find that getting older is, in general, much tougher than I imagined. Life makes less and less sense. You can already begin to see it's going to get more frightening. When you're young, you have no notion of how short your time will be.' Her father, a milkman and staunch Labour supporter, died at the age of sixty-four. Since Lucas was very close to him, the loss proved 'a devastating experience. I like to be alone, but everyone is scared of being old and getting to the stage where you start losing your friends.'

The thought clearly appalled her, for Lucas is a gregarious woman who has always relished good company. That is one of the reasons why she abhors the Turner Prize and had, she said, refused the opportunity to be included on the shortlist 'a couple of years ago'. Tracey Emin might have thrived on displaying her scandalous bed in the Turner Prize exhibition, but Lucas seemed to regard it as unacceptable territory. 'I think it's a lot of aggravation for very little,' she said vehemently. 'I would hate it, being pitted against my friends. I hate the whole circus. I don't need a medal, anyway. Who are you being judged by? I don't think anybody's had a happy time doing it. People's fascination with it is ridiculous.'

Besides, the Turner Prize, in her view, feeds the British obsession with 'the celebrity thing. I love Berlin partly because my good gang of friends there don't have this stupid interest in personal life: I find it really oppressive.' She preferred to avoid too much exposure and retain her privacy. Despite her wanderlust, she stressed that 'I really like to be at home,' and that it was important for artists 'to give more room to an intuitive side. You mustn't be too controlling, or even think too much. I make a variety of things, so that one plays off against the other. You want to surprise yourself. I have no intention of turning it into a job, or setting up a sweatshop employing other people to sew on your beads. If you want a sweatshop, why not run a real sweatshop?'

Instead, Lucas was preoccupied with the hope of 'opening things up as much as possible. I hate the idea of just getting grander. I'm not that interesting yet. Hopefully, I haven't even done my best work. The world would be a very dull place if I were complacent – and it isn't dull at all.'

Langlands & Bell

April 2003

An infamous Victorian murder was committed in the East London studio where Ben Langlands and Nikki Bell now make their art. Here, in a building that has been used over the years as a stable, a synagogue and a Christmas cracker factory, a respectable brushmaker called Henry Wainwright lured his indiscreet mistress Harriet Lane in 1874 and chopped her body into little pieces. Langlands and Bell know all about this terrible crime, and when we met they told me the story of how Wainwright had been caught, taken to Newgate and hanged. They understood that their neighbourhood had a turbulent history, punctuated by outbreaks of unrest and violence – but nothing could have prepared them for the terrible devastation they witnessed in October 2002, when a commission from the Imperial War Museum sent them on a haunting journey to Afghanistan.

Now that world conflicts are reported on television with unprecedented speed and frequency, I asked them, has the whole notion of the 'war artist' become hopelessly redundant? Not according to Langlands and Bell, who at the time of our conversation were in the midst of final preparations for their War Museum show. Based on their recent Afghanistan trip, the exhibition would confront viewers with a powerful array of still and moving images culminating in an eerie, interactive digital exploration of Osama bin Laden's house.

The unsettling experience they were offering viewers was completely different from the kind of content typically seen in news bulletins. Langlands and Bell, who had been working together and exhibiting internationally for over twenty years, were convinced that 'we need art more than ever. It doesn't have the same exigencies of time as a news report. The moment a war stops, the media coverage stops. We went to Afghanistan for two and half weeks. It was very intense, and we've been thinking about it every day since then. It's not how long you're there for, but what you get out of it and put back in.'

Before the Imperial War Museum invited them to make work based on the aftermath of September 11th and war in Afghanistan, Langlands and Bell had concentrated on images of architecture, furniture, flight patterns and airports. But their wider fascination with social systems convinced Angela Weight, the adventurous Keeper of Art at the War Museum, that they would respond rewardingly to a commission. 'We don't see ourselves as war artists,' they explained to me. 'We work intuitively, with few preconceptions. We don't have to be told what to do.'

As it turned out, the flight on Ariana (Afghan National Airlines) alerted them to the challenges ahead. 'It was an old ex-Aeroflot plane, with bits falling off the cabin ceiling,' they recalled. 'All the passengers were smoking, talking loudly, moving around, refusing to do up their seatbelts and pointing excitedly out of the windows.' Then, once they arrived, Langlands and Bell discovered a heap of wrecked Ariana planes beside the airport terminal, pulverized by American bombing. And in Kabul itself, they found that the Ariana head office 'had a huge hole torn out of its side by a bomb attack'.

The poverty on the streets was distressing. 'Injured and starving children were everywhere, and one girl had half her face blown away. There was nothing there apart from a slab of scars over smashed bone, and a void where she once had an eye. Widows asked us for bread. A lot of people seemed desperately hungry. And when we gave money to a one-legged man he hurried after us to give thanks, even though he could scarcely walk.'

Langlands and Bell were based at the Mustafa Hotel, a dusty and largely empty concrete building with barred, prison-like windows, in the foreign embassy district of Kabul. On arrival, they were told that the hotel's owner was having his stomach pumped in hospital: 'Someone tried to poison him.' But they coped with the hotel's besieged atmosphere, and it prepared them for the gruelling experiences to come. The extent of the devastation left them astounded. They kept getting lost, in a city where so much had vanished and no street names survived.

Few landmarks were left. The royal palace, hit by cruise missiles, was disintegrating in a wasteland where the homeless struggled to survive among the ruins. Seventy per cent of Kabul had been reduced to rubble. Even the proudly named Hotel Intercontinental, housing the city's only internet cafe, was now a dilapidated structure. In the brasserie, an enormous wall relief of the colossal Buddhas of Bamyan had been wrecked, poignantly echoing the plight of the ancient statues themselves. Langlands and Bell resolved to visit the remote caves where the Buddhas had stood for so many centuries, even though a British Embassy official tried to dissuade them from travelling anywhere in the country.

Before their Bamyan trip, though, they attended a murder trial in the governor's palace. The judge, shaking hands with Nikki Bell, laughed and admitted that he would never normally shake hands with a woman. But this was the only light-hearted moment in a gruesome day. Much to their surprise, Langlands and Bell were allowed to take a camera into the courtroom. In their London studio, they showed me an unsettling video of the proceedings. The camera zoomed in on a young, crouching soldier, gun at the ready as he nervously scanned the room for signs of trouble. Then the accused appeared in close-up: Abdullah Shah, a heavily bearded 'commander' during the civil war. Even in handcuffs and leg irons, he looked dangerous. His nickname, 'Zardad's Dog', had been earned when he began savaging travellers with his teeth before killing them.

Shah was accused of murdering dozens of victims, including three of his own wives. He set fire to them and threw them into a well. He was also charged with butchering five of his children by cutting off their noses and ears. On the video, in successive freeze-frames, angry and grief-stricken witnesses testified to his bestial crimes; Shah snarled at them, wagging his finger and pointing at his curiously pristine set of white teeth. Eventually the judge sentenced him to death, a verdict greeted with a loud cry of 'God is Great' from the relatives assembled in court. If he was indeed executed, it would be the first death sentence enacted by the new government. But first Shah would be able to appeal and his sentence would need to be ratified by the country's president, Hamid Karzai.

Ben Langlands expressed doubt that Shah would ever be punished, just as he wondered about the effectiveness of all the NGOs (non-governmental organizations) operating in Afghanistan. There were an enormous number of them, along with other donor agencies, active in the country. Ben showed me a silent sequence of still images dominated by acronyms: UN announced in giant capitals on a broken-down gate, CARE emblazoned on a rickety hut. The acronyms all faded into each other, creating a dreamlike sense of flux. They reflected Langlands and Bell's long-term fascination with communications signage, but the ever-shifting motion also conveyed the artists' fear that it might be ineffective.

Ben told me that a 70 per cent illiteracy rate blighted the Afghan population. One in four children died before the age of five, while the life expectancy for men and women hovered ominously around the ages of forty-two and forty-three. In an angry diary entry, Langlands and Bell had wondered what all the NGOs were doing about this. 'After what it has been through in the last twenty-three years, Afghanistan needs all the help it can get in almost every field,' they wrote, 'but there are times when it starts to seem like a final revenge. First you saturate the country with high-tech weaponry, then you bomb the place to bits, then when it's on its knees and completely flattened, you send in the NGOs in Timberland boots and brand new Jeeps.'

Because flags acted as such an important means of communication in a country without a telephone system, Langlands and Bell planned to preface their show with three flags on the Imperial War Museum's facade. Fluttering above the double-barrelled battery gun outside the building, the central flag bore three NGO acronyms:

WHO, ACTED and CARE. This would be flanked by flags bearing the words MERCY, SERVE and HOPE, repeated on either side. Taken together, the flags issued a questioning and provocative series of pleas for the future of Afghanistan as a whole.

Nowhere did the country's plight seem more parlous than in Bamyan. Determined to see the caves and cliffs that had once sheltered the celebrated Buddha carvings, Langlands and Bell rose one morning at four thirty and set off as soon as the curfew lifted. While their car's headlights picked out a path of dust, they found themselves confronted by 'a world of darkness and cold'. By mid-morning they were deep in the mountains, and their four-wheel drive battled to cope with the fissures and craters in a barely recognizable road. At last they reached Bamyan. Before tackling the caves they headed for its 'famous restaurant', although on their way they learned that it was, in reality, the town's only restaurant. Just outside the entrance, they had to step over the glistening, distended body of a goat that had been skinned and abandoned in the dust. They showed me a photograph of the repellent carcass and I understood immediately why they had been unable to stomach the bowls of rice they ordered in the restaurant, 'with small pieces of fatty meat lurking below the surface'.

Even so, the mountain-fringed Bamyan Valley turned out to be beguiling, its cliffs glowing a rich bronze in the afternoon sun. They found the empty cavity where 'the big Buddha' had once stood, over 180 feet high. Shattered boulders lying at its base offered a melancholy reminder of the Taliban's unforgiveable act of vandalism. Equally depressing were the nearby caves, now occupied by orphans and families made homeless when the Taliban destroyed their town. Carved and deeply coffered ceilings were still visible within the caves, their ancient Buddhist frescoes smothered in soot or defaced by looters and fanatics. So much had been obliterated; I found Langlands and Bell's photographs heartbreaking to look at.

Staying overnight in a UN guesthouse across the valley, they met a Special Forces soldier working with a Danish de-mining group. He told them that, of all the mine-infested countries he had visited across the world, Afghanistan was the worst affected. Someone in the country was being blown to pieces by a mine every hour of every day. On the long journey back to Kabul, during which Nikki was beginning to suffer badly from stomach cramps, they apprehensively noticed lines of painted rocks indicating the presence of unexploded mines in every direction.

Their most arduous expedition, however, was the trip to Osama bin Laden's house. Very few people go there. Largely unknown, it is situated in a remote and perilous region. Before they went, a UN representative warned Langlands and Bell against the idea. Even so, they were eager to try. The journey out took five and a half body-bruising hours, through terrain bleaker than any they had encountered before. They passed the town of Sarobi, infamous ever since four Western journalists were gunned down there in November 2001. But the landscape surrounding Bin Laden's house turned out to be spectacular. Near the village of Daruntah, it was built on a promontory jutting into a lake surrounded by tall mountains. The house commanded a 360-degree panorama, and some of the photographs taken by Langlands and Bell are hugely seductive.

In other respects, though, the Bin Laden compound was profoundly disturbing. The lake had been polluted with mercury, so nobody could eat the fish caught and cooked there. Langlands and Bell first arrived at a checkpoint guarded by a gang of local militia boys with a machine gun. Demanding a 'security fee', the boys insisted that one of them would accompany the visitors armed with a Kalashnikov. Otherwise, they warned, the guards in the house might shoot without warning. At the end of a turning, a smashed mobile rocket launcher stood in front of the house. Older, more matter-of-fact guards, who now emerged with rifles, allowed Langlands and Bell to take photographs of everything they saw. When the artists produced tape measures and began using them with forensic zeal, the guards eyed them suspiciously. But Langlands and Bell were determined to research the site in a detailed way for their interactive presentation.

Their resolve paid off: the images they showed me were utterly engrossing. Live mortar bombs littered the rough ground, along with abandoned military vehicles and rusting hardware. The three-roomed house appeared surprisingly modest, even rudimentary.

Heaps of mattresses, electric fans and clothes gave way, elsewhere in the building, to a single string bed isolated in a dark corner. Outside, a small mosque stood nearby, and Bin Laden had built the bizarre bunker beyond. Partially sunk in the excavated ground, its walls were constructed from wooden ammunition crates filled with rocks. In the roof, branches supported a layer of earth and stone capped, unexpectedly, by battered old tyres.

Bin Laden had first occupied this compound in May 1996, when he moved from Sudan to Afghanistan. He remained there until September 1997, when the presence of US agents in neighbouring Pakistani territory prompted him to find a more secure hideout in Kandahar. Four years later, the site had been bombed by American B-52s after the Taliban refused to surrender him. While Langlands and Bell were photographing the site, they noticed a couple of American Black Hawk helicopters appear from the mountains and fly low over the house – as if to find out whether its wily former occupant had returned there in secret.

Judging by the photographs I saw, the interactive digital model in Langlands and Bell's show was going to be irresistible. Using a control stick, viewers would be able to make a virtual tour of the Bin Laden house and its surroundings, rather like detectives investigating a crime scene. Although the elusive Bin Laden was nowhere to be seen, his presence could still be felt; the images seemed to bring the viewer unnervingly close to him even as they underlined his continuing ability to evade capture.

So the Imperial War Museum exhibition seemed set to confound all those who claimed that war artists were hopelessly outdated. Nobody could have been more alert to the wider meaning of their Afghan journey than Langlands and Bell, living and working in the shadow of London's principal mosque. 'We're in a Muslim area here,' said Ben. 'We hear the call to prayer three times a day, it's part of our subconscious. The people round here feel they're going to get the blame for September 11th, and they're very anxious about war in Iraq. At the same time, they're mostly family people and just want to get on with their lives. Every Friday, they hand out anti-war leaflets beside the mosque and then pray for peace.'

Langlands and Bell's familiarity with this neighbourhood helped them to view the Afghanistan people's tragedy in a particularly alert, thoughtful and compassionate way. 'We feel they need help, and that the crisis could easily get worse rather than better. The Western powers are intent on controlling everything strategically, but their commitment is minimal. It's highly unlikely that the Afghan people will ever be left in peace, and that's very depressing. Different warlord factions could easily start fighting each other. It's on a knife-edge, and might well topple into full-blown civil war.'

The concern they felt was sharpened by their deep admiration for the country. 'It's such a beautiful place, sparse and harsh. The simplicity of life there is like going back to biblical times. The people have a profound appreciation of nature. They're very devout and brave, as well as extremely stoical. They're also very confident of who they are, and where they are. The passengers on our plane were so excited to be going back to Afghanistan. They felt passionately about their country.'

Langlands and Bell had no intention of mounting a metaphorical pulpit to preach in their show. 'We won't ram Afghanistan down people's throats. What we're doing is not blood, guts and in your face. But we do want people to learn something about existing structures from our work. We'd like visitors to come away with at least a small understanding of how our lives interlock with the people over there, and how we're all enmeshed in these networks across the world. Artists can piece things together in a different way. We are optimistic, but when you see what they're up against in Afghanistan, it's hard to be hopeful about what's going to happen next.'

Bridget Riley

June 2003

On the morning when I visited Bridget Riley at her West London house, the entire city succumbed to a heatwave. At the front of a tall, white room on the ground floor, where vibrant paintings from different phases of her long and prolific career shimmered in the light, we both gazed out of the window. The view was dominated by magnificent mature trees in the square outside, and Riley clearly admired them. But she also deplored the fact that their trunks were illuminated artificially at night with strings of decorative light bulbs.

Natural light provides Riley with an increasingly fertile source of inspiration. She has responded to its potent force ever since her Cornish childhood, and takes an enormous pleasure in the garden at the back of her home. Wandering past impressive fig and magnolia trees in full leaf, we paused by a particularly luxuriant plant springing from a stone urn. 'Look at the blue reflections from the sky on these transparent leaves – they're amazing,' Riley exclaimed, before paying tribute to 'my very, very good gardening sister Sally, who lives in Dulwich. She's encouraged me and given me plants.'

Indoors, the house was full of parcelled-up pictures awaiting transportation to Tate Britain. Her retrospective there would focus on a carefully selected sequence of landmark paintings. Riley, then in her early seventies, was 'feeling excited' about the show, which spanned the period from 1961 to the present day. She darted through the tall rooms with amazing vitality. Small, lithe and animated by an impish sense of humour and a keen intelligence, she exuded a focused energy; everything she said was reinforced by eloquent gestures. Riley could not have been further from the cliched idea of the artist as a lazy, bohemian dissolute, forever tipsy and hopelessly unreliable. 'The English have a romantic image of the artist, and it's a cross we have to bear,' she said with a smile. 'It's a safe recipe, and I was always impatient with it. I love working. There's nothing like it, making something that didn't exist before. It's exciting.'

Some artists might feel daunted by the prospect of a Tate retrospective but Riley seemed invigorated by the challenge, and philosophical about the prospect of criticism. 'This exhibition is a big deal,' she admitted, 'and it takes a year out of your working life, which is frustrating. I know the knives will be out in certain quarters. But it's encouraging when you read a positive review, or meet someone who has enjoyed your work. You realize you have communicated with someone. It's a very unsympathetic time for creative arts at the moment, and dealers have a lot to answer for. The values that a real artist holds have not been in harmony with society. But I'll always remember a remark that Francis Bacon made about forty years ago. He came up to me at a party, and said: "Let them cheat you, it gives them such pleasure!"'

Riley was certainly the focus of bitter controversy when she emerged in the early 1960s. Restricting herself to black and white, she launched a dazzling optical attack on the viewer with her dynamic, impeccably organized paintings. Some critics complained about their eye-bending impact, while others censured her for entrusting the execution of her work to studio assistants. But Riley was unrepentant. Having defined her own singular vision of the world, she had no intention of diluting its fierce originality. At a time when male artists were still overwhelmingly dominant, she proved that a determined and ambitious young woman could gain international attention with swiftness. Riley soon became an iconic figure in 'swinging London'. Exemplifying tough-minded independence and verve, she refused to compromise her stance.

'I was seen as heretical,' she recalled. 'I've never been a joiner. I found that the art world was a hugely conformist place, and if you step out of line they don't like it. But I didn't do it as an act of defiance. It was something I just had to do.'

The strength of her work's visual impact became clear when Riley took me up to a big, airy room on the first floor of the 19th-century house. Here, spanning most of one wall, was a colossal painting called *Rattle*. Executed in 1973 and unseen for many years ('It's been in store for a long time,' she said), this eye-bending tour de force is an absolute show-stopper. Within a series of horizontal bands stretching across its surface, Riley unleashes a blazing sequence of diagonal coloured stripes. They bent my vision with insistent energy, and I told Riley that the painting seemed to make my eyes work in a completely different way. 'I think that may be a good thing – with respect,' she replied, laughing.

Although *Rattle* is in essence an abstract work, I found myself relating its visual sensations to the experience of looking down at surging movements in a river or moving through densely packed trees. Riley did not balk at the idea of such references being present in her work. 'Cross-currents in water, or walking through a wood, or looking at layers of cloud, may give rise to sensations which are universal,' she said. 'A particular sensation may appear in a number of different contexts, and *Rattle* may be one more place where you might find it. I never make studies directly from nature. They would get in the way. I make use of my mind in order to work.'

Even so, Riley herself did not strike me as a forbidding, cerebral artist. She was intensely physical, remaining perpetually on the move throughout my four-hour visit. Her body had the agility of an instinctive dancer, and she used her arms in a dramatic way to highlight what she was saying. 'Although I'm not particularly athletic, I've always loved dancing,' she said with a smile. 'I enjoy movement in nature, too. It's a constant delight. And it's one of the great animators, like light. Even when things look static, it's actually a momentary phase – like the experience in *Arrest*.'

Along with the other paintings that made Riley's reputation in the early 1960s, *Arrest* is a stark image. Leading me up to the top floor, past rooms in which the walls and bare floorboards were all painted white, she walked over to a large wooden table. There, spread out across the surface, was a detailed plan of her Tate exhibition. Miniature colour reproductions of the exhibits, each one carefully scaled to show how much wall space it would occupy, were already in place. She pointed out that the plan offered only 'a rough orientation – where the paintings finally hang will be another matter....Reproductions of my work are especially difficult because of the change of scale, and because they lack the physical presence of the paintings.'

Even so, this room-by-room map provided a vivid idea of how the Tate survey would affect its visitors. While Riley fetched coffee and chocolate croissants from the kitchen below, I pored over the installation. It would clearly tell a lucid, concise and stimulating story of her development since she emerged as an *enfant terrible*. The dazzle and glitter of those paintings from the early 1960s attack our lazy viewing habits with black discs, undulating lines, chequerboard patterns and diagonal bands scything across the picture surface, like seismic fissures running through an unstable land mass. Since they are fundamentally abstract works, Riley was 'severely criticized' in some quarters for avoiding titles as sternly non-representational as *Composition*, *Untitled* or *No. 1*. Instead, with typical defiance, she gave them names like *Shift*, *Breathe*, *Shiver* and *Turn*. 'Some of the titles were to do with actions of the body,' she explained to me. 'I asked myself what were the sensations involved. So I'm still the same person – I haven't changed much.'

By the middle of the 1960s, she was receiving great international acclaim. Her 1965 exhibition at Richard Feigen's gallery in New York sold out before the opening night, and she also attracted widespread attention at the Museum of Modern Art in a celebrated contemporary show called 'The Responsive Eye'. At that time the overwhelming majority of prominent artists were still men, and Riley demonstrated with spectacular verve that their ranks could be breached. In 1968 she became both the first English painter and the first woman to win the Venice Biennale's International Painting Prize.

But precocious success did not make her complacent. Refusing to repeat herself and turn the black-and-white work into a weary formula, she introduced greys and then coloured greys into her art. Finally, in 1967, she brought pure colour into her paintings. This entailed rejecting the complex intricacy of her earlier work: 'I realized that, as I went on with colour, it had to occupy a prime position in my work.' Hence the introduction of vertical stripes in contrasting colours. She used this device for almost a decade, and a painting as impressive as *Late Morning* shows how colour introduced the viewer to a world of vibrant light. She told me how *Late Morning* had been inspired by her love of the natural world: 'It came from my response to the South of France. There's a tremendous vibration when heat rises and hangs in suspended animation between morning and afternoon. The cicadas are at their strongest, and it's the zenith of the sun. Although *Late Morning* was made in England, and I'm a northern artist, it celebrates a quintessential Mediterranean experience.'

For a long time, Riley has escaped regularly to her Provençal farmhouse at Vaucluse. At this point she was typically spending about four months of a given year there, but: 'The house isn't set up for the cold – it would need what the Americans call a "makeover". I like it the old way. It was probably one of those small farmsteads parcelled out to people after the French Revolution, and I've preserved all the old fireplaces, doors and windows. But I've also got a huge studio down there, built in the early 1970s. It's a place to work, and the light is wonderful – full and strong, even if it gets too forceful in the summer.'

Although Riley's work has remained passionately involved with abstraction, there can be no doubt that the stimulus of Provençal light has played an increasingly central role in her paintings. She told me that she even found it 'magical in the depths of the winter. Underneath that very, very bright light, the browns and greys of the trees turn to bronze and silver. The deciduous oaks look like beautiful metalwork – it's ravishing.'

So were many of the paintings in the later stages of Riley's show. By introducing twisted, crossing lines and curves, which lifted off the surface of the canvas in an airy way, she had become a more lyrical and sensuous artist. Was she, I wondered, at all surprised by this change at the time? 'No, I was pleased,' she said. 'I needed to extend my range. It's sad if one is reduced to repeating oneself.' Later still, a visit to the Nile valley in Egypt and the tombs of the later Pharaohs in the Valley of the Kings transformed her colours once more. Then, between 1985 and the following decade, she began disrupting the vertical stripes in her Egyptian work with diagonal forms. These helped her open up the space and create greater depth in the paintings.

Because Riley is a methodical painter, one who admires Mondrian and Seurat, some critics imagine that her work has always developed in a steady, logical progression. But as she was quick to point out, 'The story told in this exhibition is full of loops and turns. It doesn't proceed in an orderly manner. Some people seem to think I've got it all planned until the year 2020. But you really don't know what's going to happen. If you had a pig-headed little plan, it might prevent wonderful things from occurring. Paintings can grow from one another if there is a dialogue between you and the work. One has to listen. I have a hunch that things might go in a certain direction. But sometimes they don't. You can't waste time, and one has to be ruthless, so to speak, with one's work.'

Riley had clearly never lost her radical edge, remaining quite unafraid of extreme strategies. 'Picasso believed that in order to subvert, destroy and renew art, you had to use the human figure,' she told me. 'Francis Bacon thought the same, and I have great admiration for both men's work. But you can be equally radical by taking "known things", like squares, triangles or circles conceptually fixed in our common minds, and putting them under pressures to subvert them, as it were. You need to start with a "known" if you want to make people think in a way they've not thought before.'

Anyone talking to Riley soon becomes aware of the delight she derives from her intense, thoroughgoing involvement with art. Since 1961 she has handed over the execution of her paintings to studio assistants, deciding that 'the visual experience' of her work would best come through 'unhampered by any kind of painterly handling or touch'. But she has continued to be closely concerned with the production of her art at every stage, from beginning to end.

'The working process is very important,' she said, 'and as I enjoy it, I want to include something of it in the Tate exhibition.' For this reason, a room at the very centre of the show was devoted to preparatory images of various kinds. No more than that: Riley did not want to overload her retrospective with an excess of explanations. 'I like my work to be seen uncluttered, with as little presentation as possible,' she insisted.

Her assistants all worked in the West London house, she said, and Riley spent a considerable amount of time with them. Like every artist, though, she also needed to be on her own. 'To supervise work here is one thing, but obviously I have to be alone in order to concentrate properly. I go off to my studio in the East End. Down there in Poplar, near the Thames, the skies are enormous and you can hear seagulls. I think the building was originally a kind of village hall, built by a philanthropist during the Depression as a cross between a soup kitchen, a library and a theatre.'

Although Riley revelled in the fullness of the Provençal light at her Vaucluse retreat, she emphasized that 'a great part of me is urban. I love the centres of big cities, and I'm lucky to live in a part of London that's old and generously supplied with parks.' I once came across her in Hyde Park, sitting quietly and alone on a bench overlooking the Serpentine lake. She was clearly absorbed by the scene before her, and told me how she relished catching a bus from her home to Hyde Park and walking right through it. With her mind reinvigorated, she could then turn her attention to work in progress.

Perhaps that was the reason for the exuberance of *Evoë 3*, the most recent painting to be featured in the 2003 Tate show. 'When trying to find a title, I thought of calling it *A Bacchanal without Nymphs*,' she recalled. 'But then I remembered, just in time, that I'm meant to be an abstract painter. During a bacchanal the ancient Greeks, both men and women, shouted the word "Evoë" as they danced or drank. I love the paintings of bacchanals by such artists as Poussin and Rubens, and looked very carefully at them. Maybe they have a bearing on the curve paintings I'm doing now. *Evoë 3* has just been bought by the Tate, which is wonderful.'

As well as reflecting her lifelong fascination with the art of the past, this exhilarating canvas demonstrates just how optimistic and inventive Riley remained in her seventies. Still at the height of her abilities, she seemed committed to exploring emotions as celebratory as the joyful painted paper cutout in the Matisse poster hanging on her wall. 'The spirit of this house is important,' she said. 'It faces the sun, you see. Part of the job is to work, as far as is possible, for joy.'

Antony Gormley
April 2004

Driving through the entrance to Antony Gormley's spectacular new London studio near King's Cross was an unforgettable experience. The colossal building, custom designed by David Chipperfield, reared up in front of me, culminating in a dramatic zig-zag roof-line. And the forecourt was equally epic. Straight ahead, a tall iron figure leaned forward with both arms clamped to his sides. Exposure to the rain had covered him with orange streaks that dripped down his naked body from shaven head to feet. Forlorn yet stubbornly resolute, he would be placed against the outside wall of White Cube in Hoxton Square when Gormley's new show opened there the following week.

Suddenly I heard a shout of greeting from above. It was Gormley, waving to me from the angular metal staircase jutting out from the studio's facade. Very tall and restlessly energetic, with close-cropped jet-black hair and circular glasses, he seemed thoroughly at home in his monumental workspace. Dressed in a black top and pale khaki trousers, he wasted no time in coming down to join me.

How, I wondered, would White Cube protect the iron figure from would-be thieves at night? 'There'll be half a ton of concrete under the ground to secure him,' said Gormley, showing me a metal structure that would be buried directly beneath the sculpture. It all seemed ingeniously worked out, and he commented that moving to his new premises had 'completely changed my life – I can do things properly, and there's no longer any excuse for not doing so.'

When he began making sculpture over twenty-five years earlier, Gormley had struggled to establish himself. Unusually for an artist, he had been brought up as a Catholic in a Benedictine boarding school before studying art history and anthropology at Cambridge. After training at London art schools and travelling extensively, he became obsessed with casting his own body. The young Gormley was forced to rely on his own stamina and help from his wife, the painter Vicken Parsons. Now, however, Parsons (whose work was on show in 'Edge of the Real' at the Whitechapel Art Gallery) had a separate studio of her own within the Chipperfield building, and Gormley's ever-growing international reputation meant that he could employ half a dozen workshop assistants. One of them sat outside with a mask over his face, carefully dipping pieces of metal into vessels of liquid. The other men were all busy inside the great metal doors leading through to the main studio.

It was an awesome arena. Chipperfield had designed an astoundingly lofty space, where everything was enhanced by the radiant glow from immense skylights far above our heads. Only a few sculptures stood or crouched on the floor. All the rest dangled down from the beams spanning the roof, including an upside-down man suspended by chains from a pulley. But he was the only solid sculpture among the suspended pieces, for Gormley had increasingly moved away from work as substantial as *Angel of the North*. 'The great breakthrough,' he explained, gesturing towards the work suspended over us, 'was realizing that I didn't have to make the body, that it could be a series of voids in an energy field.' Looking up at these whirling clusters of metal rods, I saw that contours of male figures could be detected inside them. 'It's like drawing in space,' said Gormley, 'and the harmonies are released from within. These interlocking spirals just hang loose. I've released them from the burden of being self-supported.'

Clearly exhilarated by the fresh possibilities he had uncovered, Gormley took me through to a darker neighbouring space where his earlier sculpture was stored. A whole cluster of life-sized figures stood in one corner, tightly wrapped in polythene and taped up. They reminded me of bandaged victims, melancholy and trapped. One of them even had black tape laid right across his eyes. The contrast between these haunted men and the work in a nearby chamber could hardly have been more extreme: here the entire white space was alive with looped, arching and tensely coiled lines of raw metal. They added up to an audacious and exuberant spectacle.

'This is the mock-up for *Clearing*, my new installation at White Cube,' Gormley explained with a quickening sense of anticipation. 'It's my attempt to liberate the room from Euclidean geometry, but you could also say it's a trapped trajectory, testing itself against the surfaces of the walls, floor and ceiling.' Either way, *Clearing* was indeed a breakthrough in Gormley's work. It demanded to be explored, so he led me into the vortex.

The same artist who, a second before, had been so meditative and verbally articulate was now transformed into a far more physical man of action. He moved so impulsively through the rods that his dusty boots were soon caught up in them. They made a loud clatter, but Gormley did not mind. 'This can take a lot,' he said, grabbing a fistful of lines and shaking them vigorously. Then he released some of the rods from the wire enclosing them. They sprang apart with an echoing noise, yet Gormley shook his head. 'They're not so good like that,' he decided, clasping them with both hands and returning them to their taut, bunched-up state. 'They'll be looser in the White Cube installation, and I'm quite interested in how people will take up positions within it. In a way, onlookers become the work once they're inside it. But if more than five people are in the room at any time, it'll be too much. It's all a bit dodgy, really, and I only hope that Health and Safety will allow it to happen.'

What, I wondered, did his dealer Jay Jopling think of such a demanding, unpredictable work taking over his entire ground-floor gallery? 'He wasn't very pleased initially,' said Gormley with a grin. 'It wasn't something he saw a lot of commercial potential in.' *Clearing* would, I thought, offer a startling surprise to visitors familiar with Gormley's previous work. They associated him, above all, with figurative sculpture. Here, by contrast, the seven kilometres of rod would soar through space without any obvious reference to the human body at all. 'You could say it's completely chaotic,' Gormley conceded, 'but it started with sine waves and a magnetic tunnel going through. The material began collapsing under its own weight, but you still get the feeling of an all-over matrix with no beginning and no end.'

Not content with making this 'psycho-spatial experience', Gormley had also been reinventing the figure in other pieces. Upstairs at his exhibition, three body forms made entirely from hundreds of steel cubes would lie, crouch and stand in a single white room. 'I'm not sure what to call him,' said Gormley, staring down intently at one of the figures stretched out in a horizontal position below us. The cube structure reminded me of ideal modernist cities by Malevich, and Gormley agreed. But he also wants this figure to 'refer to the virtual world of digital imaging', and explained that 'the strange crystalline casting technique' would take up to four months to complete.

I remarked on the strong sense of brooding isolation conveyed by each of these figures. 'The whole thing is quite dark, in a way,' Gormley said. 'They're all facing placelessness. It's a Guantanamo Bay feeling. What is the space we retreat into when there's nothing to connect with?' After I expressed interest in the reference to Guantanamo, he took me over to a large wooden box containing another hunched figure. Since most of its body was hidden from view, Gormley proceeded to crouch on the studio floor to show me the pose, with both hands clasped behind his neck. 'That image from Guantanamo, of bags put over their heads, masks over their mouths and cable ties manacling them instead of handcuffs – all that resonated for me. The crouching figure is called *Concentrate*, because it also has an allusion to concentration camps.'

Looking up at the high ceiling again, where all the linear figures still floated so freely, I realized that Gormley was exploring the polarity between their cosmic liberation and the highly controlled, oppressed bodies still relying on the ground for support. Because of his concern for the plight of prisoners, he was delighted that the thousands of small figures in his colossal *Field* sculpture were now on display at the UN's European headquarters in Geneva – especially as that exhibition, which was spread across the floors of the UN offices and theatre, coincided with a Convention on Human Rights.

By no means everything attempted by the indefatigable artist had ended in acceptance. Over tea in his large white kitchen upstairs, he astonished me by revealing: 'I've just proposed a twelve-metre-high ejaculating man for the waterfront at Seattle. But they thought I was taking the piss. The figure was meant to give an eleven-second ejaculation of salt sea water every five minutes, so there would've been a lot of people standing around waiting for it. I intended it as an ironic comment on the male figure in relation to the whole idea of a fountain, because everyone knows that the fountain is a male fantasy of permanent ejaculation. I wanted it to be a celebratory piece, but I don't know if the feminists would find it offensive.'

Nearer home, he was still optimistic about getting the go-ahead for an equally controversial proposal. 'I refused an invitation originally to do something for the empty plinth in Trafalgar Square,' he recalled. 'I thought then that it was an insult to contemporary art to take on a cast-off from Victorian militarism. But I've got my solution now. You invite twenty-four people a day to occupy the plinth, one at a time. They can carry anything up there with them, take their clothes off, talk, whatever. There'll be perverted people, converted, silent and still ones, in daylight and darkness.'

Why, I asked, did he want to make such an intensely provocative work in the heart of the metropolis? 'It deals with the whole issue of elevating the singular example in a responsible and democratic way,' he said. 'And it's a foil to reality TV – there'll be real people occupying a formally raised-up position. I'm very excited about this idea. It would work extremely well. You'd advertise for applicants, and they could be from anywhere. But a nudist, stuck up there on a freezing winter night, might become very upset.'

As Gormley went on to describe just how many projects he now had elsewhere in the world, I wondered how he coped with the incessant pressure of a large, highly productive workshop. 'I like keeping busy, and having people around me,' he replied. 'The chemistry in the studio is very important: it's a bit like having an orchestra. There's freedom within certain rules, and everyone has to be on the right wavelength.' All the same, he did not feel happy thinking about his age. 'I'll be fifty-four this summer. That seems to me very, very old. It's the same age that Vicken's parents were when we met. But I'm feeling engaged with my work, and I think *Clearing* will have a big future. It may all be a terrible disaster, but it's a very well-plotted disaster.' He paused. 'And, of course, I hope it won't be.'

Luc Tuymans
April 2004

'Welcome to Morocco Nuts' declared a brilliant yellow shopfront just before my taxi arrived at Luc Tuymans's studio. We were on the quiet, narrow street in central Antwerp where the leading Belgian painter had worked for nearly thirty years. He was waiting outside his down-at-heel studio building: a tall, grey-jacketed figure with close-cropped hair, a long Roman nose and a frown of intense concentration.

Tuymans took me inside past some noisy, laughing children and pointed out 'a new fitness centre for kids on the ground floor'. Then the climb began, up and up a narrow, tile-lined and increasingly chilly staircase to the top. The temperature was almost glacial inside his astonishingly small, derelict flat. And I had never seen such a rudimentary studio. Until lately this rented room had been the place where Tuymans, paradoxically, produced paintings that sold for very handsome prices (Charles Saatchi had recently bought one at auction in New York for a record $427,000). A naked light bulb dangled from the ceiling, threatening to hit me as I passed. A large hole and numerous extensive cracks in the plaster testified to an advanced stage of structural decay. A small, ancient heater on the floor looked incapable of combating the cold.

But dried-up heaps of different-coloured paints, all neatly laid out on circular patches of cloth near an end wall spattered with brushstrokes, were evidence of how much work Tuymans had executed in this unlikely setting. Squeezed-out paint tubes were strewn on the nearby window ledge and filled the profusion of boxes stacked on the floorboards. No easel could be detected, for, as Tuymans explained, 'I paint on unstretched canvas nailed to the wall.' Even so, this interior – its bareness alleviated only by a large, dusty mirror and a monochrome photograph of Tuymans and his sister as neat, well-groomed children – must have been a hugely stimulating arena for art.

Not any more, though. 'The romance is over,' he told me. 'It's too small, and I've had leaks through the ceiling for sixteen years. I always thought my work was dependent on it, and I clung to this room for so long. But I'm about to move to a much larger studio, and I'd be there now if the roof hadn't collapsed.' When Tuymans first came here, in the late 1970s, the small flat had served as 'my home as well, which was horrible'. But he found it strangely conducive as a place to work.

I noticed a small table in one corner heaped with Polaroid photographs taken in preparation for the work he had made here. Each painting was created, unbelievably, in a single day. The image of a toxic-coloured, violently green orchid, to be reproduced on the cover of his forthcoming show at Tate Modern, took only five hours. 'When I get going,' he explained, 'I go into the work and don't feel the cold. It's a mode you get used to. Painting is like a habit.'

Even so, the amount of tension that preceded these acts of creation should not be underestimated. 'I'm very nervous,' Tuymans admitted, taking another deep drag on one of the Marlboro cigarettes he lit up in such profusion. 'I smoke like a motherfucker, and I nail-bite.' He held up his fingers to show me with a rueful smile. 'Everything is extremely prepared before work begins, but it's still a huge relief when I start painting. It gives me a great deal of pleasure: I wouldn't do it otherwise. But I'm not very light-hearted. There's always self-criticism, and I destroy half of what I do – usually a week later.' Tuymans explained that he even had an uneasy relationship with the pictures he decided were worth saving. 'I don't keep work for myself,' he said firmly. 'It's too fetishistic, and I can't stand looking at my own paintings at home. You keep seeing the mistakes. I even turn my back on my pictures when I see them in a collector's house.'

As a result, the perpetually dissastisfied Tuymans only had a surviving total of around four hundred paintings – a modest tally for a forty-six-year-old artist with such a high international reputation. The ebullient Rubens, another Antwerp-based painter, produced a far larger output with the aid of his highly organized workshop. But Rubens flourished in an era when paint on canvas was the artist's supreme medium. Tuymans's limited body of work at this time also reflected the precarious position that painting had occupied, in his eyes, ever since he was a student. 'When I was in the Academy,' he remembered, 'painting wasn't really on call. It was a very difficult thing to do. There was a lot of talk about the death of painting, so I worked in self-chosen isolation. I got rid of a lot of work that I now regret losing, often through overpainting.' He was passionately committed to his chosen medium, even though so many of his contemporaries were jettisoning it in favour of alternative strategies.

Looking back on his difficult boyhood, Tuymans said, he understood that painting had provided him with an outlet he desperately needed. He was now an articulate adult who had no difficulty exploring the essence of his ideas in fluent English. But, he recalled, 'I was a very, very silent child, bullied at school and very closed-up. I wasn't a happy kid. I had a problem with achievers, and was extremely bored until I took action. At puberty, I turned into the exact opposite. I grew very suddenly and everything changed. At the age of sixteen I bought a canvas, and painted something I'd seen from the window of a train – a guy in the snow, poking with a stick into a red clot. It was a kind of shocking image: something was going on there that I didn't understand.'

Hindsight made it clear that the ominous, mysterious mood of that early painting had been prophetic. Tuymans pursued a similar sense of enigmatic menace in much of his subsequent work, but it did not earn immediate approval. In 1985, at the age of twenty-seven, he staged his first exhibition when a large survey of contemporary Belgian work was organized in Ghent. Its aim was to boost the country's ailing art market and make its artists more well-known to an international audience. Although the show as a whole was largely successful, Tuymans encountered crushing indifference. For one day, he hired an old swimming pool in the elegant Ostende Hotel Palais des Thermes. Around sixteen paintings were displayed on the pool's tiled ledge and surrounding walls, and he posted invitations to more than a thousand addresses – but not a single visitor arrived. A less confident artist would have felt deeply discouraged, yet Tuymans's formidable self-belief emerged from the ordeal intact.

At the time, a spectacular and splashily neo-expressionist painting was fashionable. Tuymans's work could hardly have been more out of step with this sought-after style. Unlike Anselm Kiefer or Julian Schnabel, both of whom produced monumental and exclamatory images, he favoured modestly sized paintings with a quiet, elusive air. As if in acknowledgment that the very process of applying pigment to canvas was an antiquated notion, he even coated some of his pictures with an artificially induced network of cracks so that they looked, from the start, strangely old and remote – the work of a man who still believed that 'the more distance you have from an image, the better'.

Tuymans's fascination with certain aspects of history increased this link with the past. In 2001, when invited to represent Belgium at the Venice Biennale, he filled the national pavilion with paintings focused, in their deceptively blurred and muted way, on a notorious moment in his country's history: the withdrawal of colonial rule from the Belgian Congo in 1960. 'Belgian forced labour killed ten million people there,' he told me angrily. And Patrice Lumumba, first prime minister of the newly independent Congo, was murdered. The murkiness of his death is still a sensitive subject in Belgium. Tuymans recalled, 'The royal family didn't want to see the pavilion, but my wife and I were later invited to the palace and Queen Fabiola said to me: "Why did you paint my husband in a white uniform?"'

The painting in question, a full-length photo-based image reminiscent of a late Sickert, showed King Baudouin clutching a ceremonial sword and entering his Congolese territory in 1950. Tuymans hung it at the Venice pavilion directly opposite a portrait of Lumumba, so the sense of confrontation was palpable. But he is a subtle artist, and Baudouin (whose portrait was called *Mwana Kitoko – Beautiful White Man*) looks almost as vulnerable as the assassinated prime minister. 'I think the king was traumatized from the start,' said Tuymans. 'I was invited to paint the present king. I refused, because he looks like a bartender.'

Although he realized that he was 'probably the first living Belgian to have a show at the Tate', Tuymans seemed anything but a proud, patriotic artist. He was severely critical of his native country: 'In Belgium you can only go to a Catholic school – you have no choice. I read a lot, and I think Will Self is a great writer: we had a verbal fight in the Groucho Club about Francis Bacon, and we connected because he's also an arrogant bastard. But here, I live in a country where Belgians read the least – they read newspapers and magazines but not books.' Even so, he revered Jan van Eyck, especially the Arnolfini marriage portrait in London's National Gallery. Extolling its air of stillness, he said, 'When I look at the Arnolfini picture I think, that's it, you can pack it in – because this painting is the beginning and the end. Van Eyck wrote the words "If I can" on top of his self-portrait. Under the cloak of humility, there's the most humongous ambition.'

Could the same be said of Tuymans, I asked, on the eve of a major British show that seemed likely to win him new admirers? 'I was very nervous about it,' he acknowledged, 'but not now, because I've conceptualized it and walked about the spaces. Decisions have been made, and I'm aware that the British are used to one-liners in art, obvious and clear things like your tabloid press. It's a mid-career show, not a retrospective. So it will be content-driven rather than chronological, with constellations of different works throughout.'

Eager to show me the layout of the exhibition, he phoned for a taxi. A short ride took us across the city to an utterly different building: the tall, orderly house where he lived. While our photographer, Tim O'Sullivan, took pictures of Tuymans in the stark, white-walled courtyard at the back, its emptiness broken only by a single bare tree, I looked around. Just as he had told me, there were no Tuymans paintings on the walls. Beside the grand marble fireplace sat a large wooden globe, but it turned out to contain a circular drinks cabinet. Above the mantelpiece, the dark wooden frame round an elongated mirror echoed the colour of the leather furniture in the main room. Everything seemed subdued, including a powerful black drawing by his friend Marlene Dumas in the front office. 'We are ten minutes from the centre of Antwerp, near the park,' said Tuymans, returning inside. 'This district used to be a traditional centre for lawyers, because the Hall of Justice is down the street.'

On a long white table, the ground plan of his Tate show was laid out. While his wife prepared coffee, he showed me tiny reproductions of the seventy-odd paintings to be hung there. Since he hated looking at his own work so much, I asked whether the London exhibition would prove a painful experience for him. Smiling, he explained, 'In a museum there's a lot of clarity and distance. It's been a long time since I saw certain paintings of mine, and I want to find out how they've aged and how they function. Sometimes it's shocking: they seem much cooler than I thought, or they have far more contrasts.' He also stressed that 'there are only eleven or twelve spaces in the show, and it'll be hung very generously. Nothing will feel cramped, and for the viewer that's a good thing. It'll leave question marks in the mind.'

It certainly would, for the first room plunged us into alarming territory at once. Two acid-green paintings, ominously called *Illegitimate I & II*, transformed a lamp and a flower piece into images heavy with foreboding. 'The green indicates an idea of contamination from the start,' said Tuymans gravely, talking very fast now and with a mounting sense of urgency. 'There's an element of staining the surface, and in *Illegitimate III* we have a painting of a life-sized tracksuit with no head, a doll-like experience of the younger girl, the *femme-enfant*. In the next room, there'll be images of symptoms derived from medical handbooks, and then in Room Three a still life with a lampshade made out of human skin.'

Tuymans had produced a whole series of cool yet disturbing pictures inspired by Nazis and concentration camps. They would appear at various points in the Tate show, ranging from a painting of Albert Speer collapsed in the snow to an image based on 'the inner courtyard of a transitional camp. I want to couple the gruesome and the banal.' A gas chamber formed the subject of one fuzzy, bilious work, and he would also display a portrait of Reinhard Heydrich, 'the second-in-command after Himmler and the great architect of the Holocaust's logistics. He was the most good-looking of the Nazis, and Himmler possibly had him killed.' Hitler would appear too, taking a stroll in a simply handled picture called *Walking* that Tuymans said was 'influenced by Caspar David Friedrich and Japanese prints'.

But Tuymans does not confine himself to history. By far the largest painting in the show was to be a pale *Still Life* executed in 2002, hovering like a bleached-out image of a water jug and fruit in an otherwise blank expanse of whiteness. 'My wife and I were in Chicago when 9/11 happened,' he recalled. 'I wanted to do something, but the subject was so visually strong in itself that I couldn't touch it. So I went back to an idyllic still life with a twist, like Manet in reverse, and by enlarging the banality it floats in emptiness. The whole image is there, but deconstructed and oversized, so that it's very difficult to apprehend.'

In case anyone imagined that *Still Life* was just a placid image, Tuymans intended to hang it in the same room as a small, wholly unnerving picture called *Superstition*. Here, a predatory black insect was placed in front of a naked, splayed body, covering the genitals. I told him that it looked like the product of a nightmare about suffocation or being devoured, and he said, 'I have recurring dreams, fairly abstract, about weight and the pressure on you. I can still see the bed I slept in when I was an adolescent. *Superstition* came about by looking at insects and embryos. It's heavily related to toys and dolls: I have an obsessive interest in things that are awkward or wrong, like toys that fall and break but you can't restore them.'

Tuymans's art has always been muted; as he said to me, 'I want my paintings not to remind you of sound and musicality.' But it was clear that this Tate show would have scant appeal for the faint-hearted. He showed me a reproduction of a painting of Shanghai skyscrapers in the sunlight, commenting that it looked 'like the end of the world, like Utopia that falls on our neck. My work is not uplifting.' A great admirer of the desolate mood in T. S. Eliot's *The Waste Land*, he wryly acknowledged, 'My exhibition won't seem very positive. It's not Doomsday, but maybe Doomsday in particles. I think that's the smartest thing you can be at the moment.'

Richard Long

May 2004

Back in the late 1960s, the young and precocious Richard Long began revolutionizing the whole notion of British art and the landscape. Refusing to be confined by orthodox ideas, he regarded the entire world as a potential arena for his activities. Usually on his own, Long roamed across even the most remote and deserted expanses of countryside. He made primal marks with the sand, water, earth, sticks, mud and stones he found there, recreating his epic experiences in vastly impressive gallery shows where photographs, words and floor-based sculpture invited visitors to share a potent sense of wonder. Long was the first artist of my own generation to enthral me on a profound level, and he never attracted anything except vehement scorn from the arch-traditionalists at the Royal Academy.

But now, thirty-five years later, the tables had been spectacularly turned. David Hockney and Allen Jones, who were masterminding the Academy's Summer Exhibition, had invited Long to mount a special solo show in its most prominent space: the Central Hall. His presence here was a measure of how far the Royal Academicians had developed – away from insular, mind-numbing intolerance and towards a more enlightened, open understanding of modern art at its most adventurous.

Long himself, ready for a demanding day of installation in this skylit chamber, still seemed surprised to find himself welcomed by his old enemies. But there was no time to linger on the past. Clad for action in a pale blue short-sleeved T-shirt, he was already darting round the space with a long-limbed agility that belied his age. In a year Long would celebrate his sixtieth birthday, but he showed no sign of slowing down or of opting for shorter, safer walks in locations nearer home. The most recent work on display here arose from journeys to the Sahara desert, a Japanese mountain, the Three Sisters Wilderness in Oregon, and Warli Tribal Land in Maharashtra, India.

Although his close-cropped hair was now white, this indefatigable wanderer appeared just as slim and energetic as he had been in 1971 when I'd first met him. He talked fast, gesturing with animated arms and then, quite suddenly, stopping as if overcome by shyness – for Long is an intensely private man. A natural loner, he has always been based in his native Bristol and pursued his idiosyncratic vision of the world. 'The truth is,' he said, pausing briefly between hands-on bouts of vigorous picture-shifting, 'I'm a classical artist concentrating on lines, circles and fundamental geometry. But I use lots of different media, and every stone or splash of mud is different. So I think it articulates the cosmic variety of nature.'

Unlike so many successful artists at this time, who relied on a battalion of assistants to produce their work, Long still insisted on doing it himself. 'It's all made by me, like a kind of self-portrait,' he stressed. 'The mud-works are done with my hands, and I roll the stones down the hill. It has always been like that. I'd get no pleasure from being an artist if I couldn't make the work myself. I'm one of the few artists who still lives where they were born. It's handy for all that mud on the river, so I'm still near my great natural resource.' The only help he relied on, installing his show here in the Central Hall, came from two young men called Kevin and Stuart. They suddenly arrived with a red metal ladder. As they climbed up, Long began directing them, measuring an immense white wall with tapes. Far above, a bust of Michelangelo glared down disapprovingly from a gilded niche. But Long ignored him, pacing restlessly and very quickly back and forth, assessing the space with his limbs as well as with practised eyes.

'You don't just plonk things up,' he insisted. 'Sometimes the creative way to work is to look at all the permutations. Opportunism is important, being able to use the particulars of a place which I normally don't know at all.' On two of the walls he planned to hang large photo pieces and text works printed on thick paper. But on the other two, the words would be applied directly to the walls' surfaces. 'The first piece deals with a six-day kayak ride down the Columbia River,' he said, 'and the second is a fifteen-day walk in South Africa – that'll be like a big circle of words, showing how I walked in a different direction each day and camped for fourteen nights at a borehole on Guarrie Berg in the Karoo.'

By this time, Kevin and Stuart had been given the go-ahead to place some sentences on the wall devoted to the Columbia River trip. I noticed that two of these were song lyrics, from Johnny Cash's 'I Hear That Lonesome Whistle Blow' and Bob Dylan's 'Watching The River Flow'. Did Long listen to songs while making the journeys? His bushy black eyebrows close in a frown and he shakes his head. 'I don't take audio tapes – that's too technical. They're not for me: I'm not on email or computer. But music is important to me at home, and sometimes an idea comes from having a piece of music going over and over in my head, like a mantra. I like very emotional music: I think art is very emotional. What else is there to live for? The happiest time of my life is when I'm walking. It's a great therapy, and a great time to sort things out. One function of art is to simplify the complications of life.'

So how could he bear being in a metropolis as big as London? 'I couldn't live in it, but I accept it,' he said. 'Most art is made by artists based in cities, so my work is not typical. I have a hit-and-run attitude to urban life. I do love the energy of New York, but all my work is made in completely isolated places, where there's amazing freedom.'

Out there, in the desert or wilderness, silence had to be cherished. Long did not even take a mobile phone with him. 'It spoils the walk,' he said. 'I don't want to interrupt the concentration: I'm in a private zone. Many years ago I took a radio along, to follow a cricket match. But I couldn't focus on either the game or the world around me.' For the same reason, he avoided taking books. 'They're too heavy to carry, anyway, and not as important as food. I don't like novels taking me over. If you're in Oregon, where the land is covered in volcanic dust, you don't need Jane Austen. I've never felt lonely, ever. Urban loneliness, yes, but never in a landscape.' Why? 'Because solitude is rare, and something to be savoured.'

Only by concentrating very hard in the primordial emptiness could he become fully alert, and respond to the kind of uncanny experiences behind a text work called *Transference*. Taking me over to look at it, Long explained, 'There's a phenomenon in particle physics where behaviour can be duplicated, from one part of nature over to another. It's one of the great mysteries.' *Transference* started with a three-day walk on Dartmoor, where Long noted, among other things, white butterflies, animal droppings, slipper boulders and a peat bog. Then, 'half a lunar month later', some of these observations were uncannily repeated during a seven-day walk on Mount Chōkai in north-east Japan. They made him respond 'in completely new ways', and a related urge had now led Long to use an equally fresh approach for a large new sculpture on the floor of the Central Hall.

'I'm calling it *White Mud and White Light Crescents*,' he said, moving over to a lamp resting in a corner. 'I guess I wanted a work which people can walk through. There'll be heavy human traffic in the Summer Exhibition, and visitors will cut that crescent with their feet and shadows.' Where had the idea for this unprecedented piece come from? 'It sounds corny,' he admitted, 'but I was camping and looking at the moon out in the desert. I thought, what am I going to do in this space at the Royal Academy, with its problematic trap-door in the floor? So I just decided it'd be nice to have this image of white light, with people walking through it.'

Although Long emphasized that he was 'not a literary person', the choosing of words had become a central activity on his walks. So how did he record them? 'Most of my text works start out in the margins of maps, written in pencil,' he said. 'But I do have a note-book and, in fact, I can show it to you.' Striding over to a rucksack deposited at the edge of the room, he searched inside and produced a battered little notebook with the number 4 inscribed on the cover. 'It's small because everything has to be light on a walk: that's crucial,' he said, showing me a densely written diary, lists of things he had encountered and words in capital letters, the try-outs for wall works.

Turning the pages, I found myself reading a dramatic entry from his Japanese expedition: 'Ants in dry grass. Tremor, in evening! Bigger quake around 7.13 in the morning!' During his last night on Mount Chōkai, this major earthquake had killed several people in the region. I asked Long if he had been frightened. 'No, no, not at all,' he replied dismissively, as if the question were absurd. 'I wasn't scared: I was in the middle of a forest. It's the safest place to be. Nothing can ever happen to you.'

All the same, Long had undoubtedly been a lucky traveller. He was 'almost never ill', and his worst mishap had occurred when 'I twisted my ankle on the South African walk.' No wonder he still preferred to go it alone, with nothing more than a simple tent for shelter at night. On one journey, through Spitzbergen in Norway, this supremely independent man had been ordered to employ a guide 'because of polar bears. He carries a gun and an emergency beacon, so if you have an accident he can light it and a helicopter scrambles.' But nothing went wrong, and Long continued to regard the natural world with a fundamental sense of awe.

Hence, perhaps, the luminous serenity of his *White Mud and White Light Crescents*. Later that day, high up in the ceiling, the lamp was finally attached to a circular track with the aid of a blue Genie scissor lift. The projected beam created two large curves far below. Their glow was enhanced by a layer of white mud meeting another layer of China clay, with a glistening rainbow effect all along the edges.

Watching how they scythed through space, meeting at a point of intense brightness, I saw it above all as a symbol of Long's perpetual need to keep on the move. 'The whole world is my territory,' he said, 'and the big tension in my life is finding a balance between walking and showing my work. I wish I had more time for walking.'

Doris Salcedo

September 2004

Art and politics have come a long way since Diego Rivera joined the Communist Party in the 1920s, pledging to promote social progress throughout Mexico by painting monumental murals for public settings. In 2004, the intensely political Doris Salcedo came over to London from Colombia to make a large installation at White Cube, but the final impact of the work itself was impossible to predict.

When I arrived at the gallery in Hoxton Square a colossal lorry was parked outside, loaded with hefty brown containers all marked *Fragile*. For an instant, they made me wonder if the street was about to become the site for Salcedo's new piece. After all, she had used outdoor urban locations in some of her most spectacular and powerful work. Two years earlier, she had commemorated a murderous attack on the supreme court in Bogotá, her native city, by lowering wooden chairs over the frontage of the new Palace of Justice. Old and damaged furniture, in Salcedo's work, often acts as a mute, haunting reminder of victims who have suffered persecution. In Turkey in 2003 she heaped six hundred chairs into a gap between two buildings at the centre of Istanbul. Once again, her target was the human cost of war, and the stacked-up furniture looked like a pyre awaiting the arrival of sacrificial corpses.

This time, though, she was confining her art to the inside of the gallery. And instead of deploying piled-up objects, Salcedo had concentrated solely on the walls of the main ground-floor room. They were all being hidden behind a different set of walls, and wire fencing was embedded in their pale surfaces from floor to ceiling. Ten technicians from her studio in Colombia were perched on scaffolding here, either hammering or talking to invisible colleagues at work on the other side of the walls. Their voices, combined with the hum of enormous electric fans, created a formidable amount of noise. There was tension in the air, too: they were behind schedule, even though the team had already been labouring away here for a week.

It was rapidly becoming clear that Salcedo would have very little time to talk to me, and I felt frustrated at the thought of being unable to discuss her intentions as fully as they deserved. Although we had never met before, I felt certain that she was immensely thoughtful. And in my experience, talking to artists should never be rushed: time is always needed to get beyond superficialities and try probing the centre of their intentions.

I was relieved, therefore, when this striking forty-six-year-old with her abundance of exuberantly wavy black hair managed at last to extricate herself from working in the exhibition space. I asked her straight away about the schedule for the show, and she explained calmly, 'We lost four days because of discrepancies between what we'd made in Bogotá and what we have here,' adding, 'Every millimetre counts, and it's extremely precise. The human, handcrafted surface is always what counts in my work. I was trained as a painter rather than a sculptor, and manual work is essential to me.'

Salcedo was right to emphasize the intricacy and exactitude of her installation. A closer look revealed that the wire loop stretching round the room like an immense cage consisted of many thousands of small diamond shapes – mostly filled, painstakingly, with white plaster. No wonder the containers on the lorry outside the gallery were labelled so prominently to convey the fragility of their cargo. It all added up to an astonishing feat of sustained workmanship. Salcedo, reaching out to touch the wall, told me, 'Each diamond has been made with great care. We've been constructing the walls for a whole year, and I've got thirty-eight people working for me in Colombia. They are all extraordinarily involved, but it can become ridiculously difficult. Every day I felt we were in a Beckett play, so in order to help us I put up a quotation from one of his poems: "Fail better."'

Salcedo has always been nourished by words, whether fictional or factual; she characterized herself as 'a political person – I'm so political I cannot tell you.' When we left the room and sat down for a while in a quiet space upstairs, I asked what form her commitment to politics might take. This militant woman explained succinctly that for many years she had 'kept files on concentration camps as well as contemporary versions of them, places where civilians are kept without trial'. She read a great deal, she said, explaining that the White Cube installation 'comes more from literature than art. I think of Kafka's *Metamorphosis* and the way he crawls across the wall without having any access.' Was philosophy important as well? She nodded. 'Every time I'm working, I have a thinker guiding me. In this case, it was Emmanuel Levinas, especially a book called *Totality and Infinity*. He has an extraordinary way of seeing the Other, and the responsibility one has towards the Other.'

Salcedo's vision of the world had been decisively affected, too, by her own first-hand experience of life in Colombia. 'Most of the time I'm there,' she said, 'and I keep a very, very low profile: I like it that way, the privacy.' Besides, she had to guard against potential danger. 'The spread of kidnapping means that I no longer travel around the country as much as before. But it's important to have a perspective, and I see everything from the vantage of the Third World. It's not enough to look from a comfortable position, and in Colombia they're getting poorer all the time. I think it's going to get much worse – you have sweatshops everywhere and conditions are deteriorating rapidly for people, with more violence and chaos. War has become a way of life there, a means of making a living.'

How did these desperate conditions affect other, more fortunate countries? Salcedo told me that she believed war 'casts a long shadow over all of us. In the First World, are we at war or at peace? I can give you a long list of the same type of questions, and I have no answers. Here in England, you're involved in a war I find particularly catastrophic. But we don't know what times we are living through. That is why, in this new room, I'm trying to get as close to nothing as possible.'

Salcedo said she had decided to call the White Cube installation *Neither* – a title she chose 'because of the ambiguity. I want people to experience not being able to see here, and to that extent it will become frustrating.' Might that, I asked, run the risk of cancelling out her political intentions? She shook her head. 'I'm not a message artist. I see reality in a raw, naked way, so I have to respond with my work. That's why I adore art over politics, obviously: it's where our humanness resides. But I don't think art will save us. The poet Paul Celan says something beautiful: "Art is nothing but mortality, and in vain."'

The ambiguity of *Neither* extended to the use of the enclosing white plaster, chosen by Salcedo because 'having a home is essential, and an interior is a place of safety'. But she remained aware of the 'harshness of the wire mesh, which will be left bare in a couple of places within the room'. The same wire was also, most alarmingly, allowed to jut out unprotected at one side of the entrance. She warned me that 'the mesh will be left exposed there, and it can hurt you. After all, the same material has been used at Guantanamo Bay.' This stark installation promised, in fact, to be the most extreme piece Salcedo had so far produced. 'I want to make it almost invisible,' she said. 'It's the most minimal piece I've ever done, and the only one without any objects.'

In this respect, *Neither* could hardly be more different from the finest political art of the past. Jacques-Louis David, who dedicated himself in the early years of the French Revolution to painting passionately committed images of the upheaval, focused in his most impressive painting on a single figure: the martyred Marat, murdered in his bath by Charlotte Corday. David's bleak elegy has the purged simplicity of classical art, and gains enormously in tragic impact from the mysterious area of darkness above Marat's corpse. Picasso went to the other extreme, fired by anger and pity when German bombers obeyed Franco's orders to blitz the Basque capital Guernica. This callous assault on the town's civilians became Picasso's target. He painted a battering-ram of an image filled with anguished humans and animals, over 25 feet in width. It is a terrifying and seismic denunciation. While fire assails a building, women react in horror and a speared horse's wounds are disclosed by the aggressive rays of an outsized light bulb. The most agonizing emotion belongs to a distraught mother who grasps her dead child, pushes back her head and yells at the unseen agents of death in the sky.

Compared with Picasso's grotesque, splintered distortions, Salcedo's installation struck me as eerily calm. 'I want people to feel they are walking into an empty room,' she explained, 'and you'll need silence in order to connect with it.' But the wire-fenced walls were bound to exert their menacing power, and there was no mistaking the tenacious gravity of the work.

Despite the pressure of her deadline, Salcedo had spoken with me for long enough to illuminate the nuanced thinking behind *Neither*. Now, however, we had run out of time, and she needed to get back downstairs to continue working on the installation. As we returned to the ominous room, before we parted, I commented that each of the individual plaster fragments enclosed in the cruel mesh looked breakable. Salcedo paused, considering her response, and then replied: 'That's what we are – fragile and vulnerable. I think we are all prisoners.'

Sam Taylor-Wood [Sam Taylor-Johnson]

October 2004

She seemed cool and unflappable – a woman accustomed to interrogation by journalists – but Sam Taylor-Wood was honest enough to tell me that, for her, 'being interviewed is like having root-canal treatment. I just want to hit some of the people who come and see me. They ask such insensitive questions, like a thud in the gut, to do with my illness. Sometimes I feel too open.'

Why, then, was she prepared to talk to me? The obvious answer was that her solo London show was about to open and she felt naturally eager to discuss her new work. But because 'a lot of it is about communication', Taylor-Wood was also prepared to be surprisingly frank about her inner feelings, even when they centred on the protracted suffering she had undergone as a cancer patient.

In 1997 – at the devastatingly early age of twenty-nine, and only six months after giving birth to her daughter Angelica – she was diagnosed with colon cancer. The doctor shared her sense of shock and disbelief. 'He said: "You can't have that, it's an old man's disease."' Although she recovered following the removal of one and a half feet of her colon, breast cancer subsequently hit her at the age of thirty-three. After a mastectomy and months of chemotherapy 'which wouldn't leave me completely infertile', she once more regained her health.

The entire ordeal had been so gruelling that Taylor-Wood was now determined to discuss it without any prompting on my part. 'It's important for me to talk about cancer,' she said. 'When I had it, there was no one willing to discuss their experiences as a patient, because it's a fucking tough thing to go through. But if I can help other people, by showing them you can conquer it and survive, I will. Even though I have a fear that I'm just setting myself up, and the recovery won't work. I'd love to have more children, but the doctors are divided. Some say that being pregnant could bring back the cancer, because of hormone change. But if I'm still clear after five years, which will be next April, I'll think again.'

She took me up to the top floor of her immense East London studio, a handsomely converted former stables for horses belonging to Whitbread Brewery. Downstairs, she said, the Pet Shop Boys had a recording studio. But most of the space was hers. Looking out of the ample windows, I noticed coils of barbed wire running along the tall brick wall that separated her sturdy building from the narrow streets beyond. Taylor-Wood confirmed that the protective barrier was 'very necessary'; yet here, in this panoramic space, she felt safe and hugely stimulated.

'I've only been here a year and a half,' she said, moving swiftly across the bare floorboards. Her energy was self-evident, accentuated by the slimness of a body at ease in a thin, pale green, short-sleeved blouse and blue jeans tucked into brown leather cowboy boots. 'I feel like it's the return of the Prodigal Son, because I used to live in a terrible Peabody bedsit near here with one little window. I've never had a studio before, and it's had a massive effect on me. I'm much more prolific than I was: this is a place to work hard and think in. You can breathe more. It's quite calming, and brought about a phenomenal change in my life.'

Half unrolled, in the middle of an otherwise empty floor, lay a black mat. Responding to my query, she explained that she used it for yoga: 'Three times a week, and two hours each session. But I'm so aware of time, I can't really switch off.' A strict regime, the yoga was part of her sustained, determined battle with the aftermath of illness. 'I had to make radical alterations in my mindset about life,' she said. 'I don't get pressured into things now. I used to feel that I always had to say yes to everything, because I was so privileged to be asked. But now I'm much more selective, committed to yoga and in bed by midnight.'

She was also taking great care with her food intake: 'No dairy, no meat.' Was that dietician's orders? She shook her head defiantly. 'It's my own instinct. I read an amazing book called *Your Life in Your Hands* by Dr Jane Plant. And I refused all the drugs that doctors wanted to give me for five years.' Why? 'I just felt I didn't want to take them, so I had to do something else. Doctors know how to treat cancer, but not how to prevent it. You just have to follow your own rules, and I do a lot of acupuncture. Another great book is Lance Armstrong's *Every Second Counts*. I didn't think I'd get through chemotherapy: it's the worst thing, and it basically kills every cell in your body, the good cells and the bad cells. But when you come out of it, you find you've still got that drive. And you're so grateful to have your energy.'

The visual proof of Taylor-Wood's resolve was displayed on the walls of her vast first-floor studio, a more public room where her personal assistants were working. To my astonishment, she showed me a series of austere black-and-white photographs of landscapes and remote, desolate streets. Far removed from the sophisticated, minimal interiors inhabited by so many of the celebrities in her richly coloured earlier work, they reminded me of Walker Evans and Dorothea Lange exploring America with their cameras during the Depression era. Taylor-Wood nodded. 'I liked the idea of going on the same trail as them. So in June, I went on a big road trip to the Deep South, covering the whole of Georgia, Alabama and North Carolina. It was a long journey.'

Are you fearless, I asked her, staring at the powerful images of lonely garages at night, decaying motels and empty forests? In one, a sign pinned to a tree announced in Gothic script: 'Jesus Is Coming'. 'I am in certain ways,' she said, 'and I was planning to go on my own in a big four-wheel drive. But *he* was thrust upon me.' She pointed at a blurred, grainy image of a man's hand holding a gun. 'He's Sergeant Jeff Wenninger, an LAPD cop who's head of a drugs gang detail. And

I definitely needed him. We got chased a couple of times by people who saw me taking pictures of them and got mad.' An enormous woman next to a car, visible in one of Taylor-Wood's most ominous nocturnal photographs, became unbelievably furious with her and yelled: 'Hey! You just take a picture of my ass?'

But Taylor-Wood did not approach the project as an invasive, hit-and-run photographer. 'I always ask people if I can take their picture,' she explained, 'and sometimes they say yes and then run away.' She indicated a mournful image of a town in Georgia called Unadilla. 'An extraordinary place, the most derelict and desolate scene. Do you see the little boy standing on a skateboard? That's Cameron. He's only eight, but his dad's dead and his mum's in jail. I told him: "I'll build you a skateboard park if I sell this picture."' Then she showed me a photograph of muscular Sonny Moody, stripped to the waist and fishing in a creek. He invited her to 'come up to the creek and meet my friends'. She was tempted, but cautious Sergeant Wenninger had other ideas. 'Jeff said: "No, I don't want to be shagged up the ass." He thought it might be like a scene from *Deliverance*.'

Taylor-Wood was clearly fascinated by the most unnerving aspects of the Deep South. 'The poverty was scary, and really, really frightening on the outskirts of Savannah,' she said. 'But it was most frightening at nights in the motels – they were so creepy.' Several of her most memorable photographs focus on plantation houses marooned in emptiness ('I've given some of these to Elton, to use on his next album cover'). She wandered into an eerily deserted home, only to discover that the TV set in the living room was still warm. Elsewhere, a saddle abandoned on an electric fence became the subject of a melancholy image, as did an isolated house entirely burnt down apart from its weirdly intact, upright chimney.

All in all, this haunting territory provided Taylor-Wood with an unforgettable experience. 'I went there at a time when I felt everything was closing in on me, and I felt so free for the first time in ages,' she said. 'Out on the road, with no exhibition waiting at the end of the journey. I haven't worked like this for as long as I can remember. I went back to London wanting to pare my life down and get rid of all the crap. Immediately you come back, you're asked to do this, that and the other. I don't want all this stuff, and the invitations to shop openings. I mean, they're only shops.' She sounded like an artist fired by a determination to focus on her work alone, at the expense of everything that had worn her out before the liberating trip to Georgia.

Sitting down on a bright orange sofa, she opened boxes filled with photographs. These were for *Crying Men*, the epic two-and-a-half-year project that had exhausted her before the Deep South trip. 'It was so hard doing this,' she said. 'It was an ordeal.' The images were all of prominent actors and most of them looked heartbroken. Ed Harris seemed particularly bleak; Jude Law crouched on the floor in the corner of a room; even the ebullient Robin Williams appeared devastated. 'The idea was to fight against the cliche of pointing a camera at someone and saying "Smile". I also thought about all those early paintings of martyred saints with tears in their eyes. I wanted to take these huge icons of our era and make them more human, more vulnerable.'

But how could the viewer know if the tears were genuine? For Taylor-Wood, that was the key question. 'Because they're actors you recognize, you don't know if their sadness is real or not,' she said. 'I could tell. It's to do with a change in the eye, so fractional, like a momentary flicker. None of them knew what I wanted beforehand, apart from taking their picture. And some didn't like it when I told them: "I'd quite like you to cry." They threatened to leave. But I can talk anyone into anything – it's a skill.'

Even so, didn't the attempt to focus on so much melancholy end up affecting her deeply? 'Oh, you've no idea,' she agreed. 'At the beginning, I felt like saying – you're an actor, I want you to cry, that's your job. But after the first few, I got really involved, and worried about when to say stop. How do you tell Paul Newman to finish crying? I'd come home so miserable and depressed. I'd feel intensely sad. To have big, grown men crying – people I'd been in awe of when young – is really moving.'

As we gazed at the images, I asked her about the mournful song that was playing on her sound system. 'It's Caetano Veloso, the Brazilian singer,' she said. 'I like him a lot: he has such a fabulous *tristesse*, and I suppose my work is full of it.' When I remarked that she seemed happy and positive, her reply was revealing: 'I suppose I channel my misery into my work. Sadness isn't bad, it's underrated. It's such a fantastic emotion, and it's all around us.'

Music clearly nourishes Taylor-Wood and her art. A while ago, she worked at the Royal Opera House for a year with singers and dancers including Ivan Putrov of the Royal Ballet, whom she described to me as having 'that wonderful Russian emotional heaviness – he said: "I'm from Ukraine, and this is as happy as I get."' She particularly loves opera. 'I go a lot. There's nothing like it, and it really pisses me off when people say it's elitist. You can go there for five pounds.' She darted over to her iPod. 'Today I got so excited, beyond excited, when a letter came asking: "Will you be on *Desert Island Discs*?" One of my choices, I know for sure, is *Orpheus and Eurydice* by Gluck. Oh, it's so beautiful, I must play it to you. Orpheus is standing at the graveside of his wife, lamenting her death and crying her name to the gods. It's so heart-wrenching, it brings tears to your eyes and hairs up on the back of your neck.'

How, I wondered, did Taylor-Wood's own marriage to Jay Jopling work, in terms of their professional relationship as artist and dealer? Was Jay tough enough with her? 'He can't be tough, not with me he can't,' she said, laughing. 'But we worked together first before we got together romantically, and we established the ground rules then. Jay feels he can't give me preferential treatment. He refers to me as "STW" in all his business notes, which is perfect. But never at home. Otherwise, we'd be talking about work stuff all the time. So we do manage to separate it, but I have to stand my ground and be very firm.'

Taylor-Wood could not think of any other artists married to their dealers and she acknowledged that there were, inevitably, tensions. 'I never talk about what I'm working on with him. But Jay does make demands. He'll know I'm doing something, and he gets so enthusiastic and says: "Can we show this?" And I say: "No, of course I can't, I haven't finished yet."' I have to be allowed to get on and do it, without external influence of any kind. I sometimes get irritated with him, especially at art fairs. In New York, I looked at the White Cube stand and there were five Tracey Emin works on display. I only had one little one, and one in the cupboard. So I said to him: "What's the point of being married to a dealer if there are no advantages?" Then I phoned Tracey and we had a laugh. We're so different, like chalk and cheese, but we get on really well.'

Taylor-Wood was frank about how different she was from Jopling. 'My mind races along, it drives me insane because it doesn't stop. I have to tell myself to shut up, and force myself back to the present. It drives Jay mad. But he drives me utterly insane when he falls asleep in the cinema. Art and Leeds United are his things. And he's much more passionate about art than I am – he's always going to galleries and museums, and I hate it. Damien [Hirst] says museums are filled with dead people. Jay has a pretty intense relationship with Damien, too. They talk to each other as much as I talk to him – pretty much twenty-four hours. But Damien is one of the most generous people. When I was ill, he was so over-generous with me; he'd write me notes and send me drawings and paintings.'

Like Hirst, Taylor-Wood had recently found herself increasingly fascinated by religious imagery despite having no conventional faith. She described how 'I grew up lusting for a religious base. Catholicism seemed so romantic, with the smell of incense and all those great paintings.' Ray Winstone (who appears in her *Crying Men* series clutching his grief-stricken head) was, she said, 'obsessed with William Blake, and he's asked me to direct him in a film about Blake'. Why did she agree? 'Well, the best answer is that I was reading Angelica the poem "Tiger, Tiger", and told her about the film. She said: "Who was Blake?" So I said: "He was a man who saw angels."' But Taylor-Wood's faith in Winstone must have been the decisive factor? 'We get on extremely well. He's one of the warmest, kindest people, one of the few who makes my knees go wobbly. When he asked me to direct the film, I went quiet for a very long time. But he said: "You're more in tune with me and intuitive than a lot of directors."'

She is also an artist who thrives, more and more, on risk-taking. For her extraordinary recent project *Self-Portrait Suspended*, she 'hired Bondage Master Rope Knot for the day. He came round to the studio at nine o'clock and proceeded to tie me from the ceiling beams in all kinds of different ways.' She smiled as she described the process. 'It was for art, of course, and all about making the most interesting shapes with my body in space. I took a long time working out what to wear. I didn't want to be naked, because that's a whole other focus. So with the help of my best friend, who runs [lingerie company] Agent Provocateur, I ended up in vest and knickers.'

There are eight separate works in the series, and Taylor-Wood has digitally removed the ropes so that she appears to be free-floating in space. 'You can see the change from light to dusk. Master Rope Knot said I had the most stamina of anybody he'd ever worked with. My body was covered in bruises and rope marks for weeks after, which is so not my thing. But it was about the release of adrenalin and seratonin in my body. And anyway, I now feel I can take on the cast of *Ben Hur* after doing the *Crying Men* pictures. Those bloody actors, with their teams of "people" – they weren't all as nice as pie.'

Lucian Freud

May 2005

It was dark when I approached Lucian Freud's London studio. The tall, bulky house ahead of me looked deserted, apart from a small illuminated window glowing right at the summit. I rang the bell, then pushed the front door open and started climbing, up and up the steep flights of stairs. Freud made the same journey every day so he must, I thought, have benefited hugely from the exercise since moving in twenty-five years earlier. He certainly looked slim and spry enough, holding the studio door in readiness as he waited for me to arrive, panting, at the top.

It was late, the stage of the evening when most people would have been unwinding and looking forward to sleep. But Freud seemed tense and alert. His paint-spattered clothes and boots testified to the fact that work was progressing within. And when I asked about his schedule, the answer was astonishing for a man of eighty-two. 'I work until midnight or half past twelve,' he said in his soft, low voice. 'But then I get up at four. I've never been any good at sleeping. I think: "What am I doing, lying here?" I don't really need much sleep, but I feel quite ill some of the time.'

So far as possible, Freud refused to let physical ailments get in the way of his overriding commitment to art. Painting remained his supreme priority, and no wonder: the prospect of a major retrospective, due to open at the Venice Biennale a few weeks after our meeting, had strengthened his already formidable sense of determination still further. It would be a signal honour for any artist to be given such an ample airing at the world's most distinguished international art exhibition. And Freud wanted, in particular, to finish a large, ambitious painting of a nude in time for the show, so that it could be displayed there as a manifestation of his continuing resolve.

He had no desire to involve himself in the selection of exhibits or even see the show himself. Freud was content to let his friend, the critic William Feaver, organize it, with one caveat: he did not want his monumental painting of Leigh Bowery, naked and seen from the back, to be included. Why? He shrugged. 'I didn't like it, and I don't think it really works. I painted it freely, with an innate knowledge that wasn't quite there.'

On the whole, the large body of work Freud had produced over the previous seventy years was still intact. 'I have been very lucky – I've lost very little,' he said. 'In 1944, when I was painting my big zebra picture *The Painter's Room*, a bomb went off outside. Luckily I'd gone round the corner to get something, but when I got back large fragments of glass from the smashed window were sticking into the studio. They would have destroyed the picture if it hadn't been positioned at right angles to the window.' All the same, he seemed resigned to the fact that one of his most intense and memorable early paintings, a small portrait of his friend Francis Bacon in mesmerizing close-up, could not be obtained for Venice. Owned by Tate, it had been stolen from a 1988 exhibition in Berlin and never recovered. Freud gave a stoical sigh. 'Ten or fifteen years ago there was a reward of £100,000 offered for it,' he recalled. 'Lots of people came forward, but it was all a lot of rubbish. I painted it on copper, on an old etching plate, and Bacon was a terrific hero in Germany.'

The irony is that Freud was himself born in Berlin in 1922, and grew up there before his family wisely decided to leave Nazi Germany and move to England in 1932. But when we spoke he had no desire to return to his native country, even for the briefest visit. The truth was that Freud hated going anywhere. He knew Venice: 'I had a room there with Bacon in the fifties, but I had a horrible time. I don't like anywhere except London.' Although he approved of the space in the museum where his Venice retrospective would be staged, he said: 'I won't see the exhibition, being so old and not feeling well all the time. It's bad at nights sometimes. I haven't been out of London now for two years, apart from a quick trip to Belfast for lunch. I came back here the same day, but I did go to Lulworth Cove a few weeks ago. I'd love to see it again: it's neither maudlin nor melancholy, the way the rocks go. They made me think of portraiture and facial features and I thought, this could really help me.'

When younger, Freud was certainly not averse to visiting the seaside. 'I used to go to Southend, and you couldn't see the sea for all the fat ladies and "Kiss Me Quick" signs in enormous letters. It's very, very lively there, but you felt that these are not educated people.' He fought shy of visiting his own exhibitions, though. 'The only private view of mine that I've ever attended was at the Lefevre Gallery years ago. I thought it'd be so exciting, but all I saw there were my uncles and aunts.' When we met, he had not seen his brother Clement for many years – 'my mother maintained that I bullied him when we were young' – and saw little of his other brother, Stephen: 'He became a door-knob merchant, which rather surprised me because he was a highly educated Cambridge graduate.'

Freud was, however, seeing a great deal of Alexandra Williams-Wynn, a thirty-two-year-old sculptor and daughter of a Welsh baronet. When he took me into the studio, via a corridor where dozens of paint tubes were piled high on a large trolley, she was standing by a well-lit bed in the middle of the room. Here, only a few minutes ago, Alexandra had been posing naked for Freud as he worked on a small painting of a nude with her legs apart. How, I wondered, had they met? Dark, curly-haired and wearing a simple black shirt with white trousers, Alexandra explained that she was a friend of the late Bruce Bernard, a photography expert who knew Freud well and wrote a perceptive book about his work. 'I'd always wanted to meet Lucian and never had,' she said. 'So I wrote to him, and he replied.'

The small painting on the easel was unfinished, even though Freud had been working hard on it for several months. Why was it taking so long? 'I'm suspicious of everything I do,' Freud admitted, 'and when it's quick, I think, oh, that must be wrong.'

Alexandra smiled and said, 'It keeps evolving, keeps changing. Days can go by and you look at the painting and you think, what has changed? But suddenly it can move on very quickly. And you can be quite ruthless, getting rid of things you don't like.'

Freud agreed. 'I don't think you can be severe enough, and to destroy something that doesn't seem up to your best is really important. So I scrap things.' He made a harsh, decisive cutting gesture with his arm and hand, adding: 'Sometimes it's rather like a baby that hasn't got a proper spine – it has to be scrapped.'

Expending so much time and energy on his work might well have defeated a lesser artist; but Freud was formidably resolute and knew how to pace himself. 'When I get weary,' he told me, 'I put one cheek of my behind on this high chair.' Pointing to the half-finished painting, he said, 'I'll have to enlarge this small nude.' Freud often decided, while he was working on a picture, that the canvas should be extended by adding an extra section. Most of his paintings underwent radical alterations during their prolonged gestation periods. He was the very opposite of an artist who knows, before the work even begins, how the final image will appear. His absorption in the act of painting was total, and Freud felt so driven that he even claimed: 'I don't have time to dream. But I do daydream a bit when I rest: it's to do with shapes and composition. All painting is really to do with abstract form, but you wouldn't know from this picture.'

Nor would anyone have guessed from the extraordinary number of self-portraits Freud painted, drew and etched throughout his career. One of the earliest and most important is an arresting 1943 painting that was due to come up for sale at Sotheby's shortly after our meeting. The blanched young artist stares out at us with an air of melancholy, his projecting ears as alert as his intense eyes. He holds a white feather in one hand, like a symbol of peace defiantly displayed in a time of war. But the icebergs floating around him announce a more sinister mood of glacial menace.

Gazing at a reproduction of this painting, Freud could not say what the feather meant, but he remarked, 'I always liked icebergs.' He was never an artist absorbed in symbolic meanings – quite the reverse, in fact. He became, above all, preoccupied with the empirical challenge of scrutinizing the posed human figure, out there in front of him. But he conceded that he had also done 'an awful lot of self-portraits. James Kirkman, who was selling this picture at Sotheby's, once said: "You've done more self-portraits than any other artist."'

Why did he do so many? 'I'll tell you what: I couldn't get people to sit for me. They always say how hideous I make them look. Besides, my subject matter is always autobiographical. I feel that I have to take stock of myself, although no one has ever seen themselves except in a mirror, so you've got to remember that it's a reflection and not you.' He also felt wary of most self-portraits by other artists. 'There's one odd thing with bad painters. When they paint themselves, there's a curious tension. They're more indulgent, everything is "look at me". Whereas I want my self-portraits to look as if they were somebody else. If I strike an attitude in them, I don't want people to think "here, finally, now, it's me, this is the truth".'

Leaning against a paint-encrusted wall in the studio was a recent, much-debated example of Freud's determination to study his own features. He called it *The Painter Surprised by a Naked Admirer*, and the canvas was destined to excite as much comment in Venice as it had at the National Portrait Gallery. Freud is shown in the act of painting himself while the naked Alexandra sits hunched on the floor, her right arm pressed against his leg. He looks down at her, and yet his hand points towards the unfinished canvas on the easel.

How on earth had this bizarre picture come into being? 'I was doing a self-portrait,' Freud explained, 'and first of all it was just me standing there painting, with all the paint on the wall behind me.'

Alexandra remembered watching him at work on it the previous year. 'He said that he was doing a painting about paint,' she recalled, 'and he looked completely enveloped by paint.'

But then, quite suddenly, Freud's idea changed. 'Alexi was around, and I thought, oh, she'd better be in it. So I asked her if she minded.'

How did she react? 'I was pretty surprised,' Alexandra said. 'I thought self-portraits were self-portraits.' What was it like, taking up and holding such a position for hours on end? She laughs.

'I used to complain bitterly, if I'd eaten too much supper, that the pose was uncomfortable. On the whole, sitting for Lucian is not hard labour. But *this* one!'

Even Freud confesses, 'It was difficult doing it, because she was round my legs and I had to keep stepping forward to paint the picture.'

'Once I yelped,' Alexandra added, 'but he didn't tread on my feet all the time. I should think it's going to get the feminist movement quite excited!'

She had a point. It was, after all, one of the most deliberately provocative images Freud had ever painted. But looking at it then, in the quiet of his studio around midnight, he was more fascinated by the realization that 'this self-portrait is the most distanced. I was very conscious of it being out of focus. I wanted it to be caught in movement, with her hand against my leg and static, and my hands dynamic and moving. That's something I've never really done before, treating two figures in a single painting so differently. And I wanted the white mug behind us to look as if it was falling off.'

The painting took 'probably eight months' to complete, and Freud told me that he always worked on it 'by electric light, because I couldn't see in the mirror properly during the day. It's pretty much a winter painting.' It was also, I suggested, like so many of his images, a picture about bare floorboards. He nodded. 'I did a lot of work on them. I always led a floorboard life in Paddington, even though you were supposed to have carpets. You can make much more of a mess on floorboards. I've always liked the look of them. To me, they have an anarchic excitement about them.' Then, unexpectedly, he pointed to his forehead in the painting. 'I've always had a bump there. I didn't like it when I was at school, so I went to the doctor. He said: "It's not a cyst, and it could be sawn off. But there'd be a danger of brain damage."'

I wanted to find out more about the central relationship presented so strangely in the painting. Why was Alexandra sitting on the floor in such a highly dramatized position? 'It's got a theatrical joke element,' Freud explained. 'It's supposed to be: "At last!" A bit like that. I wanted a sudden look which bore little relation to me here. My expression is ambiguous. I wanted it to be a surprise, full of movement but with her sitting steady.' I pointed out that the tone of the picture's title was quite new for Freud, who normally gave his paintings very matter-of-fact names. 'Absolutely.' So are you, I asked, laughing at yourself? 'Maybe. I hadn't thought of that. My grandfather [Sigmund Freud] used to say: "Laugh? That's the first sign of sexual attraction."'

I asked him about the chemistry of his response to the people who modelled for him. What made a session go well? 'I think it's all to do with atmosphere,' he said. 'The worst thing would be someone looking at their watch. If they don't want to be there, I couldn't go on. But if the person is prepared to sit, and Alexi is certainly prepared to, stillness is not necessary for me. I like the idea of working from people who are able to be themselves – not posing, just being.'

It was an uncanny sensation, looking at Freud's canvas in the same room where he and Alexandra had struggled for so long to bring this mysterious, tantalizing work to completion. During the quarter of a century since he had acquired this top-floor flat – and then spent eighteen months building a studio in it – the long, high-ceilinged room had become layered with accumulated paint marks. Several heaters ensured that he could 'make it very warm', although Freud still wore a thin grey scarf round his neck, 'because I get sore throats'. Without warning, he pulled a white sheet off a big mirror opposite me. I could see myself, now, in the space Freud and Alexandra had inhabited while *The Painter Surprised by a Naked Admirer* was produced. It was like finding myself lodged, inexplicably and unnervingly, within one of his images.

The pigment heaped on the studio wall behind me was so thickly applied that Freud had even been able to stick a pair of scissors into it. 'The paint on the walls is from my palette knife,' he explained. 'When working, I change the colours with every brushstroke, so I'm always wiping them off.' With tubes of paint stacked high in the studio and crushed paint rags heaped on the floor, the whole room testified to his incessant activity. But he had left a space on one of the studio walls for handwritten inscriptions, one of which caught my eye: *All systems tend towards disorder*. A quotation?

'Yes,' he said, 'it's Newton. The anarchy of it was very appealing to me philosophically. People think that they're safe with a system, but they're not.'

We went through to the kitchen, where Alexandra handed round ample cups of green tea and we all ate handfuls of almonds and cranberries. Freud suddenly rested his head on the table in front of him – but only for a moment. He soon sat up again, as alert as before. Even though it was very late, he wanted to resume work on the small nude painting. But he invited me to his other studio, in the London house where he lived, to see the large painting of a nude that he hoped to finish in time for it to serve as the final exhibit in his Venice show. He said that he would phone me when it was ready to be viewed.

A few weeks later, I went round there. Alexandra let me in. It was mid-afternoon, and in the ground-floor living room I noticed the same small nude painting propped up on the mantelpiece. Just as Freud had predicted, an extra piece of bare white canvas had been added to its right side. Why?

'Space,' he said. 'I don't mean anything mystical, but the figure seemed to demand it.' The small nude had been brought round here from the other studio because, as Freud explained, 'I've not been well recently, so I'm painting it here rather than coping with all those stairs in the other place.'

But he seemed to have no trouble leading me swiftly up to the top floor of his house. There, illuminated by brilliant sunlight from a large window, was a big canvas on an easel. The bed where Alexandra had been posing for it was positioned very near, so Freud needed only the minimum amount of movement to turn from her to the painting and back again. It was not quite complete: part of her left foot remained unfinished, and the bunched-up linen sheets below her were still a white, turbulent mass of impulsive brushstrokes. But the rest of the figure was fully defined, and highly impressive.

Stretched out on the bed, with one leg projecting upwards and the other lying out sideways, the nude looked pensive. Painted very directly, with complete anatomical frankness, she rested her head on a pillow. Pressing her right hand against the side of her face, the woman gazed in the direction of Freud's studio window. She seemed lost in a far-away reverie, yet her body was forcibly presented with great sensuous immediacy and a palpable feeling for the strong, almost sculptural presence of her breasts, stomach and limbs. Freud's handling of skin, bone and flesh was as compelling and persuasive as ever. But he never set out with the idea of imposing his distinctive vision on the figures he observed with such zeal. 'At the beginning, I have an idea about the composition,' he told me, 'but I have no idea about how it will look. I want to surprise myself.' Collaboration with the models was, for him, all-important as the work proceeded. In finding a position for them to adopt, he said, 'I use something that they find natural during the session. I want to avoid posing them: I never, ever plan a pose. I'm affected by the subject.' That was why this new painting, started around October the previous year, had 'changed a lot. I did notice that it looked surprisingly abstract for a long time. I asked myself: is that a figure? I worked very freely and abstractly on it.' Was that, I wondered, the way Freud thought his work as a whole was going, at that late stage in his life? 'Yes,' he nodded, without any hesitation at all. And what was the big nude picture going to be called? Freud smiled. 'They are nearly all called *Naked Portrait* or *Girl on a Bed*,' he said. 'They're very boring, my titles, as you know.'

I became aware, as we stood there looking at the canvas, that Freud was anxious to carry on with his painting. So as a final question, I asked him how he knew when a work was truly complete. 'Suddenly there comes a time when I feel that I'm painting into a finished picture,' he said. 'I go on until there's literally nothing more to be done. But I'd never let it out right away. I keep on looking at it.'

So did I. The painting was so hypnotic that I found it difficult to break away, even though I could tell Freud was growing more and more impatient to pick up his brush. The afternoon was turning towards evening, and he wanted above all to bring this ambitious canvas to fruition in time for Venice. 'It'll be saying to the exhibition's visitors that I'm still working,' he explained. Eventually, keen to be alone with his canvas and model, he said ruefully, 'I'm afraid I've got to throw you out.'

Leaving the studio, I sensed that he was an artist acutely conscious of how much he still wanted to achieve in the limited time he had left. We said goodbye. 'You just wait till you're eighty-two,' he said with a grimace. 'It's no joke.'

Jake and Dinos Chapman

August 2005

As soon as Jake Chapman opened the studio door, the barking erupted. Two clamorous and belligerent dogs rushed towards me, eagerly vying with each other for attention. Jake introduced them. 'That's Snoopy, a boxer, only nine months old. And the other one's a Staffordshire bull terrier. We call her Kylie.' Throughout the afternoon, these hugely energetic animals roamed around, growling and scrapping or imploring us to throw rubber bones. There was no respite even if they lapsed, momentarily exhausted, into silence: whenever Jake's mobile rang, it played the sound of yet another yapping hound.

So my visit to the Chapman brothers was far from restful. But I hadn't expected it to be. Jake and Dinos, after all, had been responsible for some of the most intensely controversial, provocative and disturbing works produced by any artists over the past decade. They had first provoked a furore with *Great Deeds Against the Dead*, a monumental sculpture in which the butchered victims from Goya's *Disasters of War* were transformed into hideously mutilated shop-window mannequins. Their later decision to paint ghoulish images straight onto Goya's prints proved even more scandalous. They were accused of attention-seeking vandalism, but the Chapmans remained defiantly unbowed.

At the Royal Academy's 'Apocalypse' exhibition in 2000, they stole the show with *Hell* – a series of enormous vitrines arranged in the shape of a swastika. Inside them, thousands of helpless figures were decapitated, disembowelled, pushed into gas ovens and impaled on trees. The mass carnage culminated in a vast pit filled with hideously damaged corpses. Taken as a whole, the massacre amounted to a relentless and despairing indictment of 20th-century savagery. The Chapmans had expended an unimaginable amount of hard, closely detailed work on *Hell*, and they told me that painting it had affected their eyesight. 'I wear lenses now,' said clean-shaven Dinos, while bearded Jake complained, 'I look like Mengele when I wear my specs.' Their immense, protracted efforts paid off: Charles Saatchi bought *Hell*, and it was widely admired by critics in tune with the Young British Artists generation. But then, with shocking suddenness, it was obliterated by the notorious 2004 fire that swept through the Momart art storage warehouse in East London.

The Chapmans' enemies took an unsavoury delight in *Hell*'s destruction, claiming that the fire was a judgment on barbaric, cynical artists. But the brothers were unrepentant. As Jake recalled, 'When journalists phoned up and said: "Is it true that *Hell* has burnt?", we said: "How could it not?" Even when people told us how sorry they were to hear that *Hell* was destroyed, we replied that it should be a cause for celebration, surely.'

Mordant humour is the Chapmans' forte. I noticed that Dinos, the older of the two, was wearing a T-shirt with a skull grinning fiendishly under a clown's hat. He told me, 'We're in the throes of remaking *Hell*, but it's completely new, not a facsimile – bigger, better and more horrible. If we didn't do that, people's expectations would exceed the object when it was finished. It's a nice challenge: the moment people say: "You couldn't possibly redo it," you're honour-bound to prove them wrong.' Indeed, the challenge appealed to the Chapmans so much that they had decided to do four more *Hells* as well. They took evident delight in telling me, with mock solemnity, what these versions would be called: 'Fucking Hell, Fucking Cunting Hell, Fucking Cunting Pissing Hell, and Fucking Cunting Pissing Shitting Hell.' Struggling to recover from this scatological bombardment, I asked them where they imagined all these works would end up. 'In flames,' said Dinos with a devilish grin.

No sign of the new, improved *Hell* could be detected in the Chapmans' studio. Located in Fashion Street off Brick Lane, a formerly run-down area of East London where property prices had gone stratospheric, it was a big, barn-like space. But *Hell* was being made with the help of five assistants in a fabrication studio over at Hackney Wick. 'That's where we do our dirty work,' said Jake, 'and this is where we escape.' The room around me was clearly reserved for drawing, watercolour work and other activities directed towards their new show. Several large, sloping desks, ranged in a row along the far side of the studio, were scattered with images in progress for the exhibition. And through the window, a panoramic view of Hawksmoor's great edifice, Christ Church Spitalfields, stirred me as ever with its redoubtable grandeur. Jake proudly mentioned that he had been married there the previous year, although he was also quick to point out that 'Hawksmoor built it after the Huguenots settled here. It was completely political, and supposed to cast a shadow over the entire area.'

How on earth did the brothers manage to work together without arguing, or secretly longing to be recognized as individuals rather than a sibling couple? 'There are lies and hypocrisy in our practice like holes in cheese,' Jake laughed, 'but that's what makes it fun. The idea of collaborative art appeals to us because it flies in the face of the cult of individual genius.' Yet why did the work they produced look so uncannily like the product of a single artist? Jake protested: 'We work together to multiply the differences, and constantly try not to do the same thing.' But the fact remains that ever since they graduated from the Royal College of Art in London, the Chapmans have thrived on each other's creative company.

Five years separate Dinos from the younger Jake, so 'we didn't really know each other before then. Our lifestyles were very different and we never coincided at school.' But Dinos 'took five years out' during his higher education, working for Gilbert and George in their photography studio. So maybe, I suggested, the idea of two artists working together began to take hold at that stage? 'Gilbert and George function as one person, in a symbiotic relationship,' Jake said, 'whereas we're quite the opposite, attempting to produce multiplication rather than reduction. It's an exponential project.' Even so, Dinos and Jake both applied for postgraduate places at the Royal College at the same time, won them and then joined forces.

They shared a disgust with the College which did not seem to have lessened with the passing years. 'It was an old boys' club,' said Dinos with a sneer. 'I never had aspirations to go to public school, and I ended up in one. It was so English, so conservative and myopic. There was such a contrast between working with Gilbert and George, who were all focused, and the College, where everything was flaccid, uninteresting and gave me nothing of use. It was obvious that the College had been put in place to employ a bunch of redundant people, and at every level it was impoverished. Like the Royal Academy, the teachers all ended up drinking in some pokey bar with other pissed, stinking old men.'

Jake was in the sculpture department and Dinos in painting. But they 'started talking quite a lot', their ideas converged, and 'the notion of collaborating emerged in a quite unpredictable way'. Why, I asked? Their answers were contradictory. Dinos said, 'I was getting more dissatisfied with what I was doing,' while Jake protested, 'I was very happy with my work, and it was much better than what I'm doing now.' But they agreed that a decisive influence had been exerted by a show called 'NY Art Now', held at the old Saatchi Gallery in 1987. Jeff Koons and Robert Gober had been among the nine young American artists displayed there, and Jake was convinced that the exhibition had brought about 'a real paradigm shift in the way art was made. It was massively influential and felt like walking on the moon. It was nihilistic, brutally misanthropic, completely negative and mesmerized by its own laughter. It raised the relationship between art and capital which, for English artists, hadn't been thought through. It was post-punk, and had teeth.'

After they left the Royal College, the Chapmans found their main inspiration in Goya. The floor of the flat in Peckham where they worked soon became 'a sediment of Goya pictures, heaped in layers', said Jake. 'I actually got burgled there, and when the police walked in they said: "Christ, they've really done a job on this place."' He showed me the first book on Goya they acquired: a large Thames & Hudson volume. All the illustrations were smeared, stained and splashed with blood from cuts in the Chapmans' fingers as they worked on the images with scissors, razors and paper knives.

Why did they become so obsessed by Goya? Jake was quick to respond. 'He was the first modernist artist, the first who has psychological and political depth. Goya arrived at a crucial point in European history, and he's the vehicle for the Enlightenment, struggling against the tyranny of the church. His *Disasters of War* series is contradictory. He's defended as being a humanist, but there are moments of pleasure here. They have an intensity, a humour and a tendency to undermine their own dignity. I don't think Goya even realized this. But he can't be compressed into what modernist historians want him to be.' Dinos agreed, pointing out, 'Goya is like the first complex artist. Looking at his *Disasters*, you think, how did he do that without being conflicted?' And Jake went further, declaring, 'In Goya's etching of three figures hung on a tree, the human body becomes a Newtonian lump. His depiction of atrocity exceeds moral observance. It's not pessimistic, it's quite a positive fatalism.'

Seconds later, Dinos brought the conversation round to the plight of our world today. 'There's no alternative to a very dystopian view of reality,' he said. 'And the news media have become adept at teasing themselves into a heightened state of panic. The TV channels don't have enough news, so they endlessly repeat bits of film. The bombing in London became over-sensationalized. It was a globally minor event, compared with the bombs in Iraq.' Both brothers had given up on politicians and refused to vote in the last general election. 'I wasn't going to vote for a war criminal,' said Jake, and Dinos revealed, 'I spoiled my ballot paper. The problem with British politics is that it's all to do with self-interest and economics. New Labour should be called New Equity.'

But they refused to lose faith in the potential of art. 'What we can hope to do is radicalize the environment you exist in,' said Jake. 'Being an artist is an odd job, and often equated with failure and stupidity. So it's already a political activity, but political on its own terms. You have the potential to be politically quite active nowadays compared with politicians.'

Their anger, however, could take surprising forms. Sometimes they took it out on the large, heavy punchbag hanging near their ping-pong table. *Everlast: Choice of Champions*, ran the inscription on the bag, and I could imagine the brothers giving vent to their rage on its dark, bulky surface while their dogs barked appreciatively in the background. Jake said, 'I punch it on the way to the toilet,' but most of the Chapmans' boundless indignation seemed to be reserved for making the images they showed me on their desks.

Etched first and then coloured in, these belonged to a new series of thirty-one rancid pictures based on banal illustrations in children's colouring books. The raw material could hardly have been less offensive. In one archetypal suburban view, a garden fence and flower pot perched on a ledge were the only objects worth noting. But by the time Jake and Dinos had had their fearsome way with it, this dull illustration was transformed into a gruesome vision. Dumbo the elephant appeared, painting at an easel in the garden, and behind the fence some of Goya's mutilated figures could be seen suspended from a tree.

Other images in the series were even more gangrenous. Beautiful, fairy-tale children had become inexplicably stricken with festering wounds. Everywhere you looked, the supposedly innocent and protected world of small boys and girls was invaded by merciless menace. To my astonishment, the Chapmans claimed that the original colouring-book pictures had been 'quite weird and malignant already'. But the brothers had travelled deep into their own nightmarish region, a place filled with repellent horrors. When I asked to see their preliminary sketches, they shook their heads: there weren't any. 'We don't mess around, we're too busy. And we like the etching medium because it's not good for second thoughts.' But they were keen to make visitors to their new show aware of the origins of the series. That was why they planned to call it *Etchasketchathon*, named after the popular toy that encourages children to draw.

The Chapmans both have first-hand experience of parenthood: at the time of this interview Jake had a five-year-old stepdaughter and a new baby, while Dinos had two children aged thirteen and eleven. 'But they don't draw much,' said Dinos, 'and anyway, art is an adult thing. It's Daddy's job. They're just as uninterested in this as they would be if I sold office furniture.'

They knew there was bound to be a lively demand for the new work when it went on display. Jake showed me a wicked little sketch of the White Cube space, with some of their pictures hanging on the wall in the shape of a brontosaurus while a nude woman looked on appreciatively. I laughed at her, but Jake seized a pen and quickly turned her into a man with very thin, predatory arms. Who was he? 'It's Jay,' he explained, referring to their dealer, Jay Jopling. 'He's got long, dangling hands for reaching deep into people's pockets.'

Then I noticed a new set of Goya images, based this time on his celebrated series of eighty etchings called *Caprichos*. First published in 1799, they show the Spanish master at his most outrageously satirical. The Chapmans had bought a complete set 'for a fraction of what they'll soon be sold for' and were now adding their own outrageous faces, animals, monsters and bodily organs to Goya's revered prints. So far, they had only finished eleven of them. 'But all will be done,' promised Dinos, pointing out, 'We've got four hands between us.' Did they work hard, I asked? 'Yes,' he said, 'we get totally transfixed by things. And when you're on a roll, you just go with it and get a lot done. The prospect of a show is an incentive, but we also have the idea that the energy in our studio is fuelled by Goya's own body spinning in his grave.'

I was beginning to understand that the Chapmans had a classic love–hate relationship with Goya. When I asked if they would have liked to meet him, Dinos replied: 'I'd like to have stepped on his toes, shouted in his ears and punched him in the face.' He showed me Goya's *The Shamefaced One*, which they were just about to start work on. The main figure's face is already hideous enough, and Goya's own vitriolic comment on this ancient grotesque was worthy of the Chapmans themselves: 'There are men whose faces are the most indecent parts of their whole bodies, and it would be a good thing if those who have such unfortunate and ridiculous faces were to put them in their breeches.' No wonder Dinos felt that the *Caprichos* were 'already quite insane. Actually, there's a risk of making them less interesting, and I'm sure we'll run out of steam before the end.' At the moment, though, a palpable sense of creative rivalry with the master was driving them on: 'We're not adding to Goya, it's less friendly than that. And we're not adding insult to injury.'

Nor did they intend to stop at interfering with other artists' work. Stacked against a wall behind the punchbag were some enormous framed etchings of their own, belonging to an earlier series called *The Chapman Family Collection*. Why were these waiting here? 'We'll do to them what we did to Goya,' said Dinos, adding: 'We often return to our old work, like a dog returns to its vomit.' Jake reacted to these words with glee. Rushing over to a notebook and writing them down, he exclaimed: 'That's great! We should call the whole show that! You can have an early day, Dinos, and go home now.'

He wouldn't have had far to walk. Dinos lived in a 19th-century house further down the street; Jake's home had also been nearby until recently, when he moved to Islington. 'We needed a bigger house and a change,' Jake explained. 'Our place here used to be a halal butcher's shop, and it was very dilapidated. When we moved in, there was no sign that gentrification would get this far east. The National Front used to hand out leaflets at the top of Brick Lane.' Dinos enjoyed making fun of Jake's relocation, claiming, 'He'll start wearing corduroy next, and move to Bexhill.' But I could not imagine the brothers ever growing apart. They still seemed, in a creative sense, absolutely wedded to each other. They chattered about their obsessions wherever they went, getting 'funny looks' when people overheard them in public 'talking about amputations'. In their shameless ability to scandalize and affront, they belonged to a satirical British tradition encompassing Gillray, Hogarth and Swift.

As I left the studio, accompanied as ever by the noisy dogs, Jake said that the yapping would make 'the perfect soundtrack for our exhibition – a kind of optional audio guide, giving visitors the real low-down on our work'. And Dinos warned me that they planned, in the long term, to make a horror film: 'It's totally impossible, but failure is underrated.' They were clearly in love with danger, and said goodbye with a story about a Tate curator who jauntily told them that 'the burning of *Hell* was quite apt'. He thought the Chapmans would be pleased with his joke, but their response was merciless: 'Well,' they said, 'we'll come round to your house and burn it down, shall we?'

Frank Auerbach and Lucian Freud

April 2006

Although Frank Auerbach and Lucian Freud had long been ranked among Britain's most outstanding painters, they shared an unwillingness to be interviewed. Both men disliked straying very far from their North London studios and valued their privacy to an extreme degree. They had little in common with so-called BritArt celebrities like Tracey Emin, who thought nothing of talking and writing about their own escapades in as many media outlets as possible. So when I heard that Auerbach and Freud were celebrating their long friendship in a joint exhibition at the Victoria & Albert Museum, my curiosity impelled me to get in touch. Would they, I wondered, mark this unique event by meeting and discussing their work with me?

To my astonishment, they agreed. Because they were both early risers, Auerbach suggested we get together in front of their paintings at eight thirty a.m. – and so, one October morning long before the V&A opened its doors to the public, I made my way to the heavily guarded side entrance. Wary officials stared at me with grim, professional suspicion. I was relieved to find that Auerbach and Freud were there already, both looking immensely energetic and alert. The long, lofty galleries and grand staircases stretched ahead of us, empty and forbidding. But both artists had often roamed through the National Gallery at night, communing with its masterpieces and relishing the silence; hence the eagerness with which they now walked through the V&A's immense spaces towards their new exhibition, happy to be ambushed by chance encounters with the collection along the way.

Freud, slim and sprightly in a pale grey suit and black shoes, darted towards a Rodin bronze portrait of Eve Fairfax. 'Look, Frank,' he said, 'isn't she marvellous?' Auerbach, equally trim in a dark green corduroy suit and brown shoes, turned towards the sculpture. The two men closed in on the furrowed Rodin head and gazed at it very intently. Friends for fifty years, they were clearly at ease with one another. Freud savoured the startled sensuousness of Eve Fairfax's head and enjoyed speculating about what the flirtatious Rodin might have said to shock his sitter. Moving on, they grinned at the cluster of pale legs in a monumental Burne-Jones painting, warmed to the vitality of Millet's dynamic *Wood Sawyers*, and lingered in front of Etty's nude woman lying upside down in a turbulent landscape. 'Etty calls this painting *Deluge*, but it's clearly been painted in the life-room at an art school,' said Auerbach, reminiscing about the time when 'you could buy Etty's work for nothing'.

Finally, we arrived at the ample room where their own paintings had been hung, with great daring, near masterpieces by Constable and Turner. Freud walked around restlessly, explaining, 'I'm very moved by Constable's work. It's more like life than Turner, and the little people in Constable's paintings are all portraits.' Auerbach gestured at the figures in an apocalyptic Turner seascape, where anxious women and a child watched a lifeboat struggling to rescue a stranded vessel. 'I believe in those figures,' he said admiringly. 'They're only little scribbled things, but they're already very much *there*.' Freud's eyes kept returning to Constable's astonishingly fresh oil study of *Water-meadows near Salisbury*: 'I'm not very acquisitive, but I wouldn't mind taking that home with me.' As a young man, Freud studied at an art school near Dedham, in the heart of Constable country. So he felt a great kinship with Constable's landscapes, and relished the dynamism in a dark, wild and thunderous painting of

Hampstead Heath. 'There were bandits on the Heath in those days,' he murmured, 'so you had to be very careful.'

Ultimately, Auerbach shared Freud's preference for Constable. 'Turner has a reckless poetry,' Auerbach said, 'but I look at Constable much, much more. My nature is mole-like, I have to burrow and dig.' So did Freud, who could spend up to a year working on one large painting. He had, he said, once been so captivated by Constable's *Study of the Trunk of an Elm Tree* that he thought: 'What a good idea.... A close-up. Real bark. So I took my easel out and put it down in front of a tree and found it completely impossible.' Eventually, Freud had managed to produce the powerful etching of an elm tree that now hung next to Constable's painting at the V&A. But the joint exhibition of new work by Auerbach and Freud was displayed separately, on the end wall of the gallery. I asked Auerbach how he felt, appraising the final hang. 'I'm actually relieved,' he said, 'because I thought my pictures would be totally overwhelmed by Lucian's and look sketchy.'

He was right to feel gratified. The show's impact was immediate and impressive. Far from feebly echoing Constable and Turner, the two friends asserted their own robust and singular identities with defiant conviction. Both men were born in Berlin, but escaped Germany in time to avoid the Holocaust. Freud, eight years older than Auerbach, moved to London with his family in 1932; Auerbach made the same journey as a boy in 1939, but without his parents. Tragically, he never saw them again and eventually accepted that they must have been 'killed in the camps'. But he firmly rejected self-pity, insisting, 'I never wished that I had parents.' Both he and Freud were British artists, and they looked thoroughly at home in the V&A context. Freud now felt, quite fiercely, that he had 'nothing at all to do with Germany. I'm not aware of it, and in my youth I always resisted the idea that I should only mix with my parents' German friends.'

They met at the moment when Auerbach, who had studied at the Royal College of Art and in David Bomberg's legendary classes at the Borough Polytechnic in London, staged his first solo show. The year was 1956, and Auerbach was only twenty-five years old.

Freud had already been a major figure in contemporary British art for over a decade, but the young Auerbach made a forceful impression with his debut exhibition at the Beaux-Arts Gallery. He was obsessed with the aftermath of the Blitz, and focused on demolition sites where the damage inflicted on London by Nazi bombs was still overwhelmingly apparent. 'It was dangerous work,' he recalled. 'Men used to push their wheelbarrows on muddy planks over abysses in the ground, and I drew them.' The city's struggle to recover from the war was painfully prolonged, but Auerbach found his walks through the battered streets hugely stimulating. 'London looked marvellous in those days,' he recalled. 'There were endless vistas in the gaps between buildings, and the sight of houses sheared away by explosions was very dramatic.'

Francis Bacon, the most talked about painter in London, introduced Freud to Auerbach. At that time Bacon and Freud were great friends, although they fell out years later and never spoke again. Bacon lived very near the V&A, and told me once that he often went there to look at its unrivalled collection of Constable oil sketches. He admired the young Auerbach's raw and impassioned attack as a painter. Now, when I asked Freud if he recalled what Auerbach's first show was like, he said: 'I remember thinking, what a lot of paint! When you're an artist yourself, you're always very aware of the technicalities. They were all heaped with paint, and done on board.' Auerbach quickly corrected him: 'Some of them were painted on canvas.' But he was clearly delighted that Freud had paid him the compliment of turning up to the opening of his first show, and said, 'I'll never forget Lucian making a very ceremonious bow at the end, when he left the gallery.'

Now Auerbach's paint was far less thick and solid than it had been half a century earlier. Aged seventy-five, he had developed a looser, wilder handling, so that his portrait heads of his wife Julia, David Landau and Catherine Lampert all seemed convulsed with a seismic vivacity. 'Only six people sit for me, and I paint them time and again,' he explained. Freud, at eighty-three, had a wider range of sitters, but he refused to disclose the identity of the fleshy middle-aged man in a painting simply called *New Yorker in a Blue*

Shirt. When I asked him why his subjects retained their anonymity, he confessed: 'I'm secretive. I like to think that no one knows what I'm thinking or feeling. I happen to be Jewish, but I don't want to go round exclaiming and tearing my hair.'

The only sitter he did identify was his assistant, the painter David Dawson, who had stripped to the waist for the biggest Freud painting on view. It was an arresting image. Over a period of nine months, Dawson had sat for up to six hours at a time with his whippet, Eli, slumped on his lap. It must have been a challenge for man and dog alike, yet Eli looked utterly relaxed and Dawson's face was caught, with vivid directness, in an affectionate grin. It was the very opposite of laborious, showing how Freud thrived on the penetrating drama of his encounters with closely observed life.

At first glance, Auerbach's tempestuous, endlessly scraped and reworked paintings seemed the very opposite of Freud's steadier, more painstaking approach. And Auerbach agreed that 'in terms of the idioms we use, there's every possible difference between us. Lucian's extraordinary curiosity and endless rifling of reality mean that, in the end, there's nothing left that hasn't been painted. But I become impatient: I repaint all the time, so what you see is very much the product of the last session.'

The longer I looked, though, the more they seemed to have in common. Both men were opposed to abstraction. They were utterly involved with the thing seen, out there in front of them, and neither of them cared what the critics thought. Freud gave a scornful smile when he predicted, 'Brian Sewell will go mad here with the sheer impertinence of it all.' And Auerbach agreed: 'I used to feel so vulnerable, but now it doesn't make a lot of difference what people think. I just hope there's something real here to cling on to, because nothing else matters.'

David Hockney

July 2006

A few days before my trip to David Hockney's Yorkshire home at Bridlington, he phoned me. 'After we've talked and looked at my new work,' he said in his inimitable Anglo-American accent, 'I'll drive you through the landscape I've been painting. It'll take about two and a half hours, but in the evening sun I promise you it'll be *fantastically* beautiful.'

On the train up to Bridlington, I wondered how this defiantly old-fashioned coastal resort had pulled Hockney away from California. After all, he had previously spent most of his time in Los Angeles after moving there in the mid-1960s. When I interviewed him in 1997, he had explained: 'I'm a bit claustrophobic, and that's why I settled in LA. I like big, white, open spaces. I used to say that I settled in California because it was sexy. But with time, you become aware of other things. I love the vastness of the American West. England is small, and I've been abroad too long to come back now.'

Why, then, had Hockney so dramatically and unexpectedly changed his mind? The answer turned out to be complex, as I discovered after his friendly Parisian assistant Jean-Pierre Gonçalves de Lima collected me from flower-bedecked Bridlington Station. In an astonishing noonday heatwave, we drove along the esplanade.

The wide, sandy beach was impressive, and everything around us seemed to have been uncannily preserved in a period time capsule. So did Hockney's capacious house, positioned near the seafront and still boasting all the extensive decorative embellishment lavished on it back in 1924.

'It's like a set for an Agatha Christie play, isn't it?' he said with a grin, greeting me in the elaborate central hall where a tanned young man busied himself hoovering the ample staircase. 'I bought it for my sister Margaret and my mother, who didn't do stairs and lived on the ground floor. She died seven years ago at the age of ninety-nine, after spending only three days in bed.' Hockney was very close to his mother, a strict vegetarian and teetotaller; every three months he would come over from California to see her and draw her. 'My mother was deeply religious,' he recalled with obvious affection. 'She was a Methodist, and knew the Bible backwards. She had a powerful look. I'm the unmarried son, so she was the woman in my life and I used to talk to her on the phone every other day. She told me to read the Song of Solomon because it's all about mothers and sons, so I did. My mum said I was a very curious child, always asking questions. She ran everything, she was the boss.'

As they were so close, her death affected him deeply. 'I was here when she died,' he said. 'It was very tough, even though she had a long life. I have the image of my mother lying in the bed, and she'd say to me: "It's no fun being old." But she'd also say: "I've not been called yet."' On one level, then, it seemed Hockney's decision to move into his mother's former home might have been bound up with a sense of loss. His sister Margaret had also settled in a house nearby.

He led me out to a spacious garden where, protected from the fierce sun by immense umbrellas, we had a light summer lunch. The wooden table was laid with plates all bearing the same quirky black-and-white drawing of Hockney's dog. He does not touch alcohol, and told me, 'I can't, because I'm prone to pancreatitis.' But he still insists on smoking strong Camel cigarettes. 'I only have two or three puffs of each one, but I like to hold them. I prefer Turkish cigarettes, really, but you can't get them here thanks to the fucking Blairs.' Angrily, he held up a packet printed with a cancer warning. 'It's the uglification of Europe,' he stormed, like a diehard campaigner. 'I'm sick of the health police.' In this respect Hockney seemed to take after his father, an accountant's clerk who threw his protesting energies into Ban the Bomb demonstrations. His son showed the same militant spirit, smoking defiantly as he told me, 'I was sixty-nine the other day, and I'm perfectly healthy.'

Hockney certainly looked trim enough. He had hearing aids in both ears and explained, without a trace of self-pity, 'I'm getting deafer, so music has gone: often I just hear a cacophony. And I don't watch TV because I can't hear it any more. Long before they banned smoking in LA, I stopped going to restaurants there because I can't stand what the noise does to me.' But he was still making a conscious effort to keep fit. 'I go for a walk every morning along the Bridlington promenade, and don't I notice the difference in the air quality between here and Kensington!' He also went to Baden-Baden a lot, taking the baths there so diligently that 'When I come back, people say: "You look twenty years younger!"'

As if to prove how energetic he was, Hockney said, 'Come upstairs,' and darted away with prodigious speed. Dressed in a blue-and-white striped shirt with workmanlike braces and paint-spattered grey trousers, he looked ready for action. And when we entered the studio he had built at the top of the house, I could immediately see just how busy he had been since the previous July. While persistent seagulls cried outside the tall, sloping windows Hockney had installed in the roof, he showed me canvas after canvas filled with his fresh, sensuous response to the Yorkshire countryside. Gesturing vigorously at a painting of an empty path leading through trees, he said: 'That one was done in about six hours – very intense, it knocks you out.'

What attracted him to this landscape, so different from the California terrain he used to favour? 'Well, I wasn't going to stay here,' he said, sitting back in a deep yellow armchair with stubbed-out cigarette butts scattered on the floor around it. 'But as things changed and the corn got golden, I realized there's a fucking good subject here. So why should I go back to LA? I'm very excited in Yorkshire. If you told me last summer what I'd be doing here, I'd have been surprised because I wouldn't have known how to paint these pictures. It's not just about landscape: it's about being in it, seeing it, it's about England. I'm painting the *real England*.'

With an emphatic sense of urgency, Hockney leaned sharply forward and stared at me over his round spectacles. Was he, I suggested, motivated in part by memories of his own Yorkshire childhood? He smiled. 'I was born in Bradford, one of the smokiest towns. And I left England because I couldn't stand the self-hatred, everyone running everything down. It's a very beautiful place, but *very* mean-spirited.' As a teenager in the mid-1950s, though, Hockney spent summers working on the farms around Bridlington. 'I was stooking corn for the harvest, and picking up the chaff. As I cycled round the rolling hills and the little valleys, I noticed how very beautiful it was.'

All these potent memories played a part in his decision, half a century later, to immerse himself in the same landscape. It had been an extremely intense year, he explained: 'I've not been social. I don't have many visitors here: it's too distracting. For days and days I haven't seen anyone. Jean-Pierre drives me out in the Toyota truck, even in the winter when we had to dress up like Michelin men to ward off the cold. Otherwise, with the temperature at zero centigrade, you're going to feel it. And if you start to freeze, you can't concentrate.'

Hockney knew precisely how to focus. 'I'll tell you this – cold makes you work fast,' he said, waving his hands restlessly before raising an index finger to emphasize the point. 'And I didn't know it was such an abundance here until I'd seen it in the winter. But I've been painting the abundance, and speed is a deliberate part of it. I'm working as quickly as possible, and looking unbelievably hard. The wind can make things very difficult. A canvas is like a sail: it can blow away, or leaves fall off the trees and stick to it. But I only get tired when I stop painting. My eyes can be so exhausted after I come back that sometimes I get into bed immediately. It's been a fantastic process of discovery, and I reckon I've painted about eighty oils here since last July – including some multi-part landscapes made up of six canvases each.'

Underpinning all this prodigious activity was Hockney's renewed belief in working directly from life, without the aid of photography, relying on his own ability to make marks. 'Damien Hirst says that the hand of the artist is nothing, but I believe the ancient Chinese saying about painting: you need the hand, the eye and the heart.' He used all three of these forces to devour the landscape in front of him. And before painting began, he would 'take a chair, with a few cigarettes, and sit there looking for a couple of hours. As I get deafer, I can see space better. You use sound to locate yourself in space, and if you go deaf, you see space more. Photography pushes things away, whereas in painting they become very close. The shadows and the shapes are ravishing.'

A selection of these new landscapes was about to go on show at London's Juda Gallery, where their feisty colours might surprise visitors expecting a more naturalistic approach. 'The previous year I did watercolours of Yorkshire, and reviewers thought I'd exaggerated the colour,' Hockney said. 'Recently, someone in LA looked at one of my new Yorkshire paintings and said: "When did you ever see a purple road?" But I do.' So he wasn't going to care what the critics wrote? He shrugged. 'I'm assuming they'll have a go at me. This is a small country with a large press, so it's bound to be bitchy. And I'm too confident to be bothered about it.'

He seemed to thrive on controversy and looked forward to the imminent publication of a new, expanded edition of *Secret Knowledge*, his hotly debated book arguing that old masters had often depended on a surprising array of mirrors, lenses and other optical devices. 'People thought I was bonkers when the first version was published,' he said with a laugh, 'but now they're coming round to it.'

The same attitude would doubtless protect him when a major retrospective exhibition, 'David Hockney Portraits', opened at the National Portrait Gallery that October. It was to include work from as early as 1954 – the date of a newly discovered self-portrait of the seventeen-year-old, dark-haired Bradford boy gazing shyly yet very intently out of the corners of his eyes. By the time he painted it, Hockney had already become aware that he was gay. 'When I was in the cinema aged thirteen,' he remembered, 'a man took my hand

and put it on his cock. I never told my parents, but I've loved the cinema ever since.'

This emphasis on the personal would run right through the 'Portraits' show. 'I only paint friends and people I know,' he stressed. 'If you don't know the subject, you're not sure you're getting a likeness. I don't like doing portraits to order. Someone asked me to draw Auden, and I agreed because I wanted to meet him. Auden was like an old schoolmaster and sat there smoking.' Did he have a favourite portrait? 'No, but I'm very aware that *Mr and Mrs Clark and Percy* is a very memorable picture.' At first glance, this wide-screen portrait of fashion designer Ossie Clark and his wife, fabric designer Celia Birtwell, seems to epitomize early 1970s London cool. But then we realize just how much distance separates the couple, physically and psychologically. Hockney was astute enough to prophesy, all too accurately, that their marriage would be short-lived.

A similar gap divides his parents in the big painting of 1977. And while Hockney's mother stares out of the canvas, his father is lost in a book. What was his parents' marriage like, I asked? 'Well,' he replied laconically, 'they stayed together.' But while he was painting them, Hockney would not have tried to ease the tension. 'I never talk to the person once I've started a portrait,' he declared. 'When I sat for Lucian [Freud] a few years ago, the sessions went on for 120 hours and I did talk to him. But when I'm painting, I never do. Nor do I ask the sitters what they think, because I don't care what they think. It's what I think that counts. I'm doing them for me. And I'm assuming that if I like them, someone else might a bit.'

It was nearly time for our drive, yet on the way downstairs Hockney darted into his bedroom to show me another Yorkshire landscape hanging on the end wall. It was a work in progress, and I noticed his brushes and paint were placed near at hand. 'I go to sleep looking at my paintings, and when I wake up – wow! – I have a completely different response to them. I always have paper by the bed, because your mind is freer then, and it's in a special state.'

After vanishing for a moment, Hockney reappeared sporting a white peaked cap, pale grey suit and white scarf. He climbed into the driving seat of an open-top Mini Cooper S, gleaming white with black leather seats. Gesturing to me to sit beside him, he said: 'You won't believe this road through the mad valleys. I've allowed well over two hours for it, and the evening light is perfect. It's quite a find for me, to discover all that at this stage in my life.' With startlingly fast acceleration, he drove out of Bridlington and turned, quite suddenly, into a narrow country road. 'This is where four policemen stopped me recently and fined me £30 for not wearing a seat-belt!' he exclaimed indignantly. 'I told them that I'm not into bondage.' Soon afterwards, he moved to the side as another car came towards us. It stopped, and a bespectacled lady wound down her window with a cheerful 'Hello, David!' This was his sister Margaret, a retired nurse who had now taken up painting. She beamed at him before driving on, and Hockney explained, 'She'll just be enjoying the view because I tell her to come up here.'

We moved on, slowly enough for me to appreciate just how irresistible this secret landscape really was. 'We're on our own now,' he said excitedly. 'There are no white lines on the road, you can drive for miles, there's never anyone in front of you and this is our private estate.' Taking a signpost for the enticingly named Thwing, and then turning off the road towards a magnificent, preening pheasant, he showed me 'a vista I painted in the spring. There was rape up there, bright yellow, and look at that purple! It's a field of borage.'

After passing through Sledmere – 'This village hasn't changed for fifty years' – we soon found ourselves curving down into an even more seductive region where round, steep hills blazed in the evening light. Hockney was ecstatic. 'See how tiny the valleys are!' he said. 'They're glacial, the shapes are lovely, and just look at the way the earth moves – it's changing all the time.' A hare leapt out in front of the car, zig-zagged along the middle of the narrow road and then swerved back into the hedge. After passing Uncleby, Pocklington and Bugthorpe, Hockney stopped and opened a gate. We got out and walked down to the edge of a very dramatic drop; minuscule sheep were just visible far, far away at the valley's bottom.

Gazing around keenly, he said with awe: 'I get very thrilled here. I could sit for hours, on a chair, right there. Look at that incredible field of barley – luminous, isn't it? And the trees are never alike.

In the winter you realize this: they're like veins, or brains. You can't beat nature, it never lets you down. We're just little creatures, aren't we? We're all part of it.' Did he still retain any trace of the Methodist faith his mother had advocated so strongly? 'By sixteen, I'd lost it, but I've never been anti-religious,' he said. 'I knew Billy Wilder very well over in Hollywood, and he said something marvellous: "It's not the pilot I'm complaining about, it's the ground crew."'

Reluctantly, we walked back to the car and started the spectacular descent to the plain of York. How, I asked, would he sum up his obsession with this empty, little-known and wholly beguiling landscape? 'I'm painting a place that I loved, and seasons I'd forgotten about,' he replied with passion. 'People don't look, do they? I'm out on my own a bit, but I'm way ahead. It's the biggest painting project I've ever done, and I've only just begun.'

The sun was setting as we approached my destination, York Station. Before saying goodbye, I asked him how he felt about getting old. 'I'm afraid of pain,' he admitted quietly, 'but I'm not afraid of death. It'll be another adventure, like this one. Isn't the opposite of fear of death a love of life?'

Annette Messager

February 2009

Although Annette Messager is now ranked among France's leading contemporary artists, she struggled against fierce male prejudice at the outset of her career. Back then, in the late 1960s, virtually all the prominent French artists were men. 'There was a lot of misogyny in France,' she recalled with an ironic shrug when we met in early 2009. 'I was told that women are babies, and that I cannot be an artist. At the beginning they would say: "Puh! Nothing! Girls' work!" But I wanted to do girls' work – I knew it could be strong.'

We were sitting in Concrete, the aptly named brutalist cafe at the Hayward Gallery on London's South Bank. Messager, whose first British retrospective exhibition was about to open here, seemed tense and almost withdrawn. Slim, with close-cropped, red-tinged hair and wearing jeans along with a simple zip-up top, she looked very private. But this guardedness was only an illusion. Immediately I produced my notebook, she exclaimed: 'You are left-handed! I was once, but my teachers at school forced me to use my right hand. It disturbed me, and that's the reason I became an artist.' Intrigued, I asked if she thought it was essential for an artist to be disturbed. She smiled. 'Oh, *everybody* is disturbed. Our new president is *very* disturbed – he is mad!'

Messager, a tireless collector of 'ordinary materials' ever since the 1960s, 'when I had no money', has never been afraid of exploring the darker side of life. In one early work, she wielded a pen to scratch out the eyes of children in newspaper and magazine photographs. And as early as 1972, in a piece called *Voluntary Tortures*, she raided magazines to expose the bizarre rituals some women underwent in their quest for smooth, slimmed-down flesh. The bandages, lamps and other electrical devices looked disturbing and at times downright macabre. But even when these images were at their most troubling, Messager also brought their titillating qualities to light.

She mentioned to me that although her work was seen by some as 'funny, droll', others found it 'very morbid, very sad'. Yet she has always embraced these contrasting extremes of optimism and suffering. She knows how to combine playfulness and melancholy – not least in a work called 'Stories and Narratives', where heaps of stuffed animals discarded from children's playpens turn out to be blindfolded. Elsewhere, she transforms coloured crayons into rifles thrusting through holes in a wall, or impales woollen gloves on long wooden shafts like decapitated trophies. Another work assembles proverbs about women across the world, ranging from 'A woman should be feared like thunder' to 'Even the walls cry when a girl is born.' Messager, who sees her own art as 'coming out of painting', is fascinated by words. She once made a work by obsessively writing her own signature thousands of times, each one alarmingly different from all the others.

'My favourite book is the dictionary,' she told me. 'For me, the word is visual. My favourite artist was for a long time William Blake, because he mixed poetry with images. I love the English because you are eccentric – especially Lewis Carroll and all those stories with spiders. In France, we are Cartesian.' She was drawn to all kinds of surprising objects containing words: 'I collect safety instructions from aeroplanes,' she said. Why? 'Oh, they are very strict, against life and reality. They are completely absurd, because life has no sense, no order – it's chaos.'

Not that Messager succumbed to mayhem in her working life. Back home, in the Paris suburb of Malakoff, she compartmentalized everything into three categories: 'Base One is where I live, Base Two is where I work, and Base Three is where my archive is stored.' Her husband Christian Boltanski, also a well-known artist, worked there too. I asked Messager if their artistic practice had ever created any unwelcome tensions in their relationship. She shook her head. 'An artist understands you better. I never go into his studio. We speak always about art, but not about our own work.' Did they have children, I asked? 'Only Lola,' she said, before suddenly pressing both hands to her face and exclaiming: 'Oh! I'm missing her! She is a very English cat, with a lot of colours.'

Messager has always been fascinated by animals, whether alive or dead. 'At my first retrospective, held in Grenoble, I felt sick in the stomach with nerves. But then I rediscovered an early work which I had forgotten, to do with stuffed birds.' And her most spectacular recent installation, which won the Golden Lion Award at the 2005 Venice Biennale, had been inspired by *Pinocchio*. I remember seeing long queues of visitors waiting to view this much-discussed work at the French Pavilion, where Messager was the first woman artist ever chosen to represent France at the Biennale. Knowing that she would be recreating part of this intensely dramatic and disturbing installation at the Hayward, I asked her what it would look like. 'It has a red curtain, and Pinocchio has become human,' she said. 'There is some kind of birth, with a lot of blood and inside plenty of organic elements and wind. You see, Pinocchio was eaten by a whale.'

Why, I wondered, had she called the work *Casino*? 'Because Pinocchio is a player, a gambler,' she explained. 'He could win or lose. His name means wood from a pine tree – or in Italy, a little gay man.' Messager laughed, revealing her infectious and subversive sense of humour. 'Did you know that *casino* means brothel in Italy?' she asked. 'One Paris newspaper, reviewing the Pinocchio work when it was in Venice, claimed that I had turned the French Pavilion into a *bordel*.'

When Messager first planned her Hayward exhibition, she wanted to 'hang a moving puppet outside the gallery, on the balcony. But it was too windy.' Blustery weather in this exposed Thameside location forced her to abandon the plan, yet inside the Hayward she definitely intended to install *The Hitter*, 'a puppet who wants to get out. He's a little mad, going back and forth on a pendulum.'

Warming to her theme, Messager described another puppet piece she had made the previous autumn for a Parisian convent garden. Seizing my notebook and pen, she made an impulsive drawing of this plastic figure – 'very simple, white like a tube and blown through its base by air' – rising up from the plants and flowers. 'Afterwards, in a little church, I attached strings to the feet and arms of real musicians playing instruments. They all went up and down.'

While she talked, Messager drank water and fondled her glass like a sculpture. She kept pulling a large ring along her finger, as if impelled by an inner sense of agitation. Where, I asked, did she think all her obsessions came from? 'Ah, Dr Freud!' she responded. 'It's difficult to say, but I compare Pinocchio to an artist who wants to travel and be free. When young I didn't ever want to work in an office. My father, who was an architect, felt very nervous. But when he painted, he was so quiet. All the time, he gave me brushes and paints. We lived in Berck-sur-Mer, a town near Boulogne in northern France, where most of the houses were destroyed by your bombers in the Second World War. It was a little macabre, full of sick people attending the hospital for war veterans. We used to say: "Berck heals the sick and kills the healthy!"'

Messager suggested that her abiding preoccupation with 'the body and books of anatomy' had come from childhood experiences 'of hospital where people were X-rayed and spoke only about the body. I like all the things inside me!' Even so, she did not seem easy to pin down as an artist. 'I became mystical in rebellion against my family, who were atheists,' she said. 'But my father would take me in his car to see church architecture, at Amiens, Arras and all over.' She has retained this fascination ever since, and yet emphasized that she liked 'to try different things, different media – I was working recently with a composer, it's new food for me'.

In France, where her major 2007 exhibition at the Pompidou Centre attracted an abundance of visitors, she has come to be regarded as highly as Louise Bourgeois. Not that Messager can be summarized as neatly as Bourgeois, whose work stems from a fundamental sense of traumatized childhood betrayal; nor is she under any illusions about the ever-increasing public interest in her work. 'The more we please, the more we displease,' she told me, before turning to her translator, conferring and then declaring: 'The more popular you are, the more people hate you!' So did she feel apprehensive about her Hayward show, given that she was at the moment far less well known in the UK than Bourgeois? She smiled. 'Well, smoking helps a lot,' she said wryly. 'My cigarettes are very thin and stupid, and I try not to smoke so much.' With that, she produced a packet and pushed back her chair. 'I need a cigarette now,' she said, getting up and heading for the winter sunshine outside Concrete. 'You could continue the interview with her,' she added, gesturing warmly towards our admirable translator. 'Her English is better than mine!'

Later, before we parted, I asked her how she regarded the future at a time when the state of the global economy seemed so alarming. Messager refused to be pessimistic about the ongoing recession, suggesting: 'The crisis will be very good for artists. It'll be difficult, but interesting, and they will have more imagination.' Ultimately, though, she stressed the importance of escaping to her studio and being alone. 'I'm always nervous there,' she confided, 'so it's very important to forget, to be empty.' She paused, then leaned forward to make a final, emphatic point. 'But for an artist, the most important thing of all is to continue.'

Tony Cragg

March 2009

The winter afternoon was waning by the time my taxi arrived at Tony Cragg's studio. This immense structure, rearing up at the end of a quiet street in Wuppertal, began life as a pair of garages for Nazi army tanks. But Cragg had enlarged the monumental building since moving in there, adding a spectacular wall of windows that enlivened its tall interior with a deep, lush and panoramic prospect of the fertile Rhine Valley beyond.

Everywhere I looked inside the studio, an overwhelming abundance of sculptural forms demanded my attention. They looked tirelessly inventive, and the same energy drove the man who leapt up from his chair to greet me. Cragg immediately suggested that I join him at a computer screen, where hundreds of new photographs by Charles Duprat provided a fast-changing, crisply defined overview of this prolific artist's sculpture and drawings. 'These pictures have all been taken for the catalogue of a new show starting at Karlsruhe and then going on to Salzburg,' Cragg explained. 'But it's just my recent work: I don't like to do retrospectives, because I'm not dead yet.'

He certainly wasn't. With a wry grin, Cragg told me, 'I'll only be sixty next year.' And one of the most arresting works he showed me on screen was called, defiantly, *I Am Alive*. Nearly a decade earlier, he explained, he 'felt really ill and [became] so thin, well under eight stone'. But after an agonizingly protracted bout of intensive care in hospital, he had recovered his former verve. Cragg jogged every day – disregarding memories of the acute pain he had once suffered when his ankle gave way during a lonely forest run, and he had to crawl for three hours in order to get home.

Now, he appeared nimble and restless near the end of a long working day. 'People think sculpture is slow, static and somewhat boring,' he said, 'so I like to stress how dynamic and fast-moving it can be.' Even so, Cragg could not be accused of complacency: 'I'm always on a knife-edge between having too much to do or nothing to do. There's loads of stuff I want to make, but any attempt to speed it up can lead to vacuous work.'

This combination of impetuous vivacity and self-critical caution has informed his attitude to art ever since 1977, when he moved from London to Wuppertal with his German wife. He had just finished a four-year sculpture course at the Royal College of Art and imagined that 'I'd only be here for a year and learn a lot of German'. But he never went back. More than thirty years later, he was an Honorary Citizen of Wuppertal with three big sculptures displayed in urban locations across the town. He had become an eminent teacher as well, holding professorships in nearby Düsseldorf and distant Berlin. Above all, he enjoyed an international reputation as a leading contemporary sculptor.

In 1979, his first London solo show at the Lisson Gallery had marked the emergence of an outstanding young talent, giving audacious new life to plastic detritus scavenged from skips, river banks and waste lots. During the 1980s he was often associated with other young sculptors backed by the same gallery: Richard Deacon, Shirazeh Houshiary, Anish Kapoor and Bill Woodrow prominent among them. They succeeded in opening up a whole range of new possibilities for British sculpture, and in 1988 I had no hesitation in voting with my fellow judges to award Cragg the Turner Prize. At once provocative, adventurous and pertinent, his work had helped to define the temper of the decade. At the same time, without resorting to pastiche revivalism, he engaged in an unpredictable dialogue with sculpture from the past. Even a classical carving as iconic as the Laocoön underwent an extraordinary transformation in Cragg's *George and the Dragon*, where discarded household objects found themselves trapped in writhing coils of plastic piping.

By the time he won the Turner Prize, though, Cragg had already begun to explore materials like steel; and now, in his vast Wuppertal studio, anything from dice and bronze to polystyrene and glass could be deployed. He was eager to show me round this enormous arena, incessantly darting forward and pointing out each twist and turn animating the works we encountered. Gesturing with vigour at a complex bronze called *Caught Dreaming* that had recently been acquired by Elena and Norman Foster, he explained, 'It's a composite of three portraits caught in motion. We see the things in the world around us as static, but they're all in motion. There are sixty-two trillion chemical reactions in the human body every second, so you're filled with bits of elements.'

As he talked, Cragg reinforced his words by moving rapidly from one part of the studio to another. Fascinated, I asked him if he was interested in dance. He nodded enthusiastically. 'I like dancing of any kind. Only last night my wife and I were out watching dancers at the Pina Bausch Festival.' Time and again in Cragg's sculpture human faces and figures turned out to be lurking somewhere in the structure, as if waiting to take us by surprise. Pausing by a big new piece, he knelt beside it and pointed out emphatically: 'There are four profiles, in two axes. Look down there!' I crouched beside him, only to realize that a giant mouth seemed about to gobble me up. 'Now come over here,' said Cragg, exclaiming as he moved round the sculpture, 'Now it's like a feather!' I told him how refreshing it was to see him circumnavigating his work with such zest. So many visitors to galleries and museums look at sculpture from one angle only. Cragg insisted, 'To actually look at sculpture is a kinaesthetic experience. People don't view it properly, but you have to forgive them because they're used to looking at a very dull, utilitarian world.'

Thinking about the way Cragg's imagination took flight, I asked him if there was a link with his father, who had designed and developed electrical parts for aircraft. Cragg smiled. 'The Comet, Trident,

Concorde and Airbus are the stations of my life,' he said, describing how, during his childhood, the Cragg family kept moving round the country from Liverpool in the north to Hatfield in the south. 'We could always hear planes taking off,' he recalled, before emphasizing that 'the designer always has a recipient in mind, but an artist has a different, non-utilitarian agenda and it opens up enormous possibilities for new language'. Had his father approved of Cragg's momentous teenage decision to leave his job as a lab technician and pursue art instead? Cragg shook his head. 'Dad didn't understand – he thought it was a waste of time. We were cleaning the car one Sunday when I said: "By the way, Dad, I'm leaving the lab." He said: "Oh yes? So what are you going to do, then?" "Well," I said, "I'm not sure, but I'm doing a lot of drawing and might go to art school." "Oh well," he said, "don't expect me to give you another penny!"'

Drawings could also be discovered in Cragg's studio, either lying out flat on top of piled-up containers or stacked in profusion against the walls. 'I draw all the time,' he said, 'and more intensely now I'm getting older. I used to stand in the studio for ten hours a day making sculpture, but now I concentrate more on drawing.' He often escaped to his studio in Sweden – 'on the coast' – to draw or paint fields and seascapes. 'It's really wild there, and I like the mood changes in the weather. I love the hard, frozen ground in the winter – it can't be too cold for me. We also have real winter snow in Wuppertal, where we're 430 metres above sea level. I'd hate to live in a country where the sky is always blue: that's a recipe for manic depression.'

We entered a portion of the studio heaped pell-mell with a jumble of tantalizing fragments. Staring at the pile, Cragg said frankly, 'These are the failures of my life. Most of it doesn't work, so I relegate it. I'm not a conceptual artist: a good idea in art can be interesting, but it's more likely not to be. I like thinking with materials: you move, it moves, towards a destination you haven't envisaged. The most rewarding thing is to come to a brand new form – what the Greeks call *poesis*. You get to a point where no one has been before.'

Sensing that our conversation was now arriving at the very nub of Cragg's imaginative concerns as an artist, I asked him why the forms in his sculpture were so fluid, so unpredictable, so bent on defying our attempts to pin them down. Grabbing a bottle and a bowl, he placed them so close together on a desk that they almost seemed to merge. 'I'm fascinated by making the middle thing, lurking somewhere between a dog and cat. You cannot say which it is. You know what a pig looks like, and an elephant. But a pigephant running towards you through the park – well, that's a new piece of reality. Between a table and a chair there are myriad things that don't exist, and this is the business of sculpture.'

As if to bear out his declaration, Cragg took me outside and led me through a dark courtyard towards another part of his labyrinthine studio. There, looming in front of us, was an immense piece made with polystyrene and glass. 'It's called *Luke*, and it's just been made,' Cragg said, adding, 'You can see the facial elements.' I could indeed, but my initial response centred above all on the sculpture's wilful instability, its apparent determination to evade any swiftly definable identity.

It was getting late now, and most of Cragg's employees were going home. 'They're all leaving,' he laughed, 'like rats deserting a sinking ship!' How many people did he have in his team? 'About twenty: it sounds a lot, but I need them all. They're a multinational outfit – Argentinian, Italian, Polish, French, German, Irish.' Why? 'Oh, it's just happened that way: I'm looking for the best people to do the job.' Were any of them artists? Cragg shook his head emphatically. 'No, if you use artists, you're bound to have conflicts. Like Henry Moore did with his assistants. I could do without it.'

As we walked through the chilly winter night towards Cragg's car, he asked if I would 'like to have an outdoor sculpture experience'. Energized by my visit to the studio, I nodded. So we climbed into his big Lexus, a quiet and energy-efficient hybrid machine heavily dependent on electricity, and shot off. The acceleration was astonishing. As we drove through Wuppertal, Cragg pointed out the dramatically lit running track where he jogged, the creaking 19th-century monorail that Gustave Eiffel had helped to plan, the imposing house where Friedrich Engels had lived for many years, and a large, exclamatory sculpture by Cragg himself, placed in the middle of a central street.

Sprawling and grimy, Wuppertal was, he explained, 'the first industrialized city in Germany'. Yet it now contained, at its heart, a magical surprise. Cragg stopped the car on a quiet hill and we walked up to gateposts announcing the entrance to a *Sculpturenpark*. 'We're right in the centre of Wuppertal, but you wouldn't know that,' said Cragg, showing me dense clusters of ancient trees and, beyond them, a vast Rhineland prospect stretching far below us. With eager and informed enthusiasm, he pointed out 'the weeping birches, oak and ash' punctuating a 30-acre site purchased recently from the heirs of a 'big paint manufacturer, Professor Kurt Herberts. After he died, it was completely deserted for twenty-four years. I negotiated with the family and bought it myself. This is what has occupied me for over two years. It'll take me a while to recover from!'

As well as adding pathways up and down the steep slopes, Cragg had planted over 300 fruit trees. 'And when old trees fall down, we'll leave them to rot,' he said, leaping forward to enfold a tall, slender tree trunk with both his arms. 'Isn't this a figure?' he asked me. 'The interplay between us and natural forms means that we're all interconnected. The human neuron is the most advanced material in the world, and it therefore has a responsibility for all other materials, whether living or inanimate. I'm not a religious person, but we have to take care of the whole thing.'

Although nineteen of his own arresting pieces were installed in the *Sculpturenpark*, they enhanced rather than detracted from the feeling of a primordial forest. Beyond the upper fence, more trees stretched for 'hundreds of kilometres' into the surrounding countryside. Respecting this wildness, Cragg had made sure that the glass-walled gallery built for special exhibitions was discreet rather than sprawling. At the moment, it housed a concise, carefully chosen exhibition of work by Eduardo Chillida, whose sculpture interacted rewardingly with the landscape bordering the gallery on every side. 'I wanted to create an indoor/outdoor situation here,' explained Cragg, waving his arms vigorously before admitting, 'I was very naive about the cost of creating this sculpture park. If I'd known how much it would add up to, I wouldn't have gone through with it. But now, since it opened a few months ago, lots of people are coming and I'm delighted.'

How did this driven and prolific artist find the time to achieve so much? Unusually, Cragg stopped talking for a moment to consider his reply. 'Well, I only need to sleep for two or three hours a night.' Astounded, I asked him if his work was affected by any dreams he might have. 'Dreams?' he echoed. 'Let's not talk about that.' But later, over a supper of roast goose at a favourite restaurant near his house, he returned to the subject. 'I've a book next to my bed, and I write my dreams down,' he said, seizing my notebook and pen in order to make a fast, dramatic drawing. It showed a land mass riven from apex to base by a violent diagonal line. 'A dream is a fault plane,' he asserted, 'shooting through the geology like a shock.'

The urgency of this analogy, in relation to his work, made immediate sense. So did the memorable moment, not long before I left, when Cragg turned to me and exclaimed: 'Solidity and flux: what's happening in your head? Whoa! It's exciting, isn't it?'

Claes Oldenburg

May 2009

Viewers are bound to feel startled when they encounter *Tumbling Tacks*, a spectacular sculpture by Claes Oldenburg and Coosje van Bruggen that sends four gigantic drawing-pins hurtling down a precipitous Norwegian hillside near Oslo. Oldenburg himself, stopping over in London to stay with his daughter before travelling on to Norway for the opening of this new work, was still excited by the opportunity presented there. 'It's the most dramatic site ever,' he said, using his arms and hands with vigour to convey the hillside 'tilting at an angle of forty-five degrees. You come round the corner in this sculpture garden at Kistefos and there, in a natural forest setting, you have *that*! It seems to have come from another world!'

Oldenburg looked surprised when I mentioned how eerily prescient *Tumbling Tacks* appeared. Viewed from the vantage point of 2009, it seemed freighted with uncanny foresight about the calamitous economic crash that was affecting all our lives. He agreed that the current financial crisis was 'far more serious than you read about in the papers, and people in the US have no idea what's going on'. But the economic climate had seemed very different when, as he recalled, 'I first went to Kistefos with Coosje in 2007. We were immediately drawn to the impressively looming structures of the red-brick mill and chimney. It's the only intact paper-pulp mill that still exists in Scandinavia, and was set up in the nineteenth century by the grandfather of Christen Sveaas, the man who has created the sculpture park on the same site. Our first proposal was going to be flowers on the same hillside.' Soon enough, this idea gave way to a vision of 'industrially manufactured tacks' careering downwards, 'each with its own distinct trajectory yet all alike'. Coosje, who had been collaborating with Oldenburg on large-scale projects ever since they married in 1977, thought that the sculpture would 'signify the transition from the mechanical, repetitive production found in the mill to a playful, free format, setting tacks loose to tumble like skiers down a hill, waving the circles and points of their poles'.

Warming to this idea with an infectious sense of energy, Oldenburg pointed out that 'everyone in Oslo goes skiing, and the forms of skis are quite fascinating. The staves are so interesting, and the points are dangerous. Skiing is dangerous, too. And *tack* is such a sharp word – it's nice!' He showed me his arresting sketch for the sculpture, where watercolour and crayon swiftly defined the tiny, vulnerable figure of a woman standing beneath the tacks. They looked as if they were crashing down on her, but Oldenburg pointed out, 'You can stand under the tack at the bottom. It's all about gravity. Everything is dependent on it, and gravity is dangerous, as I've recently found myself: I have to be careful about the stiffness in my legs. I wouldn't survive long in London, with all these steps you have to climb up and down.'

Now eighty and completely bald, the bespectacled Oldenburg still looked very trim with his blue shirt-sleeves rolled up as if ready for action. 'I try not to notice my age,' he said, 'and my father lived until he was ninety-eight. Even at the end he still had the most marvellous handwriting.' But Oldenburg wisely left the installation of the Norway sculpture to an expert team. After the *Tacks* were shipped to Oslo from Turin, where all four pieces had been made by 'a very dependable outfit', they were placed on the hazardous hillside. Each one measures 5.5 metres across and weighs several tons. Oldenburg explained that they were made with 'aluminium and fibreglass with expanding foam, so they had to be highly reinforced'. And he showed me fascinating photographs of the men on site, carefully setting the pieces down onto guiding pins 'so that the tacks are securely attached to ground-cast concrete bases travelling down several metres into the earth'.

Only artists as addicted to risk as Oldenburg and Van Bruggen would have been daring enough to propose such a work. But nearly half a century had passed since he first declared, in a rousing declaration at the height of pop art, 'I am for an art that is political-erotical-mystical, that does something other than sit on its ass in a museum....I am for an art that embroils itself with the everyday crap and still comes out on top.' He fulfilled his ambitions, too. Although London failed to respond in 1966 when he proposed erecting a cluster of pink lipsticks in Piccadilly Circus, Oldenburg later managed to install an equally phallic lipstick sculpture on the Yale University campus. And after Van Bruggen became his wife, they carried out a dizzy array of large-scale projects ranging from the 33-metre-high *Batcolumn* in Chicago and the amorous *Clothespin* in Philadelphia to the tilting *Bottle of Notes*, inspired by Captain Cook's journals, right in the centre of Middlesbrough.

In all, Oldenburg and Van Bruggen worked on more than forty major sculptures in an astonishing variety of spaces. Equally surprisingly, they did not have to initiate the negotiations for any of these commissions. People always came to them with invitations to make work for particular locations. 'These projects were never solicited by us. We were always surprised to be asked, and we never took on the ones we didn't think were right. We insisted that they were permanent, properly maintained, site-specific and related to the changing times. But we had no idea what opportunities would come in the future, and you never know quite how things will turn out. We've even made proposals in Stockholm, including a work called *Caught and Set Free*, where an orange ball emerges upwards like the sun from a basketball net. There was a very good site for it in Stockholm Harbour, and the work was carried quite far. But the project didn't get accepted. Although I've seen basketball pitches in Stockholm parks, it's not a typical Swedish sport. The rejection was disappointing, but we probably didn't do it right somehow.'

Now their tireless collaboration had come to an end. After a long battle against cancer, Van Bruggen died in January 2009 at the age of sixty-six. 'Coosje was trapped in a hotel room all through 2008,' Oldenburg told me. 'She couldn't move around and stayed in bed. But she was very alive on the phone: many of the people she talked to had no idea how ill she had become. Coosje was in on the whole thing with the Norwegian sculpture, and she would make a decision immediately. I take weeks to make up my mind.'

How, looking back, would he describe their working relationship? 'It was a unity of opposites. I tended to make sculpture symmetrical and static, but she favoured objects in movement. She would say: "This is too boring," and preferred things that moved. She loved the *Flying Pins* we made in Eindhoven, and it was an adventurous piece.' Oldenburg admitted that his future work would be 'very difficult, not just for reasons of creativity but because Coosje was so good at organizing, and contacting officials and mayors. Once, in San Francisco, we visited City Hall and went to the office of the charismatic mayor Willie Brown. He was very theatrical and witty, and asked with great drama: "Who is it that enters my domain?" We showed him our proposal, and he commented: "I think this sculpture is too big." But Coosje said: "You see that bridge behind it? *That's* not too big!" And she won him round, so in the end he said: "I like the way you think."'

Oldenburg still hoped that it would prove possible to bring their last project to fruition. 'We were going to do *Wild Flowers*, a big piece in the garden of the Indianapolis Museum of Art,' he explained. 'The director there, Maxwell Anderson, is a very, very smart guy and supportive of the piece. Although the flowers would be combined in a bouquet, Coosje wanted movement and danger. She compared it to the impact of racing cars in the Indianapolis Speedway, a big annual fixture. I hope we'll realize it – I keep saying "we" because that's accurate.'

For the time being, though, Oldenburg was still very involved with the audacity of *Tumbling Tacks*. Born in Stockholm, he spent part of his boyhood in Oslo before his father, a career diplomat, was transferred to Chicago. But the new sculpture in Kistefos was the first large-scale project that Oldenburg had ever installed anywhere in Scandinavia. And he took great pleasure in a memory of his distant days as a child in Oslo: 'When I was small, I would walk down to the harbour. There was a pier where banana boats arrived from South America. And high up on the pier, a giant long banana was positioned, made of metal and painted yellow with a silly little pigeon on top. I had never seen anything quite like it, and I must have made a habit of going down to the harbour specially to see it. I went bananas for it!'

I suggested to Oldenburg that the impact of this bizarre, outsized and flamboyant object must have exerted a formative influence on his imagination. He smiled. 'I really think that bananas are one of the great inventions of nature,' he said. 'They are naturally protected, and very good for you. I once did a huge banana for Times Square in New York. But then Coosje said: "We must do less penises." So she and I made *Flung Peel*, where the banana has been eaten but a little bit is left, and the peel is flying through the air. I have a photograph of Coosje demonstrating in graceful movement how she wanted it preserved in the sculpture.'

What would it be like working without her? Oldenburg paused, sat back and reflected. 'On the one hand, it won't be a new experience because I did work alone before we got together. But on the other hand, I'll now be alone in our big New York house, and we were so used to exchanging ideas. At least for a couple of years I'll leave our house the way it is. During the summer I'll also be preparing a memorial show for Coosje, to be held at the Pace Gallery in New York later this year. There's a danger in being focused on yourself, because Coosje always reminded me that there was a world out there. It was very good for me to have an opposite. So I'll try to remember what she might have said. Whenever we gave a lecture together, we would constantly swap mikes and contradict each other. It was kind of fun.'

Eva Rothschild

May 2009

Like so many staircases in the East London buildings where artists work in such profusion, the rough-hewn steps leading up to Eva Rothschild's studio were dark, disconcerting and punctuated by fierce official announcements on the walls. 'No Children Allowed At Any Time' insisted one notice, while another warned, 'This Building Is Under 24-Hour Surveillance'. By the time I reached Rothschild's door, though, the whole atmosphere had changed dramatically. Gazing out from her balcony into the radiant spring sunshine, my eyes were seduced by the immense sculptural presence of two gasometers asserting their industrial might on the very edge of Regent's Canal. And the panoramic view stretched far beyond Hackney to encompass the full vastness of the metropolis, dominated by Norman Foster's iconic Gherkin tower glinting in the light.

Despite the grim uncertainties generated by global recession, the city's stubborn energy was still palpable. And the sense of dynamism intensified when I entered Rothschild's white-walled studio. With her close-cropped black hair, jeans and green gym shoes, she looked ready for action. Her top was spattered with splashes of white plaster and Jesmonite, testifying to a hands-on involvement with the work in progress visible on every available surface. Two white pieces, like bleached rocks pierced by apertures, would soon be painted inside with surprising colours; Rothschild planned to balance them on slender black stands, raising these open-ended structures up to eye level and enabling the viewer to look right into them.

Having encountered 'completely toxic' materials at art school, where 'there were no precautions and the technicians must have been poisoned', Rothschild was wary. 'When painting, I use acrylic and wear masks all the time,' she said. 'I won't use fibreglass or epoxy resin – they're too poisonous. I'm always washing my hands, and I hate the feeling of clay and plaster, so I wear gloves. I've been pregnant twice while working in the studio, so I have to be careful.'

At the moment, though, Rothschild could not stop her brain focusing on a major commission. She had been invited to make an ambitious, large-scale installation for the Duveen Galleries, running right through the centre of Tate Britain. As Martin Creed, Anya Gallaccio, Mona Hatoum, Michael Landy and Mark Wallinger have all shown in recent years, the Duveen Commission can give artists the opportunity to make work with spectacular, widely discussed impact. Rothschild had promised Tate not to give away anything about the look of her installation before it opened on 29 June. 'I had to roll up some preliminary drawings before you came here today,' she confided with a secretive grin. 'They first asked me to submit a proposal a year ago, and there have been lots of hoops to jump through since then, which is good. My initial proposal was rejected, but they asked me to resubmit. It's really daunting and very exciting. The installation will be totally site-specific, involving the whole of the Duveen Galleries.'

Rothschild paused, doubtless aware that no further details should be divulged at this stage. But she was willing to tell me: 'I've spent a lot of time in the Duveen space, and realize how many people go there. Unlike Tate Modern's Turbine Hall, which is so huge it's like an outdoor site, the Duveen is more like a National Trust or an English Heritage space. I keep having dreams about my installation going wrong in terms of shape, junction and colour, or things not being ready in time. I won't be making it here in the studio: the process is different. I am quite an anxious person, but it's all quite motivating!'

Paradoxically, Rothschild showed no sign of nervousness, either in her movements or the way she talked. Outwardly calm, controlled and highly articulate, she seemed able to pour all her inner tensions straight into the work itself. 'I'm hoping to create something that will agitate the architecture of the Duveen Galleries,' she told Tate, 'tangling with your perception of the space.' So we could expect an edgy, unpredictable experience which would catch us off balance as we made our way through Rothschild's structures. She might even have been hoping to recreate the excitement that sustained her during the work process. 'When you start a piece, it's an undefined thing and the making of the work sustains you,' she explained. 'You feel your way round something. The idea of waking up in the morning and being like Daniel Buren would be hell – I'd rather work in an office! A large part of my work is looking at what I've made.' She picked up a little black stick-like sculpture and passed it over to me, so I could hold it in my hand and savour its vitality. 'It's got to live and it's got to *be*,' she said. 'And I don't like to keep things that are finished in the studio. The moment of seeing the work only occurs outside: you can't see it properly in the studio.'

Not that Rothschild was fanatically committed to outdoor settings for her sculpture. 'I'm not into plaza art,' she said sardonically, 'but it depends on the location. I love the big Richard Serra piece at Liverpool Street Station: it's in a tiny space, and yet it works so well. Some collectors have fantastic places for my pieces, but I turn down a request whenever I think it'll look all wrong. I like the idea of work being in a gallery: you go through a door and see the art properly, separate from the world. How few moments do you ever have with one thing?' Rothschild was quick to make it clear that she had no patience with 'the old image of the artist living in an ivory tower – that's completely outmoded. Artists now have to be flexible and pragmatic. But I like the idea of art being a bit apart. That interests me, although I would stop short of saying that art is magical.'

For most of her student years – first as a polemical printmaker at the University of Ulster in the early 1990s, and then at Goldsmiths College in London – Rothschild shied away from sculpture. She made 'woven pieces and works on paper' during her Goldsmiths period, and 'I thought that anyone who said "I am a sculptor" sounded so weighty, pretentious, unfeasible and grandiose.' But when she tried to explore the possibilities of painting, her body reacted negatively. 'I got RSI [repetitive strain injury]. My hands were really bad. It turned me towards sculpture.' Once she had made *Burning Tyre* (1999), a powerful work reflecting an awareness of protest culture, Rothschild's attitude towards being a sculptor really began to change.

The tyre was stuffed with incense, a surprising element that could, I suggested, surely be traced back to the Catholic religion she grew up with? 'My husband is English, and England has been very good to me. But I am Irish. The idea of believing in something, and the notion that an object can carry power, is very interesting and present in all religions.' Even so, Rothschild was quick to disassociate herself from the idea that art should be 'a force for morality. I don't feel that art is good for you. It could be bad for you! We don't go to museums to be improved – that's preachy.' As 'a responsible citizen', she went along to the climate change demonstration during the G20 week. But 'there were far too many police. I went down Threadneedle Street at one stage, and it felt overwhelmingly bad. Thank God I wasn't at the Royal Exchange! The police were putting on riot gear and, to be honest, the whole protest unfortunately lacked a real focus.'

Would she ever return to live in Ireland? 'I think about going back there every week,' she said. 'I had a very secure childhood in a happy family, and our house was near the sea in Dún Laoghaire, near Dublin. But for a small country like Ireland the future will be very difficult. The economy is a disaster now – it's like tumbleweed blowing through the streets. I do miss the sea, though. It gives you a sense of focus, and when you go outdoors it's like a compass. That's why I love being near the Regent's Canal here in Hackney. London is a great place to grow up in, too. I found this studio almost three years ago, after discovering a sign saying "Units To Rent". It's owned by a big company of Jewish landlords in Tottenham, and it's so much better than my previous ramshackle studio with a leaking roof. Having a good place does affect your work. I'm very lucky to be able to afford this studio. It can be really tough for artists who don't make a living from their work, going out to horrible, unheated places in the evenings and trying to survive in the cold.'

Looking at Rothschild's recent work, I realized that it reflected her understanding of profound instability in the world. One piece she showed me on her computer screen was called *Women of the World*. Seven ball forms were balanced precariously on top of each other, and I remarked that the whole sculpture looked as if it might collapse at any instant. She smiled. 'I'm happy about that. It's an improbable physicality, almost like being on a tightrope. It could fall apart, like the Leaning Tower of Pisa. We've become so used to digital trickery that it's great to see something like a seal balancing a ball on its nose.' Was she interested in watching animals? 'No, but snakes – yes! I'm fascinated by the muscularity and precision in their movements. I absolutely hate spiders, but snakes are graceful and may not even move for hours. They're also very primitive.' Seizing a pen, Rothschild drew a stick figure next to one diagonal line on a pink-toned sheet. 'This is a person and this is a snake,' she explained. 'Two life forms looking at each other.'

Her energy now was even more intense than before, and I could imagine how determined she must become to transfer it to the sculpture. What was her greatest hope as an artist? She replied to this with swiftness and certitude. 'At the moment, I hope that my work is exciting to be in and around. It must involve you in a dynamic experience. When one of my pieces goes well, it is like a giddiness, even a vertigo. It's like exhilaration in the physicality of something. I also hope it'll be accessible. You can't control meaning – you have to free up the artwork. When something really gets me, it's a dizzying feeling, like being right on the edge of the Grand Canyon! But whatever chaos is in the work, it's because I've put it there.'

Cornelia Parker

October 2009

As early as 1984, the young Cornelia Parker made an eerily prophetic image of major world monuments drowned in a gutter. Talking with me in 2009, she said, 'There has been a sense of the apocalyptic in my work for a long time.' Over the past few years, though, her feelings of alarm about our planet had intensified into 'terror and fear. I've been around enough scientists who are at the cutting edge to realize that it's much more serious than most people think. We could be seeing the extinction of the species. We're starting to see the effects in Australia, which supplies eighty per cent of Japanese food, and it's breaking down already.'

Everything, said Parker, was 'coming home to roost'. Recently, climate scientists had told her at a conference that 'they were battle-weary, and everything was accelerating much more quickly than four or five years ago'. According to Parker, 'We must change everything to have even a chance of pulling through.' She was angry about 'big business dealing with disinformation' and she pointed out that 'governments can't agree about anything except the most conservative reforms. We can't even adapt to lagging our lofts!'

Visiting Peru the previous year, she had admired 'the amazing terraces at Machu Picchu, which have been fed by glacial water for aeons of time. But the ambassador told me that the glaciers in Peru will all be gone in ten years.' She said, 'As an artist, I feel powerless in some ways and vocal in other ways. When you've got kids of your own, the enormity of it all seems even more staggering. I've not thought about much else for the last few years. We are the first species to know that we are becoming extinct, but we're not doing enough about it.'

In the Royal Academy's 'Earth' exhibition, she would be displaying a work called *Heart of Darkness*. Its title derives from the Joseph Conrad novel, which also inspired the film *Apocalypse Now*. 'My piece contains the burnt remains from a forest in Florida. Forestry guys do controlled burns, but then the weather becomes very windy and this fire developed there called Impassable I. Jeb Bush was governor of Florida at the time and he was deeply involved in the debacle of the election which his brother, notoriously, ended up winning.'

While remaining 'quite ambivalent about what artists can do', Parker said she was convinced that 'creativity on every possible level is what will get us out of this shit – like recycling, and growing your own vegetables. But is the government doing enough? Where are the public information films? Where's the advertising on the Tube telling us to cut down on carbon? Art is good because it continues the debate. We need a mass movement to bang on the doors of power.'

Rebecca Horn and Masanori Handa

November 2009

For both Masanori Handa and Rebecca Horn, their mentoring year spanned a momentous period that they are unlikely ever to forget. A decade ago, at the age of nineteen, Handa journeyed to India and, quite suddenly, underwent experiences so powerful and overwhelming that he became an artist. 'I had the sensation of being in my own skin among many people, but later I felt this was disappearing, and mentoring reminded me of where I began. That's what is important,' he told me during a visit to Horn's studio at Bad Konig, in spectacular German countryside.

He explained that his inspiration was derived 'from places and phenomena that are happening in me. I don't have any way of categorizing or analysing or dissecting: rather, I'm just trying to absorb what's happening in my senses.' He leaned forward, impelled by a fundamental urgency that seemed to run through his entire body. 'I use my hands,' he said with great animation, describing how, 'as I talk through my ideas, I use materials and keep changing them. I need to vocalize, and see the difference between how I change with my hands and how I change with talking. So I need somebody who can listen to me, and with whom I can discuss.'

That was why the opportunity to meet and share his ideas with Rebecca Horn had proved so exciting. As we walked through her studio, a white-painted interior converted from a textile factory building once owned by Horn's grandfather, the extraordinary range and inventiveness of her barrier-breaking work became clear. Two old wooden pianos, upended with their insides exposed and attached to wires, reminded me of her intensely dramatic *Concert for Anarchy*, a 1990 installation where an inverted piano exploded into action without warning. Elsewhere in Horn's studio, a feather moved up and down as it caressed a white goose egg nestling in a child's shoe. And upstairs, in another immense room, several large paintings charged with free and scattered marks conveyed her restless energy. She called them 'cosmic maps', explaining with great relish, 'They're all to do with the pulsation of my own body and how far I can stretch my arms to use these fantastic Korean brushes!'

Horn's physical dynamism echoed Handa's, even though they seemed in other respects very different as artists and individuals. German and Japanese culture also differ greatly, yet Horn had not hesitated to select Handa as her protégé. As a teacher for twenty years, mainly at the Universität der Künste in Berlin but also in California, she excelled at communicating with young artists; and now, having retired from teaching in February 2009, she was taking delight in the feeling that she had 'become a young artist again, or maybe even younger!'

Handa responded eagerly to her sense of empathy and free-wheeling enthusiasm, saying, 'I've been giving Rebecca lots of ideas about what I feel on a fundamental level.' Even so, he must also have understood the other side of Horn's complex personality. An ancient Chinese statue stood at one end of her studio, and she told me, 'It protects the house. I'm a Buddhist and I meditate a lot. I do yoga for one hour every day, and I have a wonderful Indian teacher.'

Her concern for other artists was so generous that she was in the process of converting the large, blue-tiled buildings around her studio – all part of her family's textile factory, sheltered by extensively forested hills on one side and a mountain on the other – into a Foundation. She was transforming them into 'a village with a museum, an archive, a space for concerts and studios for artists in residence'. The whole visionary project, which was scheduled to open in 2010, promised to be of inestimable benefit to artists everywhere. Its importance, in a world affected by an alarming economic crisis, was self-evident. And the visionary optimism behind it would be summed up by a 30-foot-high tower converted from an old factory chimney. 'We are building the tower now,' said Horn, gesturing towards it with a sense of anticipation. 'A beautiful blue light will be installed on top, so at night it will seem to levitate! That is why I am calling the whole complex the Moontower Foundation.'

Horn's own approach to art could be regarded as proof that everything was possible. Moving with supple and resourceful ease from body-extension sculpture to drawing, film, poetry and photography, she had encouraged Handa to explore even the most unlikely possibilities in his work during the mentor year. At the same time, she appreciated how hard it might be for him to break free from his native culture. Horn had first visited Japan in 1978, 'when I was twenty-nine, the same age as Handa now. I did a performance which was a mixture of traditional Western ballet and objects like a little round Japanese table. It was so strange for everyone there, but I like the way Handa has taken Japanese culture and transformed it. He hasn't become Western during the mentor year. What I like in Japanese art is their way of seeing space, both outer and inner in temples, how they use it for meditation and create their gardens. Handa has certain traditional ideas, like his constructed flying dragons in space and a traditional wood swing in a tent – this I like because it interested me when I was in Japan. But now, the new generation over there has to destroy this and make something new.'

Returning to her conversations with Handa earlier in the mentor year, Horn recalled in particular, 'He said: "I'm not so much interested in doing another sculpture, I'm fascinated by smell, wind and shadow, this kind of energy, a palm tree turning with water dripping. You have an idea and you're like a cat around the milk, trying to find the most visionary way to make things concrete." I suggested that it would be good for him to explore performance – making things exist and then disappear again. He made a drawing, and I made a drawing. This is often the way to communicate with each other.'

She also remembered suggesting that Handa live in Berlin, because it would be 'a little bit out of my comfort zone. Besides, where else should he go? I had so many connections there because of my professorship, and in Berlin he became part of his own generation and scene rather than sitting here in the countryside and watching me make sculpture.' The apartment they found for him, however, presented something of a challenge at first. 'It was on the periphery of Berlin,' Horn explained, 'and a bit dangerous. People try to break in because it is on street level, so we needed strong locks. It used to be a music shop called Half World [*Halbwelt*]. It means half hell and half heaven, but it also means red-light district. And when Handa arrived, there was nothing inside – not even a light. So I went to IKEA in a Volkswagen bus with my technicians to buy everything he needed to live there.'

Once Handa had settled in, he recalled, this strange location became very stimulating. 'Many things came back to me in Berlin,' he said. 'Memories and sensations that I thought I had lost. I was very fortunate to have Rebecca, and boundaries became blurred when I was sleeping near the street where cars rush by. I brought a big fan back from India, and all the papers were blowing round. I tested things. Before your hand touches an object, I feel the temperature and humidity of it. I was really touched when Rebecca talked about her work and described wrapping an egg gently. She cherishes these sensations, and I got a lot from her.'

Handa showed me some extraordinary new drawings, explaining that one especially apocalyptic image had been made after 'I saw there is a tornado in my room.' Another drawing conveyed his feeling that he 'was lost in a jungle, going to the bathroom in the middle of a dark night'. And the complexity of Handa's emotions grew vividly clear when he produced a drawing called *Black Mountain Black Smoke*. 'It becomes an atomic reactor,' he told me, 'and then it becomes a furnace. It becomes summer. It becomes hope.' Handa had been fired by positive emotions as well as more disturbing impulses – nowhere more than in a drawing he called *Ditch Delta*: 'The figure is in a huge room where the floor is painted like a riverscape going in different directions. He feels at ease because it's closer to the ocean. The water is not clean – there is a smell. But I grew up by the sea, and I like to "surf the world" in my work.'

Nowhere did Handa surf more successfully than in his Berlin apartment, where he made a dramatic installation towards the end of his mentoring year. 'We talked about him doing something in the apartment, moving through the space,' recalled Horn. 'He came up with transforming this very strange apartment in a totally crazy way. He pushed his bed through the window, so part of his body was in the room and part outside in the greenery, like floating in the air. And he ordered an upside-down palm tree, moving and rotating with water on top. It was a smelling sculpture. He invited the whole street in, so they decorated the palm tree like a Christmas tree – it was very Masanori!'

Handa smiled and explained with satisfaction: 'When Rebecca proposed I do this show in my apartment, I truly appreciated it. She was helping me to do it my way. It made me feel so happy, because I realized it might be a gallery space. I really felt moved by her suggestion, and I felt it was the right thing to do.'

Bettina Pousttchi

May 2012

Having grown up in Mainz and subsequently moved to New York and Paris, Bettina Pousttchi settled in Berlin in 2005. 'It's like an art village,' she told me affectionately when we met seven years later. 'And studios are much cheaper than they are in other major cities.'

Pousttchi first saw the Palast der Republik during a visit to the city in the 1990s. Aware of its history as the former East German parliament building from 1976 to 1990, she was also fascinated by the fact that it had been built on the site of the former Stadtschloss, the city castle gravely damaged during the Second World War and then demolished by the GDR government. Pousttchi soon realized that 'during the GDR period, people in Berlin had mixed feelings about the Palast. It was a governmental structure of repression, but you could also have a good time there, visiting the glamorous restaurant, the bowling alley, dancing clubs and theatre. It was a *Volkshaus*, for the people.'

After Germany's reunification, she explained, the Palast 'became an icon building for the new Berlin. And it raised an important question: can buildings be rehabilitated and tell another story? The Palast had a dark history, but the new Berlin also attempted to use this building in a new way. So there was over a decade of discussion about whether to destroy it. The big argument against preserving the Palast was asbestos, but it was mainly a problem of ideology. So eventually there was a government vote to demolish it, but only with a lot of opposition. It was cruel for people, of all kinds, to see their history obliterated. I couldn't believe it myself. It was a quiet and brutal situation, so in 2006 I felt the need to record the *Palast* before it was gone.'

During that summer, Pousttchi made videos and took photographs while the building was being demolished. 'You couldn't go in, so I only filmed the outside, but from all kinds of positions. I then started editing the images of this semi-destroyed building, but they didn't come together. The demolition took three years, and there were protest demonstrations. For certain people it had a beauty, and even for me the Palast had a very strange Eastern European modernist glamour. Half destroyed, it looked raw and brutalist – really like a wound. And then, all of a sudden, there was nothing left except a green, artificial lawn. I remember feeling a huge void after the Palast disappeared, but I also felt that it was still there, like an after-image on your retina.'

Berlin initially wanted to reconstruct the former Stadtschloss, but once it became clear just how much it would cost to build a replica of the old city castle, that idea seemed less feasible. 'Berlin is bankrupt,' Pousttchi pointed out, 'because it had to invest so much in reunification and there was never enough support from the state.' Even so, the Temporäre Kunsthalle – a temporary art gallery – was erected on a nearby site while the demolition of the Palast went ahead. 'This new building was conceived by the architect to have contemporary art on the facade as well as inside,' explained Pousttchi, 'and they asked me to make a photographic proposal.' After three days of intense thought, she arrived at her highly adventurous decision to make an immense photographic simulation of the Palast on the exterior of the Temporäre Kunsthalle. 'I felt surprised and challenged rather than delighted with the idea,' she recalled, although: 'I had a shock when I realized the building was fifty-seven metres deep, twenty metres wide and eleven metres high. I was like, oh my God, I've only got two months to do this!'

At first, she tried to use her own photographs of the Palast; but they had all been taken during the destruction of the building.

'So then I tried to find other material, and looked through the archives.' In the end, Pousttchi used 'scans from archival pictures of the Palast. I had a stressful time producing all the nine hundred and seventy paper posters, and putting them on the Temporäre Kunsthalle took two weeks. We had problems in the beginning with the glue, because the posters were supposed to stay there for six months. It was a low-budget nightmare, and people told me I was mad. But at a certain point I got a system going, and I paid a lot of attention to detail.'

Her daring and determination soon paid off. 'I was overwhelmed by the public's response,' she recalled with a sense of wonder. 'It started while I was installing. Everyone could take a picture, and I had all kinds of reactions from spectators, commentators and journalists. They were enthusiastic as well as critical, and people started telling me their memories. After all, I was dealing with their lives and the building had gone. But they recognized *Echo Berlin* at once as the mirrored bronze facade of the Palast, even though it now had a completely different shape. The original building had a coat of arms in the middle, but that symbolized the GDR and I didn't want to bring it back. So I turned it into a clock, and people became convinced that there had always been a clock on the facade of the Palast!'

After *Echo Berlin* was finished in 2009, Pousttchi spent a long time photographing it in situ. 'It was fascinating to see this fake facade in the context of Berlin,' she said. 'I didn't want to evoke sadness, but memory and respect towards the past. The Palast was a part of Berlin's history which should not be erased, even if in bookshops you can't find a record of it today. People now think that *Echo Berlin* was the Palast!'

Working on such an ambitious project changed Pousttchi's attitude towards her own art. 'Looking back now, I realize it's where everything came together in my work. Photography and sculpture became architecture in a very special place. I'm more sensitive to locations now, and my major projects are site-specific. While I was photographing *Echo Berlin*, I had sleepless nights about the posters peeling off. I also realized how vulnerable it was, and expected it to be graffiti-attacked. But I was very proud that there wasn't a single graffito, even though *Echo Berlin* had left the privileged and protected space of the museum far behind.'

The potency of the work is conveyed with great intensity in Pousttchi's photographs, which in 2011 formed the centrepiece of her remarkable exhibition 'Echo: Mirroring Memories', organized by the German Embassy in London. Curated by Sarah Hegenbart, it was held in the building known as German House at 34 Belgrave Square, the former embassy of the GDR. Pousttchi was astonished when she discovered this unexpected piece of history. 'When Sarah told me it was once the GDR Embassy, I couldn't believe my ears,' she recalled, 'because I never imagined GDR outside the borders of Germany. The state wasn't respected immediately, and not every country had a GDR Embassy.' So Pousttchi regarded 34 Belgrave Square as 'a very special location which added another layer of meaning to my *Echo Berlin* photographs. And then the guards there said: "Look at the chairs in the cafeteria." They all had yellow labels printed with the words "Property of the GDR", so the chairs were the last remaining trace of that period. I decided to make them part of my installation. They became sculpture, and my photographs of *Echo Berlin* ended up relating to their space in a site-specific way, which I thought was very exciting.'

Sonia Boyce
January 2022

Although Piccadilly felt very cold as I walked towards the Royal Academy courtyard in early January, Sonia Boyce was sitting defiantly on an outdoor bench rather than sheltering inside like everyone else. Her Covid mask did not entirely hide the smile she gave me, and her sense of welcome became even more evident as we made our way through the foyer. Boyce, who in 2016 became the first Black woman to be elected as a Royal Academician, led me up a steep staircase providing glimpses of students' lively paintings in a capacious studio space below. We both admired their vivacity, and she said, 'How marvellous it is that the RA has this art school at its centre, where students do not pay any fees!' Education is enormously important to Boyce, who is herself a professor and the inaugural chair in Black Art and Design at the University of the Arts London. But she never stops making her own work, and was due to represent Britain in the Venice Biennale later in 2022.

After entering the Academicians' Room, a lofty space lit by an extensive arched ceiling filled with windows, we settled down on a generously cushioned sofa at the far end. Such a reassuring context could hardly have been further removed from the rough, alarming and racist areas of London where Boyce grew up with parents who had immigrated from Barbados and Guyana. Born in Islington, she soon moved with her family to the East End. 'We lived near Brick Lane and my mum, who had come over to Britain as part of the Windrush Generation, trained to be a nurse. But my father was a tailor, and Mum also worked as a seamstress. So our house became filled with bagloads of patterned material. I remember making outfits for my dolls. Then I started making my own clothes, and people thought I was a punk. My mum hated it sometimes when I went out dressed in unfinished, badly made outfits with all the material pinned together!'

Although Boyce attended the enlightened Robert Montefiore School, which was 'Jewish by origin, yet multi-racial and multi-denominational', she grew 'aware of racism from a very, very young age'. As a teenager, she worked briefly as a felt packer at the Whitechapel Bell Foundry, Britain's oldest manufacturing company. 'There were old factories round the back where life was extremely rough, and because of the nearby docks there were extraordinary tensions about racial difference. The National Front was rife in East London.' So she felt immense relief when, on a very memorable day, 'My teacher said: "I think you should go to art school."' Boyce had been fascinated by images since, 'at the age of six or seven, my handwriting won me my very first book, *Charlie and the Chocolate Factory*. In a particular chapter, Willy Wonka takes an entourage into a room where he flings open the door and these cubic eyes look round. I was delighted and confused by the idea that square eyes could be round, and the wallpaper in the room led on to my interest in William Morris. This Roald Dahl book with its illustrations was pivotal, and makes me realize how enamoured I felt about perception, which was at the crux of that book. I found out recently that Charlie was meant to be a Black child – encased in chocolate and unable to get out. But Dahl's agent argued that unless Charlie was changed into a white boy, he wouldn't appeal to readers.'

In Tate Britain's revelatory and much-needed show 'Life Between Islands', which charted the fascinating relationship between the Caribbean and Britain from the 1950s to today, Boyce's most recent exhibit was a colossal vinyl print wallpaper called *Shaggy Bear*, with 'a figure in shredded rags from the Barbados carnival called Crop

Over'. Boyce also displayed a powerful two-screen video of the carnival itself, a spectacular and exuberant event she had encountered on her first visit to Barbados, her mum's native country, at the age of twenty-seven. 'Folk figures would suddenly appear at events, sometimes on stick legs, and everyone accepted them. I was amazed! Why is nobody else batting an eyelid, I wondered.' In the *Crop Over* video exhibit, boisterous carnival scenes are poignantly juxtaposed with melancholy sequences filmed at Harewood House in Yorkshire, where a solitary yet defiant carnival figure strides around the vast estate gazing at the magnificent surroundings and gravely remembering where all this wealth came from. Harewood House was built with the immense sugar fortunes made by the Lascelles family in Barbados during the 18th century. 'They were the largest British slave owners,' Boyce explained. She responded to an invitation from a curator at Harewood House to visit the Lascelles archive and discover how the family's wealth was amassed.

One of the most powerful sequences in Boyce's *Crop Over* centres on scenes she filmed at a grand Barbados mansion that had once been lavishly inhabited by the Caribbean plantocracy. Carnival performers mime the grandiose behaviour of its former owners. 'The cleaner of the plantation mansion was really angry,' she recalled, 'because carnival celebrators wouldn't have been allowed in such highly esteemed places.' Yet the truth is that enslaved people did indeed mock the luxurious excesses of the plantocracy. Boyce expressed her delight that Barbados finally 'became a republic at the end of November'.

The earlier works she exhibited in 'Life Between Islands' are equally potent. Executed during the 1980s, after her graduation from Stourbridge College with a BA in Fine Art, they show how eloquently Boyce could work with a mixture of watercolour, oil pastel and crayon on very large paper sheets. *Missionary Position II* impressed the Tate so much that, in 1987, she became the first Black British woman artist to enter the collection. Another outstanding work from that period shows with exemplary frankness the complexity of her life as a twenty-four-year-old. It is called *She Ain't Holding Them Up, She's Holding On (Some English Rose)*. And the young

Boyce, standing upright against a wallpaper backdrop, looks at once vulnerable and defiant. Her raised arms appear to be supporting the family ranged above her head. Although acutely aware of life's hazards, she looks determined to survive as an independent force. I was very impressed when first encountering this iconic image in a 1989 exhibition at the Hayward Gallery, soon after Boyce had become actively involved with the Black Art Movement.

She told me how, by the 1990s, 'I'd got really tired of drawing myself rather than other people.' She also began experimenting at that point with performance, sound and music, creating works that reflected the immense breadth of her interest in alternative media. Over the last twenty years Boyce has displayed a fruitful engagement with many different kinds of music, including the admirable achievements of Black British female singers. And in an ambitious project called *For You, Only You*, performed initially at Magdalen College Chapel in Oxford before embarking on a tour, she brought the early Renaissance work of Franco-Flemish composer Josquin Desprez into an astonishing marriage with the provocative voice of Greek sound artist Mikhail Karikis. Boyce worked on this daring and wholly unpredictable encounter 'at the same time as my *Crop Over* project, and I learned a huge amount about bringing together seemingly different forces and discovering what they were doing. Mikhail talked to me about influences like Dada and Ella Fitzgerald's jazz. That led me to think about how Dada and jazz were happening at the same time, and influencing each other – although we don't think so! They were two forms railing against tradition and rational thought. I wondered why they were kept in separate spheres: up until the mid-twentieth century, jazz was seen as "devil music" and in many places banned as an uncivilizing force.'

Boyce also remembered how, as a restless teenager, 'I actually wanted to be a dancer and went to dance school while at East Ham College of Art and Technology – where I attended a life-class drawing session when, suddenly, there was a man standing on the floor with no clothes on!' She 'loved movies' as well, encouraged no doubt by the fact that her father's 'first job in London was as a cinema projectionist. My family got all dressed up to go to the cinema – it was a major event!' Looking back, Boyce said, she realized that 'cameras were a way of shaping imagination. The first musical film I saw at the cinema was *Oliver!*, not only because it was about London – the choreography and songs will stay with me for ever.' She was only six when *Oliver!* came out, and 'I realized later that racism lay behind the way Scrooge was presented. But *Oliver!* draws on all your emotions: fear, hope, despair and the question of the poorhouse.'

Even so, Boyce felt equally fascinated by cinematic humour. 'One of my favourite films is *Passport to Pimlico*, a classic Ealing comedy and definitely a film for our post-Brexit times. You get to see bombed-out London and kids playing in the ruins. By accident they detonate an unexploded bomb, and it reveals a tunnel where an old, buried royal charter says that Pimlico belongs to the Duke of Burgundy. So it becomes a kind of free state in London. The film is hilarious, telling you so much about the nationhood question and having a mixed heritage. They call themselves Burgundians with the right to be British. It's a beautiful, complex film relating to where we are now and our relationship with Europe.' She feels very strongly that 'Brexit was about inventing a past that never was – an amnesia, and also you've got to have an adversary. The British Isles have always been about change while keeping their character. We wrestle with all of these things, and Brexit doesn't make sense in a good way at all. It breeds a constant fear factor about people we don't know, but if Covid tells us anything, it's that we're all connected. I've got two girls, and they have no problem about being here and staying in touch with the rest of the world. We all share a planet that's very fragile.'

Towards the end of our meeting, I realized that the opening of the Venice Biennale was only four months away. How did Boyce feel about receiving the invitation to represent Britain there? She grinned. 'How could you not love Venice? I got the invite in December 2019, so it was like a Christmas present. Then Covid postponed everything for a while. I'm still not allowed to say anything about the work I've planned for the British Pavilion – apart from, it's going to happen! Because of Covid it's been like pulling a juggernaut along, coordinating people being in the same space together. Apart from Zoom meetings, it's difficult to all meet up, but the joy of seeing them is great.' I remarked that it must feel weird not to be able to tell anyone about her Venetian plans, and she agreed, 'Yes, *very* funny. I feel like a member of the Secret Service who musn't divulge the information.'

With admirable honesty, she admitted, 'Of course I'm incredibly nervous as well – it means an enormous amount to be given this opportunity, and I don't know whether I'll live up to all those people's expectations. Yet it's exciting, too. When I visited Venice in the past it never occurred to me that I would exhibit there one day, so the invitation was a complete surprise. My nerves are evident, but I know they are about adrenalin. I'm addicted to taking risks, which is sometimes scary.'

She mentioned the widespread media reaction to work she had made for Manchester Art Gallery's public events programme. Uneasy about the way gender was represented in the gallery's 19th-century collection, she had singled out John William Waterhouse's 1896 painting of the doomed Hylas being fatally lured into a pond by hungry and vicious semi-naked nymphs. So the picture was temporarily taken down from the wall and replaced by a space in which questions were displayed to invite responses from the public. Boyce rapidly found herself at the scandalous centre of loud journalistic outrage. 'Mass media coverage is not something I'd recommend,' she told me wryly. 'We're not built for the "look at me" spotlight, and we're not trained to handle it. We're not necessarily equipped to be exposed to all that. Much of the art world has intimate and manageable audiences, not splashed across broadsheets. We're a bit more like a cottage industry.'

Even so, Boyce was clearly feeling very energized by her Venetian commission. 'I'm going there once a month,' she said, 'and Venice is much stricter than London in terms of security in public spaces. It is weird being choreographed away from contact with Covid, but we need to keep people safe. I'm certain that Venice will continue to safeguard and be much more consistent than us.' Regarding her work in the British Pavilion, she observed, 'I've been working across the media for a long time. Although I'd never underplay my love of painting, I decided fairly early on that I didn't want to be a painter rather than an image-maker.'

As we get up to leave the Academicians' Room, she smiled and said, 'Talking, I love. I get that from my mum. When I was young, it used to annoy me that she'd be talking to everyone we came across in the shops and on the streets. I felt like, I'm carrying all the heavy shopping, so why is she doing this? But now I love having a good chat with people. I find it really uplifting.'

ACKNOWLEDGMENTS

All the artists in this book deserve my thanks for responding so well when I invaded their spaces. Looking back now on these diverse and unpredictable encounters, I feel delighted that such robust individuals were willing to share their hopes, frustrations and fundamental ambitions in highly articulate ways.

I am also grateful to the newspapers and magazines which originally published many of these interviews. My first thanks are due to Simon Jenkins, who appointed me as Art Critic of *The Times* soon after he became its Editor. A considerable number of the interviews were written for *The Times*, and I salute as well the arts editors at the other newspapers and magazines who commissioned me: *The Financial Times*, *Art Review*, *RA Magazine*, *Apollo*, *Art World*, *The White Review* and *Rolex Mentor and Protégé*. The BBC deserves to be thanked for producing and broadcasting my interview with Helen Frankenthaler. At Thames & Hudson, Roger Thorp has been very supportive throughout this project, along with his admirable colleagues Dinah Drazin, Mohara Gill, Robert Heath and Camilla Rockwood. Immense gratitude must also be expressed to Cornelia Parker, for contributing her invaluable Foreword. Great thanks are likewise due to Norah Perkins, my agent at Curtis Brown.

I have been lucky enough to feel immensely stimulated and enriched as well by the loving encouragement of my closest family members: Vena, Adam, Polly, Katy, Joe, Katriina, Lumi, Bruce and James.

TEXT SOURCES AND CREDITS

Pablo Picasso: *The Times*, 8 July 2006.
Helen Frankenthaler: BBC Radio programme, summer 1986.
Francis Bacon: *The Times*, May 1991.
Louise Bourgeois: *The Times*, May 1999; *Sunday Times*, 30 September 2007.
Rachel Whiteread: *The Times*, 1 June 2001.
Anish Kapoor: *The Times*, 28 September 2002.
Tracey Emin: originally published in *Art Review*, 53 (November 2002). © *Art Review*, republished by permission.
Sarah Lucas: *The Times*, 23 November 2002.
Langlands & Bell: 'Inside the house of Osama bin Laden', *The Times*, 15 April 2003.
Bridget Riley: 'The Talented Ms Riley', *The Times*, 25 June 2003.
Antony Gormley: 'Wired for vision', *The Times*, 17 April 2004.
Luc Tuymans: *The Times*, 1 May 2004.
Richard Long: 'His name is mud', *The Times*, 29 May 2004.
Doris Salcedo: 'Down to the wire', *The Times*, 11 September 2004.
Sam Taylor-Wood: *The Times*, 23 October 2004.
Lucian Freud: 'The master and his muse', *The Times*, 28 May 2005.
Jake and Dinos Chapman: *The Times*, 8 October 2005.
Frank Auerbach and Lucian Freud: 'Two old masters', *The Times*, 3 May 2006.
David Hockney: *The Times*, 2 September 2006.
Annette Messager: 'Annette Messager at the Hayward Gallery', *Financial Times*, 28 February/1 March 2009.
Tony Cragg: *Art World*, April/May 2009.
Claes Oldenburg: *Financial Times*, 29/30 August 2009.
Eva Rothschild: *Art World*, June/July 2009.
Cornelia Parker: *RA Magazine*, Winter 2009.
Rebecca Horn and Masanori Handa: *Rolex Mentor and Protégé*, December 2009.

INDEX

This book is dedicated to my darling granddaughter, Lumi, with all my love.

Page 8: David Hockney and Richard Cork, East Yorkshire, Monday, 17th May 2006 © David Hockney. Photo: Jean-Pierre Gonçalves de Lima

First published in the United Kingdom in 2023 by
Thames & Hudson Ltd, 181A High Holborn, London WC1V 7QX

First published in the United States of America in 2023 by
Thames & Hudson Inc., 500 Fifth Avenue, New York, New York 10110

Designed by Dinah Drazin

British Library Cataloguing-in-Publication Data
A catalogue record for this book is available from the British Library

Library of Congress Control Number 2023939387

ISBN 978-0-500-02510-9

Printed and bound in Slovenia by DZS-Grafik d.o.o.